Lyrical Strains

ELISSA ZELLINGER

Lyrical Strains

Liberalism and Women's Poetry in Nineteenth-Century America

The University of North Carolina Press *Chapel Hill*

This book was published with the assistance of the Authors Fund of the University of North Carolina Press.

Set in Arno Pro by Westchester Publishing Services
Manufactured in the United States of America

The University of North Carolina Press has been a member of the Green Press Initiative since 2003.

Library of Congress Cataloging-in-Publication Data
Names: Zellinger, Elissa, author.
Title: Lyrical strains : liberalism and women's poetry in nineteenth-century America / Elissa Zellinger.
Description: Chapel Hill : The University of North Carolina Press, 2020. | Includes bibliographical references and index.
Identifiers: LCCN 2020015456 | ISBN 9781469659800 (cloth : alk. paper) | ISBN 9781469659817 (pbk. : alk. paper) | ISBN 9781469659824 (ebook)
Subjects: LCSH: American poetry—19th century—Women authors—History and criticism. | Lyric poetry—19th century—Women authors. | Liberalism—United States—History—19th century. | Politics and literature—United States—History—19th century.
Classification: LCC PS152 .Z45 2020 | DDC 811/.04099287—dc23
LC record available at https://lccn.loc.gov/2020015456

Cover illustrations: *(Left to right)* Frances Sargent Osgood, from Henry Coppée, *A Gallery of Distinguished English and American Female Poets* (Philadelphia: E. H. Butler and Company, 1860); E. Pauline Johnson/Tekahionwake, from a promotional bill for the American Chautauqua Tour (courtesy of the Rare Book and Manuscript Collections, Cornell University Library); Frances Ellen Watkins Harper (courtesy of the Library of Congress Prints and Photographs Division, LC-USZ62-75978). *(Background)* light watercolor © iStock.com /Miodrag Kitanovic.

Portions of this book were published in a different form. Chapter 4 appeared as "Edna St. Vincent Millay and the Poetess Tradition," *Legacy: A Journal of American Women Writers* 29, no. 2 (2012): 240–62, and appears here courtesy of the publisher, the University of Nebraska Press. Chapter 5 appeared as "E. Pauline Johnson's Poetic Acts," *ESQ: A Journal of Nineteenth-Century American Literature and Culture* 65, no. 2 (2019): 73–122.

To Ben

Contents

Illustrations

Acknowledgments

I would first like to acknowledge the institutions and archives that supported this project. A Research and Scholarship Grant from the Office of the Provost and Academic Affairs at Armstrong State University (now Georgia Southern University, Armstrong Campus) as well as a Research Support Grant from the Maine Women Writers Collection at the University of New England helped accelerate this project. An Alumni College Fellowship from the Humanities Center at Texas Tech University also provided support in the project's crucial stages. Finally, the English Department at Texas Tech University has offered encouragement and accommodations for which I thank Brian Still, Department Chair.

I sincerely thank the University of North Carolina Press for its support. In particular, editor Lucas Church's expertise, patience, and humor helped ease anxieties about the publishing process. Both Lucas and Andrew Winters have attended to my many, many questions; to their eternal credit, they did not flinch when I brought twin toddlers to their offices. Thanks also to my readers whose thoughtful and generous feedback strengthened this work immeasurably.

This project began in graduate school at the University of North Carolina, Chapel Hill, where I had more fun than probably any graduate student should. This was due to a cohort of people who were, and continue to be, wonderful friends, consummate colleagues, and miniature therapists. I would like to thank Lynn Badia, Corinne Blalock, Anne Bruder, Angie Calcaterra, Leslie Eager, Lauren Garrett, Nick Gaskill, Jamie Jones, Jen McDaneld, Will Nolan, Elena Oxman, Kelly Ross, Aaron Shackelford, Robin Rudy Smith, and Harry Thomas. In addition, faculty members provided not just intellectual guidance, but professional and personal support. I sincerely thank Robert Cantwell, Gregg Flaxman, and Jane Thrailkill for their generosity inside and outside the classroom. In addition, Matthew Taylor's extreme patience ensured that I actually landed on my feet.

I am lucky to have stumbled into a field whose scholars are just cool people eager to support work at any level of achievement. I'd like to thank Michael Cohen, Jenny Kassanoff, Jennifer Putzi, Alexandra Socarides, Claudia Stokes, and Christa Holm Vogelius for their friendship and mentorship. In addition,

I have found a new and similarly cool group of people in the Texas Regional SSAWW Study Group, whom I am fortunate to see once a semester. I'd like to thank Desirée Henderson and Theresa Strouth Gaul for the warm welcome.

After (many years of) graduate school, I have been fortunate to land in departments surrounded by the most welcoming colleagues. At Armstrong State University, I want to thank Beth Howells, Jane Rago, and Jack Simmons for creating an environment that made faculty meetings fun. I doubt one could find friendlier, funnier, and kinder colleagues than those I am honored to call mine at Texas Tech University. I want to thank Mike Borshuk, Katie Cortese, Julie Nelson Couch, Michael Faris, Kendall Gerdes, Ryan Hackenbracht, Matthew Hunter, Callie Kostelich, Marta Kvande, Roger McNamara, Wyatt Phillips, and Jessica Smith among the many other English Department faculty members who provided support and friendship. I have been fortunate to work with a number of graduate students whose own scholarship enriched my own, and I'd like to thank Taryn Gilbert Howard, Apryl Lewis, and Meghan Self. In addition, TTU boasts the Women Faculty Writing Program, which provided the time and space for successful writing; thanks to Elizabeth Sharp and Kristin Messuri for organizing, and to my Friday afternoon group ("The Best") for all the encouragement and snacks.

This book would not exist without support from the world beyond the academy. I'd like to thank Roni Cohen for helping me to harness my inner resources. Portions of the manuscript were written while sitting in the NICU at the University Medical Center in Lubbock, Texas. I would like to thank the outstanding neonatologists and NICU nurses for their care during that time. In addition, Monica Birdwell has provided loving childcare, which has enabled me to be a better scholar and parent.

Eliza Richards has seen this project from its very (very) humble beginnings as a first-year master's student who didn't quite understand how to do graduate school. Eliza has gone above and beyond the support of any advisor in history; if that wasn't enough, she has offered me the full embrace of her warm and wonderful friendship. I get through my day by asking myself, "What would Eliza do?" I cannot thank her enough for her enrichment of my work and my life.

My family has offered both boundless encouragement and a gently critical perspective that kept my feet on the ground. My parents, Michael and Sandra, didn't blink when I quit my real job to move home and pursue a PhD in the Humanities. I thank them for their trust in me and for always providing a safety net. My brother, Boz, has faked interest in my research for over a decade. In doing so, he has provided keen perspectives that helped me understand how boring stuff can find a broader audience. My twin sons, Arthur and Oscar, made their appearance just after I embarked on the tenure track. Rather than derail a thing, they have created greater stability and joy. Their toddler tyranny is somehow delightful and has granted me a new perspective and patience.

Finally, this book is dedicated to Ben Rogerson, my husband, who read the manuscript more times than I can count. I forget this fact on a daily basis, along with all the other wonderful things he has done and continues to do. Let this dedication serve as a reminder of how lucky I am, and of my unending gratitude to him.

Lyrical Strains

Introduction
Lyrical Subjects and Liberal Publics

"I am Crispian's Crispian and I belong to myself." So begins *Mister Dog*, a 1952 children's book that treats self-possession as a strange refrain throughout its brief text. Written by Margaret Wise Brown and published as part of the beloved Little Golden Book series, *Mister Dog* describes a day in the life of a dog named Crispian's Crispian: he wakes up, takes a walk, plays with some other animals (dogs, cats, and rabbits), and meets a boy. Crispian introduces himself to the boy in unsurprising fashion—"I am Crispian's Crispian and I belong to myself"—only to have the boy respond in kind: "I am a boy . . . and I belong to myself" (Brown 2003, 9). This reply gives Crispian such pleasure that he invites the boy to live with him (9). It appears that the boy agrees, because they go to a butcher shop and then to Crispian's house to make a bone soup for dinner. Afterward they go to sleep, each in his own bed, dreaming his own dreams.

Given this clear emphasis on belonging to yourself, *Mister Dog*, we can conclude, is less about the "*Dog*" than about mustering the self-possession necessary to be considered a "*Mister*." Presumably this book was meant to teach young readers that they belong to themselves, that is, that they should know that no one has power over them (except, doubtless, their parents). Understood as such, the book *Mister Dog* is legible as an odd but nevertheless unmistakable entry in the tradition of American self-sovereignty, which is also the primary concern of this book. The establishment of Crispian's very name on the first pages teaches young readers a concept so embedded in U.S. culture that it is difficult to single it out as one that Americans ever consciously learn: namely, the idea that people belong only to themselves and that no other entity is sovereign over them.

In other words, *Mister Dog* exhibits the influence of liberal thought on U.S. culture; more specifically, the book serves as a primer on the construction of the liberal subject. In its emphasis on self-ownership, *Mister Dog* models for readers liberalism's circumscribed subject and abides by a narrative of self-making found in liberal philosophy. Starting with the tenet that individuals have property in themselves, *Mister Dog* demonstrates that this selfhood is first forged in the private sphere, a conviction reinforced by the images of

Crispian's bedroom and kitchen that accompany the opening statements. Indeed, in its freedom from pernicious outside influences, the ostensibly private realm is the seat of authentic self-development.

After it establishes such privacy, canine or otherwise, *Mister Dog* models the next steps in the construction of liberal selfhood by testing the soundness of this self-sovereignty in the public sphere. Leaving behind his little doghouse, Crispian "took himself for a walk. And he went wherever he wanted to go" (Brown 2003, 4). While readers enjoy the novelty of a dog taking himself for a walk, this scene speaks to the liberty accorded to the liberal subject who may likewise take himself wherever he wants to go—that is, until such doings infringe upon another individual's liberty. Crispian teaches us that public circulation establishes the boundaries of individual selfhood by acting to check its impermeability to outside influences and its own rational restraint. Only consider how neither Crispian nor the boy imposes on the other's liberty. When Crispian makes a soup out of his own bone to share with the boy, the boy "didn't give Crispian his chop bone" (11). Because boy and dog alike are sovereign over their own selves and property, the former is not obligated to throw his bone into the bone soup. Indeed, he instead chose to "put some of his bright green vegetable in the soup" (11). This ownership even extends to the property of the mind, the next liberal lesson this book has to impart. After dinner, the two go to sleep, and Crispian "dreamed his own dreams. That was what the dog who belonged to himself did." Likewise the boy "dreamed his own dreams. That was what the boy who belonged to himself did" (22). The liberal self, therefore, is free as long as that freedom doesn't inhibit another's liberty—even in dreams.

Yet this depiction of Crispian's perfect freedom obscures a number of concerns: the reasoning that would grant him and the boy such freedoms, the permeability of the public/private divide, and the exclusion of raced and gendered others from liberalism's rights. In short, *Mister Dog*'s assumptions duplicate the blind spots of liberal philosophy in the United States and its privileging of the white, propertied male as the only social identity worthy of the full rights of selfhood. Crispian might be a dog, but in both the title of "*Mister*" and the emphasis on private ownership in these opening pages, he is legible as male and propertied, which is to say, as the only kind of person who qualifies as a liberal self. In fact, the charm of this story emerges against a disturbing history of social and political discrimination in America. The self-reflexive verbs in the opening of the story—"he woke himself up," he "gave himself some bread and milk," "he took himself for a walk"—suggest the delight the reader should find in a "funny old dog" who takes care of himself rather than receiving help from humans (Brown 2003, 2, 4). Crispian can do

Bone soup with the boy's vegetables (15). Illustration by Garth Williams from *Mister Dog* by Margaret Wise Brown, copyright © 1952, renewed 1980 by Penguin Random House LLC. Used by permission of Golden Books, an imprint of Random House Children's Books, a division of Penguin Random House LLC. All rights reserved.

all these things because of the single fact that he "belonged to himself." The implied novelty here stems from our glimpse of autonomy where it should be absent. Thus, in order to make sense, *Mr. Dog* draws on a shared history of injustice: dogs, like women, the enslaved, and Native peoples in the nineteenth and early twentieth centuries, were never thought to "belong" to themselves. After this opening, the book retains its emphasis on gendered and raced belonging. Crispian meets dogs, cats, and rabbits, but it isn't until he meets a white boy that he hails his social equal, which he confirms by inviting the boy to come live in his home.

Indeed, the story reiterates its exclusion of raced and gendered others when the boy and the dog prepare for bed. The narrator describes Crispian's Crispian as "a *conservative*" because he "liked everything at the right time" and "he liked everything in its own place" (Brown 2003, 18). It's hard to know what the word "conservative" might have meant to children in the 1950s, but the book seems to imply that Crispian's ways follow established practice. I would amplify that implication to argue that Crispian's investment in preserving the status quo does the work of "conserving" liberalism's established practices—that is, the practices regulating who could have self-belonging and who could not. One might be enticed to consider this picture of a self-owning dog as an open invitation to others to share liberal selfhood. But, with the exception of species, Crispian evinces the usual exclusionary practices of the liberal tradition: he embodies white, able-bodied masculinity, he boasts his self-possession and asserts it in public, and, most importantly, he excludes other genders and races from joining him in the freedoms of liberal selfhood. Liberal selfhood is best illustrated by what *Mister Dog* leaves out.

I bring up (and perhaps over-read) *Mister Dog* here to establish the ubiquity of liberal philosophy and its model of selfhood in the United States. Notions of self-ownership are so ingrained and seemingly straightforward that children's books can apply them to narratives about self-owning dogs. Having used *Mister Dog* as an unlikely starting point, I want to trace a genealogy of American liberal selfhood. *Mister Dog* taps into ideas about liberal self-possession that had been circulating in the U.S. literary public sphere for more than a century. Its depiction of self-ownership in 1952 constitutes part of a belletristic legacy depicted in American literature from the prior century. Notions of selfhood evolved over the "long" nineteenth century in different public, literary forms, and I focus on what, I argue, is a literary technology specifically suited to imagining selfhood: lyric poetry. Unlikely as it is, *Mister Dog*'s explicit adherence to the tenets of liberalism makes it an ideal primer on the selfhood that underpins lyrical poetry in the nineteenth century. As I will explain more thoroughly in this introduction, poems were the literary tools that nineteenth-century readers and writers used to imagine the sovereign selfhood that is eventually on display in *Mister Dog*. The little white boy in *Mister Dog* was automatically assumed to possess such selfhood, just as white men were afforded the full political, economic, and social rights associated with selfhood in the nineteenth century. For those raced and gendered others who were denied such rights, lyric was, I argue, a technology at their disposal to advocate for their subject status. While such advocacy is beyond the scope of *Mister Dog*, the text shows the pervasiveness of these foundational constituents of liberal logic.

Lyrical Strains: Liberalism and Women's Poetry in Nineteenth-Century America will examine how lyric and liberal theories informed the conceptualization, communication, and, ultimately, consolidation of interdependent forms of selfhood in the nineteenth century. There was a pressing need for just such consolidation, as the nineteenth-century United States was undergoing a series of overlapping crises in ideas of selfhood, especially concerning the persons eligible for or barred from selfhood, the rights attributable to selves, and the exigencies responsible for distributing these rights. During the dynamic century from 1820 to 1920, I show how lyric guided readers in liberal self-making as political, economic, and social pressures were shaping lyric expression. By focusing on this continuity between the liberal and lyrical self, this work not only contributes to current critical debates in lyric theory but also reveals connections that reshape our understanding of political philosophy and aesthetic forms.

As these myriad crises in nineteenth-century lyric and liberal selves suggest, there was a fundamental instability within the concept of individual, sovereign selfhood that was not entirely fashioned by an individual but created by acts of external recognition. Just as Crispian's Crispian's self-ownership was secured in the recognition of an equal, that is, the boy, the self was sovereign because some other body or bodies granted that sovereignty. This reliance on external recognition was not unique to liberalism. Likewise, the figured lyrical subject, which was ostensibly constituted by the private utterance of a self-possessed solitary speaker, only existed if others read it. What this mutuality reveals is striking parallels between liberalism and lyric. While concurrently fashioning versions of an ideal self, both liberalism and lyric were assuming that same self's stable preexistence, a contradiction most evident in their similar attempts to base self-enclosed individuality in collaborative, communicative exchanges. Which is to say, both liberalism and lyric sought to create the self's interiority by making it public. Of course, such paradoxes are especially poignant in the United States, which championed the contradictory ideals of individualism and democratic union—all the while actually restricting these supposed universals, and the subjectivity that subtends them, to white men. Liberal subjectivity was not a universal right; rather, such autonomous individualism was created by excluding women, the enslaved, and Native peoples, and denying them the political and social freedoms enjoyed by those identified as full liberal subjects.

In this work, I contend that these same excluded groups clarify liberal selfhood by poetically contesting its assumptions during this crucial period of crisis. For that reason, this book will focus on women writers, as well as on the intersections of gender with race, in order to survey the poetics of the excluded. Lyrical poetry, I argue, was the technology that allowed disenfranchised others to address the ideologies of the self-enclosed, self-reliant, self-possessed liberal subject. By articulating a fantasy of lyrical subjectivity through poetry, the genders and races excluded from liberalism's freedoms could publicly establish themselves in relation to its ideals. In other words, lyrical subjects imagine liberalism's publics in the nineteenth century.

Nineteenth-Century Lyric

In what follows, I argue that the lyric ideal offers us the prospect of a dynamic, historical mode of reading poetry that is intimately connected to the fantasy of stable selfhood put forth by liberalism. Whether striving to achieve or laboring to contest the notion of a circumscribed, stable self, the poems I discuss uniformly attest to the ongoing and myriad crises of selfhood that were erupting across the years 1820–1920. In the face of so much social, economic, and political tumult, the lyric ideal of unified selfhood becomes an aspirational genre, one perpetually chasing the liberal promise of autonomous individualism. Drawing on what Michael Cohen calls the "social life" of poems, I argue that lyric existed in the nineteenth century as a reading practice whose social function included determining the boundaries of the self (M. Cohen 2015, 9).[1] I will thus deliberately read poems in the "long" nineteenth century as social experiments in selfhood that tried to achieve, critique, or reject the promise of the liberal subject.

However, lyric's social utility stems not from its practicality, but from its very unattainability. The lyric is an impossible ideal: no poem can ever actually be a lyric. Poems, however, can be lyrical inasmuch as they conspicuously display the idealized qualities of the genre or, as is more often the case, aspire to them. "Lyric," in other words, is a normative description of a genre; "lyrical" describes poems possessing some of the qualities of that genre.[2] The circulation of lyrical poems in the nineteenth century spoke to the era's struggles to define selfhood; that is, despite its nonexistence, the lyric ideal demonstrates its social utility through the presence of lyrical "strains" in nineteenth-century poems. In other words, "strains" of lyric definitions were present in the poetry of the nineteenth century. Or, to continue to tease out the metaphor, a "strain" of lyric infected nineteenth-century poems.

As I will explain further, lyric was a nineteenth-century exercise in social experimentation because its connection to expression was inextricable from its claims to signify subjectivity. Even if they did not explicitly define lyric as such, nineteenth-century readers and writers encouraged the association of lyric with person and poet with poem. Indeed, lyric comes to be associated with subjectivity because readers adopted the genre as a way to think through the contested meaning of the self across the long nineteenth century. But, as current scholarship has argued, perhaps this sequence is flawed. Critics have suggested that we flip the underlying assumption that lyric merely taps into the depiction of subjectivity, and, in so doing, they turn the very idea of subjectivity into an inescapable by-product of lyric. For instance, Virginia Jackson and Yopie Prins argue that "perhaps a properly historical approach to the lyric would entail imagining the terms of subjectivity as themselves quite lyrically generic, particularly by the latter part of the nineteenth century" (V. Jackson and Prins 1999, 523). This approach certainly encourages us to rethink the question "Which came first?," but such questions are not the focus of this book. Instead, I will treat the relationship between nineteenth-century lyric and subjectivity as mutually constitutive. I see no reason to insist on prioritizing one or the other. In fact, the interanimation between lyric and subjectivity further proves how impossibility had social uses. Readers and writers aspired to one by engaging the ideals of the other; as I will show, writers could employ the devices of lyrical expression to aspire to the selfhood they were denied, while notions of selfhood relied on the circulation of interiority evoked by lyrical expression.

This collaborative approach addresses not only the relationship between lyric and subjectivity, but the critical history of these concepts. Recent scholarship creates a false divide in lyric's history by arguing, on the one hand, that lyric is a twentieth-century construction, or, on the other, that nineteenth-century lyric has no resemblance to modern definitions. By maintaining this connection between nineteenth-century lyric and notions of selfhood, I concentrate on what was lyrical in poetry during the period before lyrical poetry had consolidated into its modern definition. Nineteenth-century poems do contain, I contend, flashes of the idealized subjectivity attributed to twentieth-century constructions of lyric. Instead of dismissing such flashes as merely anachronistic retroprojections, I will discuss how twentieth-century ideas of lyric serve nineteenth-century purposes.[3]

No doubt the most influential critical position is the theory of "lyricization," which considers lyric as an artifact of twentieth-century critical practices. According to Jackson, lyric as we know it—the figured expressive utterance of a solitary speaker—is "a retroprojection of modernity, a new concept artificially treated to appear old" (V. Jackson 2005, 8). In other words, lyric is a twentieth-century construction projected backward onto the nineteenth century. As Shira Wolosky explains, this process of lyricization began with turn-of-the-century literary editors and critics; she writes, "The notion of poetry as a self-enclosed aesthetic realm; as a formal object to be approached through more or less exclusively specified categories of formal analysis; as metahistorically transcendent; and as a text deploying a distinct and poetically 'pure' language: these notions seem only to begin to emerge at the end of the nineteenth century, in a process that is itself peculiarly shaped in response to social and historical no less than aesthetic trends" (Wolosky 2003, 14).[4] According to such scholarship, this definition of lyric is not eternal but originated in the late nineteenth century. At this time, literary editors and critics constructed a lyric ideal by describing lyric poetry as a transcendent, timeless form that gave "voice" to a speaker's pure feelings.[5] This imaginative frame was an attractive one—so attractive, in fact, that other ways of thinking about poems were ignored. Thus, lyricization was born. By endeavoring to read any and all verse as "a short, nonnarrative poem depicting the subjective experience of a speaker," so many poetic genres with historically distinct purposes were collapsed into the idea of lyric (V. Jackson 2008, 183).

By calling attention to how a twentieth-century reading practice was projected backward onto nineteenth-century verse forms, this scholarship helps us identify contemporary critical tendencies to read lyrically.[6] Prior to the turn to historical poetics, earlier twentieth-century scholarship persistently assumed that lyric was a universal form and, for that reason, such scholarship reads it as an ahistorical genre. Scholars who define lyric as such believe that these subjective musings tap into a universally recognizable poetic genre. Consider the example of Jonathan Culler, who writes that "the historical study of different poetic practices should be joined to a revival of the idea of the lyric as a poetic activity that has persisted since the days of Sappho, despite lyric's different social functions and manifestations" (Culler 2001, 202). Likewise, Mutlu Blasing argues, "The lyric is a foundational genre, and its history spans millennia; it comprises a wide variety of practices, ranging in the West from Sappho to rap" (Blasing 2007, 4). According to recent scholarship in lyric theory, these examples show that lyric as it has been understood in the twentieth century is a figment of scholars' imaginations, and one whose reading practices threaten to erase the historical existence of other verse genres.

But whereas Jackson and others, in their most polemical moments, nearly disavow the existence of lyric altogether, other recent scholarship more closely attends to how the processes of lyricization have obscured the historical existence of nineteenth-century lyric itself. But in recovering the existence of nineteenth-century lyric, such studies strive to sever lyric from its twentieth-century construction; according to this scholarship, when we put such retroprojections aside we find that the nineteenth-century lyric had little to do with the subjective expression of a figured persona. For instance, work by Cristanne Miller finds that lyric did in fact exist in this era, but it barely resembled the most commonplace modern definitions: "Nineteenth-century American definitions of and references to 'lyric' rarely mention subjectivity, address, or temporality—the characteristics centering virtually all twentieth- and twenty-first-century discussion of this genre" (C. Miller 2012, 21).

In the first half of the nineteenth century, Miller argues, "lyric" lent itself to a wide category of poetry. It was, as she writes, "any poetry that was not distinctly dramatic, epic, or narrative, that was harmonic or musical in its language, or that was conceived as song" (24). Basically, lyric was any and all verse that was not already another genre.

As such scholarship demonstrates, the complex relationship between lyric and poetry in the nineteenth and twentieth centuries is difficult to untangle. But one thing is clear: the triumph of lyric, which is to say, its eventual synonymity with poetry, has impoverished our understanding of not just what specific verse forms meant to earlier readers but, as I argue, lyric's social function for readers and writers during that era. Lyric's victory is, in a sense, pyrrhic: it became poetry but at the expense of its own historical specificities. In other words, the process of lyricization cost lyric—not just discrete verse genres—its very relevance. However, this book proposes to return to nineteenth-century lyric its social existence and, in so doing, to reconsider the historical forces that made lyricization so appealing. When we stop with Jackson, Wolosky, and others at discovering the practice of lyric reading, we overlook the social utility of lyrical ideals in the nineteenth century. Conversely, when scholars such as Miller solely address the meaning of lyric in the nineteenth century, they lose sight of how nineteenth-century lyric fosters later definitions. In sum, such scholarship is indicative of a tendency in contemporary lyric studies to regard lyricization as a process that is purely scholarly and editorial, and not a nineteenth-century social one that was responding to the promises of an emerging liberal order. With this historicization in mind, I nevertheless dive back into lyric reading. I will "lyricize" poetry in the nineteenth century in order to demonstrate how poems confronted liberal selfhood during this time. To that end, I am proposing a new methodology that, at a glance, perhaps seems contrary: namely, I continue to read lyrically while remaining aware of historical reading practices. I do not believe that my interpretations will collapse under objections of anachronistic lyric reading. I come to nineteenth-century poetry from a twenty-first-century vantage, and this study is aware of this vast historical difference.

Cristanne Miller is right to claim that "the lyric poem as such was not a much discussed genre in the mid-nineteenth-century United States" (C. Miller 2012, 49). Yet "subjectivity, address, or temporality"—the qualities Miller argues are rarely mentioned in nineteenth-century lyric definitions—were, I argue, nevertheless present for the purpose of creating and debating models of selfhood during an era when the status of the self was unstable (21). I connect the seemingly disparate concepts of the lyric in these eras by focusing on nineteenth-century poetry's "utopian horizon" (V. Jackson and Prins 2013, 4). In the face of so much social, economic, and political tumult, the lyric ideal of unified selfhood becomes an "aspiration," and, I argue, one perpetually chasing the liberal promise of autonomous selfhood (4). However, according to Jackson and Prins, a problem occurs in the twentieth century when lyric becomes not an "ideal to be aspired toward" but "a real genre" (4). As we can see, they and critics in a similar vein tend to identify such idealism only to build a case for twentieth-century lyricization, effectively eclipsing the contemporary function of lyric's aspirations. I will argue that lyrical poetry's utopian horizon had historical utility; its aspirations to universality constituted the outlines of a "real genre" because such aspirations served poets' social and political ends throughout the nineteenth century. In other words, poetic striving toward or struggles with the lyric ideal were the practices that marked nineteenth-century lyrical poetry.

This idea of lyric as the subjective expression of a singular speaker was, as twenty-first-century critics have asserted, not uniformly recognized as the primary definition of lyric until the end of the nineteenth century. But put these academic disputes aside to browse the pages of popular periodicals and anthologies across the nineteenth century, and it becomes apparent that nineteenth-century critics knew lyrical poetry when they read it.[7] I maintain that when these writers do discuss lyrical poetry, they define it by one quality: its expressiveness. Nineteenth-century authors and audiences thus participated in lyric reading, which recent critics claim was a twentieth-century practice. Such assertions are glimpsed in accounts across the long nineteenth century, such as when the *Western Recorder* (Utica, NY) reports that "sentimental feeling is the first requisite in lyric poetry" in 1825 or when Charles Moore asserts in 1915 in the *Dial* that "lyrical poetry is usually the expression of emotion" (*Western Recorder* 1825, 132; C. Moore 1915, 401).

For instance, the *Vermont Chronicle* in 1832 ran twin articles titled "Essay on Lyric Poetry" only three weeks apart. While the articles disagree on what exactly constitutes the content and tone of a lyrical poem, the definition of lyric is explicit. The first article declares, "The aim of all lyric poetry should be to express emotion," and, a few weeks later, the second article doubles down by asserting that "every sentence should be constructed so as to express emotion" (*Vermont Chronicle* 1832a, 136; *Vermont Chronicle* 1832b, 148). Such accord is not limited to local American papers. In the preface to his internationally popular 1861 *Golden Treasury*, Francis Palgrave calls lyric "the colouring of human passion" (Palgrave 1992, 5). Palgrave writes that "each [Lyrical] Poem shall turn on some single thought, feeling, or situation" (5).[8] Palgrave's influence was felt elsewhere, and these accounts suggest a loose consensus surrounding lyric's meaning by the mid-nineteenth century, if not earlier.

These writers even lyricize, demonstrating how lyrical strains could be found in all types of poems. Indeed, according to Palgrave, "narrative, descriptive, and didactic poems" qualify as lyric if colored by "human passion," and in an 1874 piece in *Littell's Living Age* discussing Palgrave, J. D. Rees argues that "the kind of inspiration that prompts [lyric] is to be found in the Ode and in the Song, in the Elegy and in the Sonnet" (Palgrave 1992, 5; Rees 1874, 195). By 1877, critics elsewhere would seem to agree. An article in the *Boston Daily Advertiser* distinguishes lyric from drama and epic by repeating this basic lyric contention multiple times: "Lyric poetry is the expression of strong feeling in brief form in language fit for singing"; "The lyric is subjective"; and, finally, "The subject [of lyric] is coextensive with the range of human passion" (*Boston Daily Advertiser* 1877, n.p.). At the same time that it distinguishes lyric as a unique genre, this article blatantly lyricizes, claiming that "pure lyric includes the song, hymn, ode, lyrical ballad, idyl, elegy, dirge, and epithalamium" (n.p). This reading practice suggests that lyric's compass of specific verse forms was actually a feature of nineteenth-century definitions of the genre, not a twentieth-century misattribution.

Nineteenth-century critical associations of various verse genres with lyric also suggest that lyric's ahistorical idealism had a purpose. Both readers and writers hoped to fashion their own selfhood through the expression of subjective emotions that presumed to tap into a shared human nature. For instance, H. T. Tuckerman argues in 1850 that the popularity of lyric owes to a recent preference for universal, humanist sentiments—which, perhaps unexpectedly, emerges from a study of the individual. "Lyric poetry is thus in vogue" he writes, because "sensibility to the universal and quiet facts of human nature, renders the poetic records of an individual's experience singularly attractive" (Tuckerman 1850, 105). Tuckerman articulates a key connection between lyrical inspiration and individual expression that, I argue, makes lyric poetry the literary technology for creating and understanding nineteenth-century selfhood. Lyric's emotional expression was linked, as these texts demonstrate, not only to a subject, but to the creation of this subject for readers. Tuckerman even connects lyric to self-development. Lyric benefits its readers by "awaken[ing] the springs of genius," which is to say, lyric reveals to readers their own internal, natural powers (109). The dissemination of lyric via "the gazettes and school-books of the country" has "induced" "virtue" and "refinement" in "the minds of millions" (109). By 1900, this type of lyric reading becomes more emphatic, at which point critics were insisting that "lyric poetry is preeminently the expression of the individual" (Heydrick 1900, 618). With such a premise, it was a small step for the editor Benjamin A. Heydrick to advise readers who wanted to further study lyrical poetry to "read a biography of the author. If possible, get a volume of his letters: the true life of a man is usually found there" (618). After all, the lyrical expression of emotion on the page depicts verisimilitude just like a letter: both forms were, in the long nineteenth century, understood to be the seemingly sincere profession of interiority for readers.

Lyric's exposure of individual emotion was not merely sentimental; it was also instructive. By imagining a self and, just as importantly, an audience who recognized that self, lyric's idealized expression of emotion helped construct liberal selfhood. Poetry thus had public, political import in the nineteenth-century United States: the public reception of that interiority registered those who were and were not granted the full rights of selfhood.

Liberal and Lyrical Selves

It is no accident, I think, that any discussion of lyrical poetry and liberal political philosophy leads us back to the single thinker who arguably defined both: John Stuart Mill. The nineteenth-century English philosopher's contributions to liberal philosophy are a matter of scholarly consensus; in the words of Alan Ryan, "Modern liberalism is exemplified by John Stuart Mill's *On Liberty*" (Ryan 1998, 292). Indeed, Ryan relies on that 1859 treatise to provide the "most plausible brief definition" of liberalism, which centers on "the belief that the freedom of the individual is the highest political value" (292).[9] The liberal subject "is by natural right, or by something tantamount to it, sovereign over himself, his talents and his property," and contemporary theorists provide similar definitions that emphasize this subject's self-possession, autonomy, rationality, and self-government (302).[10] Meanwhile, current theories of lyric employ Mill's 1833 publication, "What Is Poetry?," as a touchstone. Such scholarship, I argue, describes the lyrical speaker in the same terms as the liberal self. Indeed, David Russell claims that "Mill's aims for liberalism are to be found not in his description of eloquence, but of poetry" (Russell 2013, 21).

Given these apparent points of conceptual overlap, it's striking the extent to which the influence of poetry on Mill's political works has been underestimated. *On Liberty* completes a lifelong disquisition on selfhood that Mill had begun to describe in "What Is Poetry?" Indeed, Mill is instrumental in forging the conceptual connections between selfhood and poetry because he personally experienced the power of poetry as a technology for constituting selfhood. After suffering a nervous breakdown in his twenties, Mill recuperated by reading widely in poetry.[11] Writing in 1840, John Bowring, Jeremy Bentham's secretary, observed that Mill "read Wordsworth, and that muddled him, and he has been in strange confusion ever since endeavoring to unite poetry and philosophy" (qtd. in Russell 2013, 11).

Scholarship on Mill tends to neglect the essays on poetry written in his youth and to disconnect them from his older and, in the words of Russell, more "important stuff" on political philosophy (Russell 2013, 10). But this important stuff, as scholars such as Russell correctly contend, emerged from his thoughts on poetry. Granted, political theorists are not the only academics guilty of neglecting parts of Mill's oeuvre. If political philosophy tends to ignore Mill's earlier work on poetry, then poetic theory tends to ignore Mill's later work on political philosophy. Due to this inattention, scholars conclude that Mill's "What Is Poetry?" proffers an ahistorical interpretation of poetry.[12] While these thinkers have turned to Mill for definitions of lyric's timelessness, I argue that we should look to his writing to understand how poetics and politics mutually influenced the development of lyrical and liberal selves in the nineteenth century. When we read the essays on poetry alongside Mill's works on liberalism, we gain a more specific, nineteenth-century understanding of the self and how poetry proposed to shape that self for the decades to come.

The self that Mill envisioned in *On Liberty* (1859) was defined by self-sovereignty and liberty, two closely connected concepts. Self-sovereignty implies a state of freedom in which the individual has the liberty to govern all that concerns him. Yet even though an individual's decisions about himself are unqualified, the expression of such freedom cannot inhibit the freedom of others. Mill explains this complication by distinguishing between an individual's own private doings versus his interactions with society: "In the part which merely concerns himself, his independence is, of right, absolute. Over himself, over his own body and mind, the individual is sovereign" (Mill 2002, 12). Limits on individual freedom are therefore necessary to prevent one from infringing on the development of another person's selfhood. Or, as Mill succinctly puts it, "The liberty of the individual must be thus far limited; he must not make himself a nuisance to other people" (58).[13] Here the public/private distinction, a crucial premise for the formation of liberal ideology, begins to develop: Mill's nuisance-free private space of self-rule has a clear end in a society where this self interacts with others. The individual, Mill insists, must not feel pressured to conform to beliefs that are not original or authentic to the individual. After all, the external pressures of social conformity could "fetter the development" of authentic, stable selfhood, resulting in "individuality not in harmony with its ways" (7). Mill's statements suggest that the authentic, unfettered self is the end result of solitary fashioning; "the part which merely concerns himself" is forged in the private space of the body, mind, and property (7). In sum, Mill's theory rests on an underlying understanding of—and an anxiety about maintaining—a divide between public and private life, where the individual "in harmony" with himself is created in private, away from the "tendency of society to impose" (7).

More than twenty years earlier, Mill articulated a similar notion of autonomous selfhood that relied on the presumed public/private divide underpinning *On Liberty*'s sovereign self. That essay, "What Is Poetry?," is more often understood to provide a founding definition of the lyrical poem. Only consider Mill's most famous statement about lyric poetry: "We should say that eloquence is *heard*; poetry is *over*heard. Eloquence supposes an audience; the peculiarity of poetry appears to us to lie in the poet's utter unconsciousness of a listener" (Mill 1976, 12). Mill's description of poet and poem also anticipates what he will later sketch as ideal liberal selfhood.[14] The poet's obliviousness to the possibility of any listeners suggests a circumscribed self whose interiority is fashioned in private, alone and free from impositions. Just like liberal theory, lyrical poetry even stops at the point of interfering with others. We have eloquence and not poetry, Mill argues, "when the act of utterance is not itself the end, but a means to an end,—viz., by the feelings he himself expresses, to work upon the feelings, or upon the belief or the will of another" (13). Eloquence aims to disrupt the development of the sovereign subject or reader.

In *On Liberty*, Mill is then suggesting that the individual needs protection from eloquence. When a poem tries to influence another person, when it tries to intervene in the development of another subject's self-sovereign interiority, it ceases to be poetry. Conversely, lyric is essentially a product of the liberal subject. As the pure expression of the poet's interiority, lyric is created neither *by* the influence of nor *to* influence others—"no trace of consciousness that any eyes are upon us, must be visible in the work itself," Mill insists (Mill 1976, 12).[15] Since poetry is the expression of private feeling "overheard" by a public audience, the poet can traverse the public/private divide. The poet validates his self-possession by displaying his private self in public without unduly influencing others or suffering the inauthentic impress of others on his self. The poet, then, is the consummate liberal subject, one who is sovereign over body and mind in private or public.

Mill was not the only nineteenth-century intellectual who understood the connection between lyric and liberty. His depiction of the self-sovereign individual in *On Liberty* and "What Is Poetry?" aligns with other questions about selfhood that were being posed by thinkers across the Atlantic. The correspondence between figurations of liberal selfhood and lyrical selves that we see represented in Mill and other Anglophone nineteenth-century authors (such as Samuel Taylor Coleridge, Margaret Fuller, Henry Wadsworth Longfellow, Walt Whitman, William Wordsworth, and the subjects of the following chapters, to name a few) attests to the mutually constitutive relationship between poetics and political philosophy in the nineteenth century. For example, Mill's *On Liberty* and "What Is Poetry?" call into being a self that is mirrored in Ralph Waldo Emerson's figures of poetic genius and transcendental self-reliance described in essays such as "Self-Reliance" and "The Poet." I will focus on Emerson because of his influence on the poets I discuss in this work, such as Elizabeth Oakes Smith. Emerson's writings form the center of both American literary traditions and American liberal philosophy. He mentions Mill in his journals as early as 1833, and like him, composed theories of poetry and political philosophy (Emerson 1910, 182). Importantly, Emerson makes explicit what Mill implies: namely, the overlap between lyrical and liberal subjectivity.

Whether they address poetry or personhood, Emerson's essays have been understood to articulate a model of rugged American individualism. In the 1841 essay "Self-Reliance," Emerson affirms the individual's freedom to construct his own interiority by advising readers to disregard external influences and "to believe your own thought, to believe that what is true for you in your private heart is true for all men" (Emerson 2001, 121). Neal Dolan argues that "Emerson preached self-reliance because the self was the locus of reason as he understood it" (Dolan 2009, 13). Self-reliance therefore allowed the individual to discover his authentic self by banishing society's illusions; "only through the independent exercise of reason" argues Dolan, could one "free oneself from the falsehoods promulgated by tradition and come to grasp real truths about nature, the self, and the cosmos" (13). Like Mill in *On Liberty,* Emerson was concerned with the undue influence of outside forces on self-sovereignty. For example, Emerson complains that "society is a joint-stock company, in which the members agree for the better securing of his bread to each shareholder, to surrender the liberty and culture of the eater. The virtue in most request is conformity. Self-reliance is its aversion" (Emerson 2001, 122). In other words, Emerson worries about society's ability to prevent or pervert the authentic development of the liberal subject. But a discovery of one's own "aboriginal Self on which a universal reliance may be grounded" leads a person to his own nature (127).[16]

As George Kateb observes, "The idea of self-reliance is everywhere present in Emerson's thought" (Kateb 1995, 1). We can locate the liberal subject of "Self-Reliance" in the lyric subject of "The Poet," an essay in which Emerson aggrandizes the Poet into the ideal expression of liberal selfhood. In so doing, he warns that American selfhood has so far failed in its aspirations. In "Self-Reliance," Emerson laments that "we are become timorous desponding whimperers. . . . Our age yields no great and perfect persons" (Emerson 2001, 131). Conversely, the Poet "knows and tells," communicating to audiences the aspirational, autonomous selfhood that Emerson saw largely lacking in antebellum American life (185). Not a whimperer but an emperor, the Poet achieves greatness because he relies on his own perception in order to constitute his self: "He is a sovereign, and stands on the centre . . . the poet is not any permissive potentate, but is emperor in his own right" (185). In an echo of Mill's liberal subject and lyric poet, Emerson's Poet is beyond the influence of others and seeks not to influence others in his poetry. But because the Poet's authentic self-construction makes him "representative . . . stand[ing] among partial men for the complete man," Emerson hopes that his example will inspire readers' self-reliance (184). For Emerson, the Poet's poetry is the primary technology for communicating that individualism. By "tell[ing] us how it was with him," the Poet creates lyrical poems that promote individuality in their expression of interiority (186). Poets therefore have the ability to become "liberating gods" who "are free, and they make free" because they "yielded us a new thought" (194). Their poems spark the authentic self-knowledge that then frees readers from societal illusions.

Such self-reliance may suggest a solitary self-fashioning, but as we can see in the Poet's communicative imperative as "the sayer, the namer," the self-reliant individual cannot be solely constituted in private, away from society (Emerson 2001, 185). Rather, lyrical expression, or the public circulation of the supposedly circumscribed self, actually makes selfhood possible. This public/private participation puts to rest any claims that the Emersonian self is antisocial; after all, notions of expressive selfhood in the nineteenth century rely on holding in balance the interior and exterior, the public and private. Emerson's famous "transparent eye-ball" metaphor from *Nature* evokes this unity: "I become a transparent eye-ball; I am nothing; I see all; the currents of the Universal Being circulate through me; I am part or particle of God" (29). Although the eyeball creates boundaries to establish itself as an "eye" or the Poet's "I," this self is nevertheless "transparent" and therefore receptive to exchange. Likewise, the Poet's expression maintains boundaries between interiority and exteriority but only by traversing that divide to show how the self-reliant individual is permeable yet circumscribed.

In other words, even Emerson reproduces the public/private divide familiar from Mill's liberalism. But as Emerson makes explicit in the example of the transparent eyeball, the public/private separation that constitutes authentic selfhood only exists because it is constantly crossed. In spite of Mill's and Emerson's skepticism about pernicious external pressures, their works also assert that liberal and lyrical notions of selfhood rely, in fact, on others. Indeed, as Emerson argues in "The Poet," "all men live by truth, and stand in need of expression. In love, in art, in avarice, in politics, in labor, in games, we study to utter our painful secret. The man is only half himself, the other half is his expression" (Emerson 2001, 184).[17] As Emerson suggests, the self is "half" constituted by a social, public space that recognizes and thereby affirms it as a distinct, autonomous entity. Even Mill's formulation indicates not just solitary self-fashioning, but a communicative exchange in which the speaker performs interiority for an unacknowledged eavesdropper. When we recast Mill's "overhearing" as an excuse to draw a listener closer, we can see that the lyrical address implies that its self only exists through its tacit need for communication. Between Mill's lyrical eavesdroppers and Emerson's half-expressive Poet, we see how even the supposedly autonomous liberal subject is always formed by the social sphere. We only recognize this subject, and this subject can only recognize himself, because he circulates in society. The Poet is, in other words, the quintessential liberal subject, the subject that, as Brian Connolly argues, "was fully realized in the constant movement between the public world of markets, politics, and sociality and the private life of the family" (Connolly 2014, 2–3). Lyrical and liberal theories of the self share this open secret, but lyric poetry, I contend, foregrounds the "constant movement" that liberalism obscures. After all, lyric is thought to give voice to authentic, private feeling, but it cannot be recognized as such until it is transmitted to or "overheard" by the public sphere. The supposed self-enclosure of the lyric subject that reflects the self to itself actually occurs through a poetic pretense—an invited yet inadvertent exchange with an unavailable addressee.

Lyric and Liberal Histories

The permeability of the public/private divide was a symptom of the ongoing crisis of the nineteenth-century self, one supposedly stabilized by liberalism's impermeable, self-sovereign individual. This crisis was felt in Mill, Emerson, and the poets of the nineteenth century, and in the ways their works shaped figures that aspired to a universal, ahistorical ideal of selfhood. Rather than turning its back on political, social, or economic upheaval, this idealized self actually registers historical and cultural conflict. In other words, the poets and poetics discussed in this book sketch the history of an ideal that was actively working to dissimulate its history.

Here I would like to briefly trace the ironic relationship between liberalism and the historical forces that were motivating the desire for and belief in autonomous selfhood. At least in part, liberal thought flourished in the United States because it offered notions of stable selfhood at the precise moment that transformation of the national political economy contravened those very same ideas. From 1820 to 1920, liberal thought offered Americans a way to make sense of what often seemed senseless and to make important what seemed globally irrelevant.[18] As we will see, it's a deeply ironic moment, as liberalism gives with one hand what it takes away with the other.

This book begins on the cusp of the Jacksonian era, or the years from approximately 1820 to 1840. However, the Jacksonian era did not inaugurate the widespread economic upheaval that, I argue, assailed notions of the self. By 1820, American lives had been destabilized by the country's industrialization for nearly half a century. Such changes can be traced in part back to 1788, when the United States embarked on a thirty-year period of prosperity that was fueled by population increases in Europe (Appleby 1992, 263). Since European agriculture could not meet the demands of its growing populace, America supplied foodstuffs, and, in turn, this new, "completely commercial mode of agriculture" altered not just the American economy but its landscape (270). America needed more farmable land, culminating in the purchase of the Louisiana Territory in 1803, which doubled the size of America (McDonald 2001, 8). A second conflict with Great Britain helped to assert America's economic independence. The War of 1812 offered "an opportunity to promote internal commerce" by "lessen[ing] dependence on overseas manufacturers" (9). This autonomy was fortified by expanding domestic demand for manufactured products, expanding international demand for cotton and grain, and expanding mobilization of capital to support these demands (Dupre 2006, 264). Of course, such self-sufficiency was not sustainable. The "postwar bubble burst in 1818," triggering the Panic of 1819. Large-scale economic shifts such as falling agricultural prices and the "contractionary monetary policy" of the Second Bank of the United States ushered in the first economic depression of the century (264).

As this historical synopsis suggests, antebellum ideas of stable selfhood emerged from conditions that were anything but. The changes in political economy that supposedly solidified the nation's independence also worked to rattle its citizens' sense of self. Liberty—for white, able-bodied men, that is—did not necessarily entail stability. For instance, the Panic of 1819 threw American identity into disarray, "shaking people up" and "shatter[ing] the prosperity and confidence of the postwar years" (Dupre 2006, 264). According to Chris Castiglia, the antebellum era's "colliding ideological regimes—and the resulting social associations" impacted interiority, rendering it "a realm of disruption and attempted order" (Castiglia 2008, 4, 3).

As the century advanced, liberalism's idealized self-reliance continued to work as a buffer against the very experiences that suggested an individual's dependence on and powerlessness in the face of historical conditions. The massive economic transformations of the long nineteenth century required not just an optimistic doctrine of democratic individuality, but a method for countering social and cultural change with fantasies of self-control. Notions of autonomous individualism were imperiled by broad shifts in the composition of American labor from self-employed farmers to a populace whose only property was their labor. Indeed, myriad and major economic crises characterize the precariousness of an individual's labor power across the century—the 1837 panic saw layoffs of "tens of thousands of wage workers"; in the 1870s, there was the "sudden collapse of the midcentury economic boom"; and further panics flashed in 1884, 1893, and 1907 (Sklansky 2002, 49, 24). In addition to the abolition of slavery, the Civil War wrought major changes; the redistribution of wealth "into the hands of financiers and manufacturers" resulted in "the spectacular industrialization of the postbellum era" (105–6). Furthermore, expanding markets created "cutthroat competition," leading employers to "reduce wages or increase productivity through mechanization" (112). In turn, these actions not only sparked additional economic crises, but widespread worker unrest and strikes started in the postbellum period and continued through the end of the century (112).

By the turn of the twentieth century, the notion of a liberal political and social system that protected the self from outside influences was no longer even feasible.[19] Liberalism's efforts to ensure individual stability during the major upheavals of the postbellum era countered the sense that people still felt that "the power to affect one's own destiny had been removed from the individual, the family, and the local community," and instead "concentrated in a complex maze of interdependent, impersonal forces" (Hilkey 1997, 8). Self-sovereignty and liberty, the cornerstones of the liberal self, were continually undercut by "the impersonal laws of supply and demand and survival of the fittest" (Sklansky 2002, 138).[20] Perhaps paradoxically, a new social welfare state was thought to ensure the liberty of liberalism by allowing people to be free from fear and other life-limiting afflictions.[21]

As we can see, liberalism's triumph in the United States, seen in its promise of stable, sovereign selfhood, attempted to erase its own sensitivity to social, political, and economic change. Like the lyric, the story we tell about liberalism collapses competing modes of political thought into the one story of its own rise. Shklar argues that "to speak of a liberal era is not to refer to anything that actually happened" (Shklar 1989, 22). Liberalism may project itself backward to be the only political theory of nineteenth-century America, but liberal thought "was hardly the dominant intellectual voice" (22). Appleby agrees that "American history shed illiberal elements" in order to create its narrative of progress (Appleby 1992, 4). Liberalism did not exist as such in the nineteenth century but has since retroprojected such an image, we might say, through its processes of "liberalization." Indeed, scholars emphasize that accounts of liberalism are historical and that "we should be seeking to understand liberalisms rather than liberalism" (Ryan 1998, 292). It is easy for us to look back at political thought and liberalize the same way we lyricize because both have aspirations to the utopian. As I hope to show, when we lyrically read nineteenth-century poems with liberalism in mind, its seemingly ahistorical aspirations to ideal selfhood reflect the history (and ahistory) of liberalism in the United States.

The Private Problem

As the term "liberalization" suggests, liberal philosophy also covers up its own historical conditions and, with them, the people who challenge its philosophy. To even consider liberalism "powerful" in the nineteenth century requires ignoring the many people who could not access the liberty it described, namely, those raced and gendered others socially situated in the invisible private realm (Shklar 1989, 22). Appleby points out that the "triumph" of liberalism "leeched from the record any curiosity about those men and women who could not be given parts in the drama of improvement and discovery" (Appleby 1992, 8). While liberalism ensures "freedom from the abuse of power," those who enjoyed such freedom—white, propertied, able-bodied men—existed at the expense of others who were suffering "institutionalized cruelty" (Shklar 1989, 27, 29).

Whether one experienced liberalism's freedoms or cruelties was determined by his or her relationship to privacy. Indeed, privacy was instrumental to white men's public autonomy; the perceived domestic sphere was where they were free to develop the self-possession that withstood what Mill called the "tyranny of the prevailing opinion," or what we could anachronistically call "inner resources" (Mill 2002, 7). With these fundamental changes to many of the basic premises of social and political life in the United States also came diverging notions of public and private; by the 1830s what was civic unity split into the public sphere of the social and the private sphere of the domestic. To compensate for this shift, the private would now become associated with morality and virtue and, furthermore, was "protected by a political code of public noninterference" (Shamir 2006, 4). But "noninterference," political and otherwise, was impossible to maintain during this era. The ideal privacy that fostered the self became increasingly desirable even as it was recognized as an impossibility. In fact, such a "narrative," Elizabeth Dillon explains, "describes citizens as subjects created and fully constituted in private, familial spaces who subsequently emerge into the public sphere" (Dillon 2004, 6). However, liberal bootstrapping fantasies obscured the other peoples in this supposedly invisible private realm upon whom the white, male liberal subject depended for his existence. The American liberal public sphere developed by excluding the presence of those who were thought to possess too much privacy, that is, women and nonwhite peoples. These groups were crippled by the privacy that supposedly made them; they were *too* private and, for that reason, unfit for autonomous self-possession. Because they exist in this "prepolitical" space of the private, women were denied subjectivity; as the "apolitical" objects of private property, slaves could not be considered people (18).

Indeed, women's most personal attributes, their "very bodies and psyches," prevented them from participating in this public realm. Their "penetrable" bodies were "understood to be inherently lacking in autonomy, conjoined to children and dependent upon men" (Dillon 2004, 12). Women were thus assumed to be naturally disabled, while propertied white males were considered "able," that is, possessing the physical and mental capacity to function autonomously in the public sphere (Welke 2010, 7). Disabled as such, women were too "encumbered" to sustain existence beyond the home.[22] They were thus situated within a set of cultural obstacles: the seemingly sloppy female body lacked the firm boundaries of self-sovereignty—attached to children, dependent on husbands, penetrable in their bodies and minds—and these supposed vulnerabilities rendered women restricted, encumbered. Because women could not shore themselves up, that is, they could not fully contain or circumscribe their selfhood, they were confined to the domestic sphere, where their self-dispossession was protected—and, just as importantly, where it served a purpose.

Women produced the material products and conditions that supported the appearance of white men's public autonomy; they performed "the 'invisible,' nonwaged labor of nourishing, housekeeping, and reproducing that serves as the prerequisite to men's ability to function 'autonomously' in the public sphere" (Dillon 2004, 15). Yet the home was not construed as the site of women's work; as the realm of true liberty and authentic self-development, as a space of freedom from economic necessity and social pressure, no "work" could be done in the private realm. It was instead the site of women's love. Here women were supposedly free to act of their own volition, and their actions were interpreted as evidence of their own liberty and love. Under such circumstances, women may have worked, but this work was not considered labor because love could not be a burden (201). At the same time that their so-called physical disability denied them access to liberal rights, women's excessive privacy transformed labor power into love and, in so doing, divested women of any property in their own being.

These problems with work and place stemmed from American legal precedent, which was, in turn, derived from English common law. Or, more accurately, interpretations of common law, as William Blackstone's *Commentaries on the Laws of England* became "the foundation from which American treatise writers would then expand" (Welke 2010, 27). Blackstone's interpretations were especially influential for domestic relations, and his assertions served as the basis for the doctrine of coverture applied by American courts. Such laws basically attributed the rights of married women to their husbands by treating husband and wife as the same person. This exclusive locating of legal agency in the husband was not inconsequential. In effect, Welke argues, "married women's loss of legal personhood under the law of coverture augmented men's personhood; her dependence defined his independence" (28). A married woman's labor, earnings, and children were the property of her husband; she could have no residence separate from her husband; and she could not enter into any legal agreements such as contracts or wills (27–28). Even after reforms to coverture, the legacy of such legal practices would influence women's public and professional autonomy for the rest of the century.

Married women might not have been considered "full-rights-bearing individuals," but, as Welke points out, "they could, at least, marry" (Welke 2010, 67, 66). The enslaved were denied even that right because they were not "understood in law to have the capacity to consent" (66). Once again, this denial of rights serves to buttress the personhood of white men. The same "biological essentialism" that would denote black minds as insufficient enabled the belief that enslaved people were "a form of property that *produces* the political personhood of the white, male, liberal subject" (Dillon 2004, 17). In other words, liberalism is as raced as it is gendered, a point that Charles W. Mills makes when he asks us to recognize that "racial liberalism or white liberalism" is "the actual liberalism that has been historically dominant since modernity (Mills 2008, 1382). While liberalism aspires to be "colorless" in theory, in reality it is "a distinctively white (not colorless) abstraction" that seeks to draw attention "away from Native American expropriation and African slavery and from the role of the state in facilitating both." To discuss the freedoms of liberalism, then, means to overlook the "racial sociopolitical oppression" at its core (1387). A second bitter irony emerges. Liberalism employs a rhetoric of universal equality to silence those who are denied its freedoms; the people whose example disputes supposed liberal inclusivity are oppressed by actual liberal exclusivity.

Lyrical poetry, I argue, thus becomes a tool for recognizing those people who are confined to and concealed by liberalism's private realm. Because it stakes itself on the visibility of privacy, nineteenth-century lyric granted access to this overlooked, supposedly invisible private realm and, in doing so, revealed all those people on whose exclusion the creation of liberal subjectivity depended. In other words, lyric offered the means to develop a poetics of the excluded. To that end, I will focus on women writers and the intersections of gender with race during the crisis of selfhood that led to liberalism's aspirational and political prejudices. By engaging lyrical practices, these women fashioned poetic selves that exposed the very assumptions about selfhood that denied them the political and social freedoms enjoyed by white men. In turn, women used this lyrical expression in order to have a public "voice" where they would not otherwise have one. By figuring the expression of privacy, lyrical poetry allowed women to traverse the public/private divide, demonstrating that they were already present in and equipped for the public sphere. Their poetry registered the struggle to be recognized as autonomous subjects, and in doing so these works reveal the historical shape of the century's most idealized aspirations.

The practices I discuss were not simply a matter of symbolizing women's inequality in lyrical laments. Rather, women writers exploited the contexts surrounding their poetry in order to register their efforts to access or contest liberal ideals. Indeed, the publication and reception of poetry by women in the nineteenth-century United States points to a set of social expectations that shape the co-development of liberalism and lyric. Specifically, I will focus on public expectations that associated women's poetry with the highly feminized, morally pure figure of the Poetess. Recent scholarship by Virginia Jackson and Yopie Prins, Tricia Lootens, and Eliza Richards has taken up the relationship between lyric and the Poetess. Generally speaking, their respective work historicizes approaches to lyric and the Poetess as matters of subjective expression. Indeed, Poetess poems were extremely popular across the long nineteenth century because they were understood to provide the reading public with imaginary access to women's idealized and private interiors, and therefore to their presumably inviolable and pure souls or spirits. The problem with this, as Eliza Richards points out, was that the "uncanny affinity between poetesses and lyric media marked them as vehicles of cultural transmission" (Richards 2004, 3). Likewise, Jackson and Prins have argued that "[the Poetess] is not the content of her own generic representation" (V. Jackson and Prins 1999, 523). Rather than see this reception as limiting, I argue that Poetess poetry's lyrical expression of interiority provided a unique technology for revealing the gendered forms of inequality inherent in America's self-reliant individualism. In so doing, Poetess poetry debates the limits of liberalism's imagined publics.

Critical concern with the term "Poetess" has focused on this collapse between poet and poem. Only consider Paula Bennett's suggestion that it might "be more accurate as well as less confusing to speak of Poetess poems or Poetess thematics, rather than of Poetesses per se" (P. Bennett 2007, 270). Nevertheless, the association of public women's poetry with the fictional Poetess figure means that a strict distinction between the empirical author and the imagined Poetess persona is difficult to maintain. I therefore use the term "Poetess" to refer to an imaginary public persona associated with the names of biographical women writers whose poems shaped what readers interpreted as their personalities.

What I am trying to suggest is that, like the nineteenth-century lyric, the Poetess was an ideal whose historical reception revealed the social expectations surrounding selfhood, specifically the liberal selfhood denied to women and people of color. As an idealized persona created by a nineteenth-century literary public sphere, the Poetess was not a biographical person, yet women writers were measured against this abstraction whether they liked it or not. The reception of their works was thus inevitably connected to the cultural expectations associated with the Poetess figure. Poetess poems could be written by women and even men, but when written by women, readers *thought* these works were written by Poetesses and read them for the qualities that were attributed to idealized femininity. Because nineteenth- and even twentieth-century readers so enjoyed consuming this ideal through various poems and images, literary stakeholders—editors, reviewers, publishers—

promoted women writers as Poetesses by actively blurring the line between biographical author and feminized ideal. Women's writing was therefore packaged and received as if its authors were living embodiments of an abstraction. As a result, these authors' public personas were entities that they could only partially control, as the Poetess figure was created by the two, at times opposing, forces of authorial intent and readerly reception. Women authors essayed to position themselves in the public sphere by deploying the conventions of the genre, at the same time that readers understood these works within the horizons of an ideal.

As you can see, when I refer to "Poetess," I am referring to a tangled host of tensions between biographical women writers, fabricated personas, and public expectations. Like nineteenth-century lyrical poems, Poetess poems mediate between ahistorical abstraction and historical reception; these texts retain the trace of the biographical author plus the imprint of readerly desires. I hope to further clarify the links between the Poetess's persona and poetry in chapter 1, but I bring up the Poetess here because the figure reflects the conditions of the public sphere in which women's writing circulated. To that end, my discussion of women poets in the nineteenth-century literary marketplace draws on a Habermasian notion of the public sphere, and here I will turn to Nancy Fraser, whose scholarship has revised some of the conceptual problems within the German thinker's work. According to Fraser, Jürgen Habermas's notion of the public sphere is limited inasmuch as he "fails to examine other, nonliberal, nonbourgeois, competing public spheres" (Fraser 1992, 115). The omissions that Fraser identifies also offer an opportunity. I approach his idealized concept as an occasion to locate those excluded others who nevertheless shape the contours of the public sphere precisely because they are left out. For Fraser, the Habermasian public sphere "designated a theater in modern societies in which political participation is enacted through the medium of talk. It is the space in which citizens deliberate about their common affairs, and hence an institutionalized arena of discursive interaction" (110). The public/private split is often oversimplified, and, as Fraser warns, it is easy when one is employing a feminist methodology to condense different valences of "public" into one vaguely "not domestic" sphere. Distinct from the state or the economy, the public sphere can, in the words of Fraser, "keep in view the distinctions among state apparatuses, economic markets, and democratic associations, distinctions that are essential to democratic theory" (111). This space helps distinguish these disparate public "apparatuses" and, I contend, also provides those excluded others with a point of access into otherwise closed networks. In other words, the discursive space of the public sphere provided the background against which these writers could fashion the lyrical subjects that confronted liberal philosophy.

Because Poetess poems were wildly popular, I examine how the circulation of these works within a liberal public sphere foregrounded the contradictions implicit in this discursive site. The figure of the Poetess strains the boundaries of belonging that liberalism set for itself by entering into the public sphere and making a place for herself there; she overcomes the divide that women were deemed unfit to cross. As I have established, the self-made, autonomous liberal subject is built on a (blurry) public/private distinction. Dillon provides a succinct overview of this constitutive tension: "On the one hand, privacy is the site of freedom; on the other hand, privacy must be made publicly visible in order to perform the cultural work of representing the freedom of the liberal subject" (Dillon 2004, 235). Liberalism might disguise the permeability of the public/private divide, but Poetess poems put the exchange into stark relief because they relied on the lyrical expression of private feeling in public. Such exposure allowed the Poetess to travel widely in the public sphere, imagining a public identity for the private female persona.

In the words of Bennett, "women used their writing, in particular, their poetry, to demand, model, imagine, produce, and defend reforms that ultimately led to their acquisition of civil free agency and hence, as they defined it, to their modernity" (P. Bennett 2003, 10). The very commercial success of these works performed a public, political critique. In my examination of how Poetess poems and personas entered a literary public sphere, I will extend the project that Bennett describes by emphasizing how American women's poetry "function[s] as a form of *public* speech addressed to concrete, empirically identifiable others" (5). Indeed, such political advocacy was created by working through and with mainstream cultural conventions and not, for the purpose of my argument, explicitly subversive politics. I am more interested in the ways that Poetess poems were aimed at the larger, popular literary marketplace. In contrast, Fraser's description of "*subaltern counterpublics*" exemplifies the arguments and methodologies that I am eschewing in my discussion of women writers. Fraser proposes that these are social groups who create "parallel discursive arenas where members of subordinated social groups invent and circulate counterdiscourses to formulate oppositional interpretations of their identities, interests, and needs" (Fraser 1992, 123). Certainly Poetess poetry participated in these "counterdiscourses." However, I examine the ways that women's writing was still consumed and enjoyed by a broad readership of both women and men in United States at this time.

In order to reach these audiences, the lyrical subjects of the poems I discuss reflect both the efforts of individual poets and the sociopolitical practices of the nineteenth-century public sphere. In what follows, I demonstrate how lyric formally bears the strains of its struggles against or efforts to achieve liberalism's ideal self. For that reason, the word "strain" takes on a complex metaphorical and self-reflexive significance that describes a struggle both with selfhood and with gendered poetic conventions. In order to depict this endeavor across the nineteenth century, I discuss four poets—Elizabeth Oakes Smith, Frances Ellen Watkins Harper, Edna St. Vincent Millay, and E. Pauline Johnson—whose gender and, in the case of Watkins Harper and Johnson, race meant they were socially denied the status of selfhood. I examine how these authors engaged lyric's technologies across the long nineteenth century in order to create a space for selfhood that renegotiated the division between private and public. These poets reveal that nineteenth-century poetry models forms of subjectivity in dynamic relation to history.

Chapter Summaries

Over the next five chapters, I link the history of the liberal self in the nineteenth-century United States to women's lyrical production. I begin this work in chapter 1, "The Poetess and the Politics of Profession," arguing that women's writing, specifically poetry in the "Poetess" genre, exposes the tensions that wrack both the ideal liberal and lyric selves. The self-made, autonomous liberal subject was built on a permeable public/private distinction; public circulation confirmed one's circumscribed, and therefore sovereign, interiority. With its expression of private feelings, Poetess poetry was thought to demonstrate the opposite—namely, women's inability to exert liberal self-possession in public and, by extension, their dependent social status and the necessity of confining them to the domestic sphere. In order to illustrate how the literary public sphere enforced these conventions over time, I compare popular texts that rehearse the expectation that women poets were not professional writers but amateurs: they could not help but profess sincere feminine emotion in their poems. In so doing, these authors inadvertently offered up their interiority for public consumption. But rather than belaboring the limits of such a legacy, I argue that authors writing Poetess poems could turn amateurism into a kind of public "profession" (both line of work and declaration), and thereby push against the boundaries of belonging that liberalism had set. I explore this process with the example of Frances Sargent Osgood, whose poetry self-consciously trades on exposing a feminized interior in public. In poems specifically about the profession of the Poetess, Osgood's poetic persona reached beyond the social restrictions placed on women.

While Osgood was only thirty-eight when she died in 1850, she was one of the most famous poets of her time, so beloved that her works continued to be reprinted into the early twentieth century. In my discussion of her literary legacy in chapter 1, I hope to illustrate the standards that women writers in the nineteenth-century literary public sphere had to navigate. Each chapter in the rest of this book focuses on a single author in order to chart the development of these standards across the long nineteenth century. Individually, each writer's protracted career exposes how historical shifts in the Poetess ideal corresponded to historical struggles to fashion American liberal selfhood. In fact, the very public nature of each author's career makes plain the political-economic forces threatening the fantasy of a stable, possessable self. Through their professional persistence and publicity, these authors offer exemplary depictions of lyrical strains—which is to say, both expressive poetry and struggles to depict selfhood.

The very celebrity of these Poetess poets constituted a critique of women's supposed dispossession in public. I argue that the continued presence of these women in the public sphere—from the lyceum circuit to the Chautauqua circuit, from gift anthologies to radio broadcasts, from the Civil War to the brink of World War II—marked a form of resistance against prevailing assumptions about how liberal selfhood was embodied. Indeed, Oakes Smith, Watkins Harper, Millay, and Johnson were popular figures who used their fame for political advocacy. Their advocacy relied, in part, on their emphasis on performativity, which had the effect of troubling the transparency associated with the Poetess persona. Playing off the assumption that women's poetry was essentially privacy rendered public, these authors' performances unsettled any neat distinction between a supposedly insincere public identity and an authentic private one. Such performances had another effect as well. While women's public, poetic performances could enact their self-dispossession, performance could also call attention to a manipulated public persona whose supposedly pure, private form was ultimately unavailable. The authors I discuss handle this realization in historically distinct ways and, in so doing, illustrate how the Poetess persona develops across the century. Overall, each chapter addresses how these poets deployed the Poetess in order to access and exploit the slippages that performances offered.

Oakes Smith and Watkins Harper, whose careers span nearly the entire nineteenth century, worked through the public presence of the Poetess in order to advocate for equal rights. Their arguments relied on the assertion that women possessed the ability to both constitute and circumscribe their liberal selfhood in the American public sphere. Chapter 2, "Elizabeth Oakes Smith's Lyrical Activism," discusses Oakes Smith (1806–93), the lecturer, journalist, novelist, poet, and women's rights activist, whose literary career began in the 1830s and stretched well into her old age.[23] She was an outspoken women's rights advocate—her series Woman and Her Needs appeared in Horace Greeley's popular *New York Tribune*, and she was the first woman to lecture on the lyceum circuit. These works asserted that women, not just men, had the right to develop their own lives and pursue their own interests as equals. While her poetry, as one might guess, is very different from her essays, this chapter highlights the political aspirations that underpin Oakes Smith's poetics. By representing women's genius, her poems, I argue, endeavor to symbolize women's fundamental right to self-sovereignty. This argument expands the discussion of Emerson's "Poet" begun in this introduction, as I contend that Oakes Smith (who was Emerson's friend and colleague on the lyceum circuit) tries in her poetry to rewrite the terms of her reception—not as a generic female writer, but as the lasting, liberal poet. While Oakes Smith rejects the term "Poetess," she does not, however, reject the practices associated with the genre. Unlike Osgood, who embraced the conventions of the Poetess persona in order to cleverly critique their stipulations, Oakes Smith adapts the conventions marking Poetess poetry to anticipate a different reception for herself, and, in the process, a different status for women. By exploiting the expectations regulating the Poetess's accidental exposure of interiority, Oakes Smith's poetry acknowledges the intimate emotions of its figured speakers but, crucially, refuses to excavate them for readers. In so doing, Oakes Smith purports to reveal her self-sovereign genius through her full control over what she sees and says.

As my study of Oakes Smith demonstrates, social and political conditions made asserting sovereign privacy a difficult task for women writers. Self-ownership was impossible, however, for enslaved women. The Poetess's exposure of privacy and her subsequent dispossession continue to inform the issues I discuss in chapter 3, "Frances Ellen Watkins Harper's Two-Body Problem." I examine how Watkins Harper (1825–1911) deployed motherhood—in which the mother's body becomes "two" via her child—to advocate for African American women's equality. Like Oakes Smith, Watkins Harper had a long, prolific, and public career. In the 1850s, Watkins Harper became a lecturer on the antislavery circuit, where she recited her poems and made them available in pamphlets. She toured in the Deep South after the Civil War, which resulted in the publication of her poetry collection, *Sketches of Southern Life*, in 1872. Two decades later, at the age of sixty-seven, Watkins Harper published one of her best-known works, the novel *Iola Leroy*. From 1893 to 1900, she published many revisions and reprints of earlier works. As this very brief biography demonstrates, Watkins Harper's oeuvre charts lyrical and liberal shifts across the antebellum era, Reconstruction, and the turn of the century. She employed the concerns of the Poetess to display how slavery blighted the public/private distinction essential to liberalism, and, after emancipation, continued to use the two-bodied rhetoric of motherhood to assert freedpeople's self-ownership.

Critics have argued that, in her poems about the traumatic sale of slave mothers, Watkins Harper models forms of textual possession that urge readers to recognize enslaved persons as equal, sovereign individuals. However, I concentrate on two complications in Watkins Harper's poetry that trouble this conclusion and that speak to how violent forces dismantle or differently assemble the individual: first, slaves were private possessions, not people; and, second, encumbered or extended by their children's bodies, mothers were forbidden the self-circumscription that constituted liberal selfhood. By reflecting how mothers' bodies and the children attached to those bodies were broken down into publicly saleable parts, Watkins Harper's poetry contravenes liberalism's notions of singular self-possession. Rather than focusing on the institution of slavery and its denial of such self-possession to African American women, this chapter dwells with Watkins Harper on how the connection between disembodiment and motherhood results in multi-bodied mothers who exceed the boundaries of a singular subject. By expanding the terms of liberalism's singular self-possession, Watkins Harper symbolically gathers up the maternal body and all the other bodies it supports into a sovereign whole through the "body" of the poem.

While chapters 2 and 3 discuss Oakes Smith's and Watkins Harper's respective efforts to assign autonomous liberal subjectivity to raced and gendered others, the next two chapters concern the false liberal promise of a self with sovereign privacy. By the end of the nineteenth century, Millay and Johnson employed the inheritance of the Poetess tradition to thoroughly dissolve the figure into the very public sphere that created her. Their work—both printed and performed—revoked any sense of difference between publicity and privacy. This revocation took the critique of women's inability to constitute selfhood and extended it to the very notion of liberal selfhood in

America. The authors treated in these chapters expose the liberal fantasy of private self-possession by explicitly "performing" the Poetess in public. Millay's and Johnson's investment in Poetess performance not only depicts the continuing relevance of the figure in the early twentieth century, but also suggests a shift from earlier authorial efforts to embody the Poetess to the critical distance that performance enabled.

Chapter 4, "Making the Modernist Poetess: Edna St. Vincent Millay," explores the legacy of the Poetess's paradoxical mandate to publicly perform the social imperative of feminine privacy. Born when Oakes Smith's and Watkins Harper's public careers were reaching their end, Millay (1892–1950) directly inherits the practices of the Poetess tradition and deploys them in her poetry. Her literary fame was established with the publication of "Renascence" in 1912, and, as with Oakes Smith and Watkins Harper, her celebrity enabled her to be outspoken about public issues—most notably when she published poems about the Sacco and Vanzetti trial and America's isolationist stance on the brink of World War II.

By mobilizing the Poetess to confront the problem of modern selves and souls, Millay unveiled the problem that faced the woman poet: the self-diminishing, if not nearly impossible, practice of professing privacy. Muddying the emotional objectivity of modernism, Millay troubled not only the sanctity of the woman poet's privacy but also the more fundamental idea of sovereign privacy on which individual agency depends. The forms of Millay's poetic mediation—in print, performance, radio, and photography—flaunt the tension between the promise of perfect lyrical availability and the utter absence of the figure they purport to produce. By manipulating this tension, Millay showed that modernism's concern to preserve individual agency in the face of deindividualizing culture was a fool's errand: an essential, stable selfhood was always already impossible. This chapter concludes with a discussion of how Millay, on the eve of World War II, extends this dissolution of essentialist ideas to American foreign policy; the fantasy of an isolated self, her poetry suggests, translated into a similar and dangerous fantasy of isolated nationhood.

Such poetic exaggerations of gendered expectations were not limited to poetry written by white women. Chapter 5, "E. Pauline Johnson's Poetics Acts," demonstrates how the Canadian Mohawk poet deployed her performance of "Indianness"—that is, a fantasy of Native identity that was dictated by and performed for white audiences—in order to prove that the seemingly authentic, sincere lyrical voice was a fiction. While Johnson is primarily known and studied within a Canadian context, I situate her specifically within the United States in order to focus on how American perceptions of Indianness influenced Johnson's performances—and, in turn, how Johnson manipulated these stereotypes in order to show that American selfhood was, likewise, a received idea. By drawing attention to the exclusionary logic of liberal selfhood, Johnson's poetic presentations proved that all selfhood, was, like Indianness, ultimately a performance.

Johnson (1861–1913) first achieved literary prominence in Canada in the 1880s. In 1892, a dramatic reading of her poem "A Cry from an Indian Wife" in Toronto initiated a fifteen-year performance career—she toured Canada, the United States, and England, performing as a Native princess and a Victorian lady. While I focus on Johnson's performances on the Chautauqua tour in 1907, the poetic works she performed there were published in the 1880s. To her early twentieth-century American audiences, Johnson appeared to be a real Indian princess. But this appearance had little to do with bloodlines. Her performance dress was a bricolage of accessories and garments modeled on Minnehaha, the iconic Indian princess in Henry Wadsworth Longfellow's *The Song of Hiawatha*. By adopting the tools of assimilation, Johnson's poetic acts reclaimed autonomy for Native Americans in the U.S. commercial public sphere. Appearing as and speaking through the familiar figure of Minnehaha, Johnson exaggerated the idea of a Native "voice" to foreground the performativity of such a persona. But Johnson was following the imperatives of a cultural marketplace that had dissolved the distinctions between authenticity and performance. In so doing, Johnson proves that Native American selfhood was not subject to notions of fixed identity. Rather, Johnson created public space for a new embodied and vital Indian presence, thereby short-circuiting any easy equivalency between authentic Native subjectivity and white, Minnehaha-derived fantasies. By performing Indianness, Johnson insisted on the ongoing existence of Indians precisely because they could not be equated with these commercial figures.

Conclusion: Lyric Failure

"The fate of the poor shepherd, who, blinded and lost in the snow-storm, perishes in a drift within a few feet of his cottage door, is an emblem of the state of man," writes Emerson in "The Poet" (Emerson 2001, 194). Unlike the poor shepherd, the Poet is not blinded by this snowstorm, and Emerson insists that the self-knowledge he imparts would save us, leading mankind to "the waters of life and truth" (194). But, as Emerson famously laments, "I look in vain for the poet whom I describe" (195). Emerson's dissatisfaction speaks broadly to the potential limitations of the lyric, with its self-possessed Poet, to actually help anyone recognize their full selfhood. Here, then, is the irony of lyric: lyrical poetry is an aspiration to success at the same time that it is an acknowledgment of failure.

In fact, twentieth- and twenty-first-century critics and poets seemed to agree with Emerson. Recognizing lyric as a project doomed to failure, they did not participate in Emerson's search and instead resisted what was already understood to be lyric poetry's idealization. Indeed, disputes over the idealized lyric began as early as Mill's definition of poetry and continued to the end of the nineteenth century. Herbert Tucker explains that, to poets like Robert Browning and Alfred Tennyson, "the sort of lyricism Mill admired must have seemed 'overheard' in a sense quite other than Mill intended: heard overmuch, overdone, and thus in need of being done over in fresh forms" (Tucker 1985, 227). Prins has amplified Tucker's basic contention with her argument that "Victorian verse" does not warrant reading "as an intensely subjective, personal utterance that is heard or overheard (*pace* Mill) but as the public performance of 'voice inverse,' an inversion of the figure on which lyric reading is predicated" (Prins 2008, 230). Discussing Decadent poetry, Marion Thain likewise qualifies lyric's supposed acceptance by nineteenth-century writers. Thain argues that, through the pseudonymous figure of "Michael Field," Katherine Bradley and Edith Cooper strove to avoid the singular lyric speaker; rejecting "post-Romantic lyric solitariness," their work instead privileged "the regeneration of an older, and perhaps less solipsistic, form of Elizabethan lyric voice" (Thain 2007a, 94, 93).

Despite the perception of lyric as transcendent, the existence of a kind of lyric fatigue across the nineteenth century demonstrates that poets and critics wrestled with a troublesome lyric ideal. Indeed, some poets felt the sting of failing to achieve its perfection, others rejected it outright, and some attempted to adapt its ideals to historical conditions of selfhood. Yet this fatigue may have been responsible for making lyric such a dynamic poetic form. Thain suggests that this gap between abstraction and reality "gives lyric an undeniable energy as poetic form strains against impossible content" (Thain 2007b, 226). While Thain focuses on the Decadent tradition in 1890s England, her comments articulate the notion of lyric that this book will illustrate. Lyric is a study in failure, a definition that is not coherent, a concept in conflict across the nineteenth century and into the twentieth. Lyric's "impossible content" was both implicit and, importantly, crucial for readers and writers. In fact, the poems I examine fail, and in doing so, they resist the idealism of the perfectly circumscribed yet expressive subject. Their lyrical strains do not prove that lyric was already a tired and overheard reading practice, or an exhausted and exhausting collapse of discrete poetic genres, but that lyric contained dynamic tensions within itself.

Women poets in the nineteenth century are uniquely positioned to stress these tensions. As they contend with the expectations of the Poetess persona, these authors illustrate the chasm between an imaginary ideal and historical realities. Indeed, the women writers I examine faced the impossible task of trying to create autonomous, circumscribed selfhood by communicating it. That said, these poets practiced a poetics of failure meant to revise the poetic, public, and ultimately abstract self. Antebellum poets such as Osgood, Oakes Smith, and Watkins Harper are not naïve in their promotion of a self-enclosed subject; rather, they believed that transmitting the possibility of selfhood could forge solidarity or even freedom. By the end of the nineteenth century, Millay, Johnson, and other poets had evacuated the promise of ideal selfhood that their predecessors articulated; even so, they still upheld the unity that was inspired by *belief* in the self, and in the hope of reconstituting selfhood for a modern era. In other words, these authors essay to constitute community through the mutual recognition of the self's collapse. They approach the self with the hope that failure will still enable a productive union of deficient people—and that such union will spur social change.

CHAPTER ONE

The Poetess and the Politics of Profession

If the number of citations is any indication, Virginia Jackson and Yopie Prins's 1999 article "Lyrical Studies" has definitively diagnosed the problem of the Poetess.[1] "The Poetess exemplifies the theory of her own apparent historical obscurity," they write, because "she is not the content of her own generic representation: not a speaker, not an 'I,' not a consciousness, not a subjectivity, not a voice, not a persona, not a self. The history of her generic obscurity has not yet been written because of a tendency to read 'the lyric' as a genre defined in terms of subjective expression" (V. Jackson and Prins 1999, 523). Jackson and Prins provide a framework for understanding why there are so many recursive readings of Poetess and lyrical poems. Over the course of the twentieth century, they argue, the legacy of lyric reading exacerbated the Poetess's obscurity. The Poetess is "generic," Jackson argues, because she is "an essentially empty figure that circulates in lyrics as a vehicle of cultural transmission" (V. Jackson 2005, 210). She was—and continues to be—displaced from her own writing. The result is a figure "forgotten in the very process of being remembered" (V. Jackson and Prins 1999, 521).

To make matters worse, the Poetess substantially contributed, Jackson has recently argued, to the elaboration of the lyric subject—in other words, the Poetess created her own obscurity. In fact, Jackson suggests that we may have the Poetess to blame for lyricization's idealized, ahistorical subjectivity. At the same time that "an idealized figure of the Poetess emerged," over the course of the nineteenth century, "an idealized genre of poetry progressively replaced most social (including didactic or pedagogical) uses of verse" (V. Jackson 2011, 58). The Poetess came to presage lyrical reading practices inasmuch as she was increasingly understood as a figure whose poetry offered no "protocol of genre" (68). Given the figure's idealized emptiness, it is hard to imagine actual women writers as Poetesses.[2] Indeed, Jackson concludes that "neither Sigourney nor Wheatley (nor any other historical person) could actually *be* a Poetess anymore [*sic*] than any writer before the late nineteenth century could be a lyric poet" (68).[3]

But for all these claims about the genericness, emptiness, and obscurity of the Poetess, how do we account for the fact that Lydia Sigourney's and Phillis Wheatley's works *were* read as Poetess poems? These poems were understood to be written by an imagined Poetess persona tied to historical names.

Indeed, Poetess poems encouraged readers and writers to imagine all the human forms Jackson and Prins identify: a speaker, an "I," a consciousness, a subjectivity, a voice, a persona, a self. The Poetess's problem was not her detachment from subjectivity but, I argue, the opposite: her problem was that she was too closely identified with the imaginary "I" of lyrical poetry. In fact, she was so closely identified with this ideal "I" that the imaginary was taken as reality. The Jackson/Prins critique of the Poetess's lyrical idealization anticipates a critical complication: the Poetess simultaneously existed and exists as an individual identity and a literary abstraction. Alexandra Socarides perhaps best summarizes the difficulty of navigating this division; she writes, "It is the great challenge of all investigations into and explorations of the poetess, then, to balance the fact that real women wrote real poems throughout the nineteenth century and that they were, even at the very time of writing, already being abstracted as well as abstracting themselves" (Socarides 2018, 131).

This chapter grapples with the disjunction between the biographical poet and the full-blown imaginary Poetess. What seems to be missing from critical accounts of the Poetess is the answer to why nineteenth-century literary culture desired what Prins calls "the figure of a figure" (Prins 2012, 1052). By attending to the poetic practices that signaled Poetess reading and writing, I attempt to delimit the specific social and political historical purposes that the Poetess served. In other words, this chapter identifies some of the commonly held beliefs that constituted the generic and idealized figure so that we might understand the social utility of the abstraction. I will not put an end to the vacillation between Prins's "figure of a figure" and Socarides's "real women," but hopefully make the moves clearer.[4]

Unsurprisingly, these contemporary critical complexities were unimportant to nineteenth-century readers, for whom the Poetess was a recognizable persona and poetic practice in much the same fashion as lyrical poetry. Just as lyrical poems directed readers to imagine overhearing the intimate thoughts of a self, Poetess poems encouraged those same readers to imagine that they were inadvertently granted access to the interiority of a feminized poetic persona. But due to the cultural assumptions attached to women writers, accidental access to a feminized poetic privacy was seen as actual, not imaginary. These poems did not just articulate imaginary situations and feelings, but appeared to directly reflect the emotional states and true womanliness of their authors; this "I" was no fiction but on some level the author herself speaking. These practices resulted in the tension between abstract figure and biographical poet described above, as readers collapsed the distance between poet and poem. Indeed, biographical markers were taken as fodder for the abstraction of individual writers into the generic Poetess. For instance, the names, images, and even signatures of women poets were often printed and circulated right alongside their poems. Such material "is not 'the poetess herself,'" Prins writes, "but a reflection on her personification . . . simultaneously empty and infinitely productive" (Prins 2012, 1052). The distinction by name, image, and signature exists only to place women poets in the same generic category and render them indistinguishable.

To put it another way: biographical markers became evidence of universal womanly feeling, or grist for the Poetess mill, so to speak. Individual women poets were received as the generic and idealized Poetess whether they liked it or not due to this collapse between poet and poem that turned individual names (and faces) into generic personifications. Reception as an abstraction caused both short- and long-term problems for women writers. Despite the similarities between Poetess and lyric, the Poetess was not understood to figure the self-possession of lyric's idealized subject. The figure of a figure or reflection of a personification echoed a similarly feeble, ephemeral selfhood attributed to women in nineteenth-century U.S. society and politics. What critics perceive as the Poetess's abstraction actually speaks to the working premises of transatlantic liberalism across the nineteenth century. This chapter will address the liberal selfhood that has been left out of discussions of the Poetess, arguing that it is the background against which the genre emerged. In other words, the Poetess is based on the liberal selfhood that women were denied. Only consider the ease with which the expectation that women lacked self-sovereignty was reiterated in the widespread perception among critics and readers that female poets inadvertently exposed their interiority. In which case, we can see how poetic practices corresponded to political philosophy. Because they were understood as abstractions voicing generic feminine feeling, the poets who were read as Poetesses could not be considered self-possessed public personas, echoing American women's own experience of the same political dissociation.

Seen in self-reflexive poetic practices and in the critical conversation surrounding her, liberal ideology is baked into the Poetess. Crucially, the Poetess genre does not simply rehearse the political disenfranchisement of women. Rather, I argue, women poets engage with the public Poetess persona in order to contest the expectations that shaped the discourses and institutions of literature and liberalism alike. Gendered assumptions—the association of female poet with poem and utterance with interiority—actually allowed the Poetess to manipulate the terms of her reception. By fashioning lyrical moments that encouraged readers to gaze upon the feminized interiority of a figured Poetess, Poetess poems either assert woman's fitness for or expose the fantasy of the liberal, self-possessed ideal. Far from signifying a simple, sentimental figure of feeling, the Poetess served a political purpose inasmuch as she foregrounded the rights of women and considered poetry to offer a form of resistance. Jackson's empty "vehicle of cultural transmission" (V. Jackson 2005, 210) appears to have a more politically motivated purpose; as Lootens asks: "Defining, separating, politicking the innocent, domestic fantasy 'hearts' of nations: what processes could be more public, more political—and, in this, more likely to prove deeply contested?" (Lootens 2016, 8). It is no coincidence that the women who wrote Poetess poems also took a stand for women's rights, abolition, Native American rights, and many of the other progressive social issues of this era. In fact, print publication and public circulation provided the means to stake a claim to public autonomy. As Elizabeth Dillon argues, "Print—a medium in which bodies are, precisely, absent because only words remain present—theoretically produces the writer as an abstract liberal subject" (Dillon 2004, 25). By foregrounding the supposedly pure privacy associated with the Poetess persona, the writers I examine were attempting to translate prevailing forms of public possession into female self-possession. For women in a public sphere that would not grant them the status of liberal subjects, this genre's publicity offered agency—with the caveat that this agency was achieved as the imaginary, abstract Poetess.

Charming Sisters of Song

This endeavor on the part of women poets to reshape the contours of the liberal subject was made possible, in no small part, by the wild popularity of women's poetry at midcentury.[5] Indeed, the wide circulation and subsequent reprinting of anthologies—examples include John Keese's *The Poets of America* (1840), Rufus Wilmot Griswold's *Gems from Female Poets* (1842) and *The Female Poets of America* (1849), Caroline May's *The American Female Poets* (1848), and Thomas Read's *The Female Poets of America* (1848)—attest to the existence of a "steady contemporary readership" (Socarides 2017, 186). But this popularity came at a cost, as the anthologies' criteria for selection worked to perpetuate the abstraction of women writers in the public sphere. As Socarides puts it, anthologies of women's poetry did not enshrine women poets as autonomous artists but "positioned these poets both everywhere and nowhere" (186). Furthermore, these anthologies make clear their preference for a specific subset of conventions in Poetess poetry—in particular, for the poetic practices that underscored culturally held expectations regarding the non-autonomy of women poets and speakers. Such conventions were both restrictive and enabling: on the one hand, threatening to dissolve the agency of individual women writers into an indistinct cliché and, on the other hand, making clear the devices that women writers would need to deploy in order to stake a claim for female self-possession.

The nineteenth-century publishing industry contributed to the Poetess's problems by divesting female authors of their professional autonomy even as it established their public presence. As the spread of anthologies suggests, poetry was ubiquitous in nineteenth-century America, and most poetry appeared in popular, widely circulating periodicals such as newspapers, magazines, and gift books. Once published, each of these pieces was then available to be reprinted and circulated by other publishers in other publications.[6] But republication occurred without crediting or compensating the author. Because the venues for publishing poetry were so scattered, obtaining a copyright was not a viable solution. In the antebellum era, a copyright on a poem would restrict "the author's right in a work to the words on the page," which was useful in the case of a work written entirely by one author, such as a collection of poems (Homestead 2005, 156). But because poems often appeared singly, obtaining a copyright for each individual piece was nearly impossible for publishers and authors (156).[7] Editors were expected to at least credit the source of these items, but this did not mean that the poet herself was attributed, and the poet was certainly not paid.[8] These copyright conditions applied across genres and genders—male writers experienced the same problems.[9] But as Melissa Homestead points out, "A women writer's problematic relationship to publicity and property" made these issues harder for women to address (153).

Indeed, women were not recognized as autonomous authors because they were legally denied the rights attending proprietary selfhood. As Barbara Welke explains, "Women entered public life in the nineteenth century not as full-rights-bearing individuals as men were, but as help-meets of the state through marriage" (Welke 2010, 67). Under the laws of coverture, "a woman's legal identity was 'covered' by her husband's identity at marriage" (65). As her lack of legal personhood might suggest, a married woman was barred from acquiring or owning property. This injustice was amplified for the married female author, whose "literary labors" and "property produced by those labors . . . [was] vested in her husband, not her" (Homestead 2005, 28). Legal injustices continued even after mid-nineteenth-century reforms to coverture, which could not overcome the ongoing expectation that women's work in the home was not work, but a labor of love (Welke 2010, 66; Dillon 2004, 201). Homestead argues that this state of affairs—in which the "courts were reluctant to grant married women control over their own persons and their labors, especially labors in the home"—was not without consequences for women writers (Homestead 2005, 33). After all, it was the home that "was . . . for the nineteenth-century woman author, the primary site of literary production" (33).

Publishing and legal policies were not the end of women poets' troubles. To further complicate matters, the Poetess had professional reasons to be wary of success. Or, as Jennifer Putzi puts it, her very professionalism "becomes a potential liability" (Putzi 2012, 780). Because fame could trigger accusations of profligate self-promotion, the more a Poetess published and the more popular she became, the more she was required to practice a modesty that often edged toward self-abnegation. "To deny writing for public consumption" was, Angela Sorby explains, "a common feint among nineteenth-century sentimental poets, particularly women" (Sorby 2005, 429). Willingly or not, professionalism was to be denied, for it was better to be thought an accidental and honest Poetess than an unscrupulous businesswoman out to make money. The writing that often accompanied women's poetry in print, such as editors' introductions or commentaries, rehearsed this feint; editors dismissed professionalism under the assumption that women poets could not help but profess sincere feminine emotion in their poems and, in so doing, inadvertently offer up their interiority for public consumption. Of course, what is also clear is the predicament that such dissimulative practices generated for women poets—even as the popularity of the Poetess allowed women writers to advocate for their sovereign selfhood, the lack of professionalism associated with this figure also contributed to their obscurity.

Take, for example, *A Gallery of Distinguished English and American Female Poets*, also referred to as the *Gallery of Famous Poetesses*, by Henry Coppée, published in 1860 (Duyckinck 1881, 810). Coppée, a canny self-promoter, writes in the introduction's first sentence that his "design" is "to bring together, in one illustrious company, the most charming sisters of song" (Coppée 1860, xi). Coppée's introduction illustrates how the literary institutions working to define and promote the genre were also responsible for the Poetess's professional dilemmas. Consider one of Coppée's typical usages of "Poetess," a term he often uses in his rhapsodic flights about women poets: "Passing to the poetesses whose works are here so radiantly exhibited," he writes, "we are at once attracted into some philosophic fancies as to the sphere and characteristics of woman in the world of literature" (xiii). Admittedly, Coppée's own conceptual slippages make this a difficult task; his tendency is to consider all women as Poetesses and to merge all female poets with their poems. But some distinctions do emerge: in his telling, what appears to distinguish the Poetess specifically from the female poet more generally is the former's publicity. Poetess poets are authors who have achieved the status of publication and some name recognition; in other words, they are poets with a public presence. But this public presence doesn't speak for itself, and Coppée seizes the responsibility to teach readers the value of women's poetry, a value explicitly on display in his collection. Here, readers will find "finer feelings" and "nobler sentiments" from which they can "gather new strength and vigor" (xviii). His editorial prescriptions for readers arrogate Poetesses' power to legitimize their poetry to himself, inherently an act of amateurizing these writers.

Indeed, what made women's poetry so attractive to readers, Coppée suggests, was its amateurism or, put another way, its offer of women's publicity precisely in the absence of professionalism. What this amateur publicity promised to readers, then, was an irresistible—because it was, on the poet's part, seemingly inadvertent—peek into the interiority of women writers.[10] Such peeks stopped short of salaciousness; after all, it was understood that what women's poems primarily offered was spiritual insight. Nevertheless, the idea of an invasion, no matter how modest, intensified the allure of these poems. In other words, this allure depended on the effacement of the writers' professional skill. Motivated by their own interest to become legitimators of culture, editors such as Coppée instead embraced the rhetoric of natural affinities. For instance, the idealized Poetess was "gifted with the spirit of song, and the power of impassioned utterance," and her poetry is "the voice of Nature and of God" speaking through her (Coppée 1860, xiv, xii). The Poetess's poetic powers were not hers to claim or control, nor for that matter was the exposure of her interior. According to Coppée, the inadvertent expression of privacy—"the story of her heart"—was as unconscious and involuntary a process for a woman poet as "her respiration" (Coppée 1860, xiv). It is an uncontrollable act of self-treachery, "betraying to us unconsciously her own identity" (xiv). The appearance of unprofessionalism was, paradoxically, the mark of the profession because this appearance worked to guarantee the poetry's sincerity. Coppée therefore asserts that the women included in his anthology lacked professional aspirations; he reports that "many would repress [their heart-melodies] if they could" (xv).

While advertising the amateurish qualities of his collection seems counterintuitive, comparison with the male poet's professional acumen allows

Coppée to foreground the purity of the Poetess's accidental achievement. He writes, "Longfellow, and Lowell, Whittier, and Holmes, are poets by name and profession. They stand before the world, each with his innumerable constituency expectant and admiring; and thus, like the orator's, their work, although inspired by nature, is essentially the work of art. Much of the voluminous writings of the great poets becomes mechanical. But, from secluded homes, from the midst of household duties,—woman's truest *profession*,—the daughters of song send forth, bird-like, sweet heart-melodies, which can no more be restrained than the voice of the morning lark, or the plaintive sounds of the nightingale" (Coppée 1860, xiv–xv). Male poets are professionals; they demonstrate a craft and skill that qualifies as art. Coppée's recognition of "poets by name and profession"—Holmes, Longfellow, Lowell, Whittier—suggests that professionalism grants male artists a legacy and a name. His simile, "like the orator's," reveals the logic of gender, genre, and publicity at the heart of this historical moment: it is an effort to align male poetry with the distinctly public genre of oratory, whereas women's poetry is private and, well, just poetry. Nevertheless, masculine artworks can become "mechanical," or formulaic, bearing the marks of intentional production. Meanwhile, women's fitness for domestic duties means that their poetic utterances are unpolished but, for that same reason, more natural. Because women poets were, Coppée writes, "often unlearned in criticism, unskilled in rythmic [*sic*] rules, the intuitive soul of the poetess comes forth like the incantation of the hidden oracle" (xv). As an anonymous member of the domestic sphere with no "expectant" readership, the female poet has a different "*profession*" in both line of work and declaration. Despite not naming a single female poet in the quote above, Coppée nevertheless endeavors to highlight the celebrities whose works are featured in his anthology, a process that occurs in the apparent absence of professionalism. Here we can see the primary problem of being a Poetess: the very publicity that constitutes the Poetess also contributes to her generic forgettableness. In other words, a "name and profession" only served their male counterparts.

Women poets could not claim individuality when they "enact[ed] a naturalized art performed as if flowing through them" (Lootens 2016, 4). As a result, Lootens argues, "to sign 'Poetess' is, then, to practice signature as a form of erasure: it is to sign 'Nobody'" (3–4). As one who cannot help but expose her interior, and one whose artistic merit is attributable to other forces working through her, the Poetess becomes a nameless and therefore generic literary product. Individual women poets were famous—indeed, a town in Iowa is even named for Lydia Sigourney—but the qualities that made them popular were the same ones that made them generic and forgettable (Kramer 1940, 166). In fact, Coppée's efforts to distinguish his Poetesses by "outward form and appearance" speaks to how specificity perversely becomes obscurity (Coppée 1860, xv). Coppée includes "striking and excellent portraits" of these women writers, as well as reproductions of their signatures (xv). All these individual markers attest to the belief that Poetesses were made for public consumption. Their very image and interiority, and even their signature, did not evince their artistic self-possession but rather their public self-dissolution into inherently womanly—and not individual—qualities. A glance at an anthology's table of contents conveys as much, as the "sheer number of poets included in these books" suggests that editors "were not interested in whittling the mass of women poets down to a special few through whom the nation could define its female poetic tradition" (Socarides 2017, 188). For Coppée, each author's portrait may give a sense of the Poetess's "identity"; but "when the writing of many are taken together, they are the exponent of woman's general character" (Coppée 1860, xiv). It is easy for Coppée to construe the Poetess poem as an emanation of woman's "general character" precisely because the Poetess is "general" by design, figured only by the accidental expression of her womanly emotion. Coppée appears to give voice to the flourishing of the Poetess as a persona bereft of any historical particularity or professional legacy.

We can be forgiven for thinking that the Poetess's case sounds hopeless. Critics tend to agree. According to Lootens, if the Poetess "does anything gloriously, it is to fail; if she belongs anywhere, it is on the edge of dissolution" (Lootens 2016, 4). Yet, I argue, this critical consensus has missed something productive in her "dissolution." The ways that professional self-abnegation, publishing industry protocols, and public consumption of privacy shaped the Poetess all speak to the consequences of liberalism on political life in the United States. And as a result of public, professional, and publishing demands, the Poetess was positioned to strain against the boundaries of belonging that liberalism had set. Even in the pages of Coppée's collection, "the poetesses . . . so radiantly exhibited" were also exhibiting a selfhood that responded to women's unsuitability for liberal subjectivity (Coppée 1860, xiii). Despite their being denied professional autonomy, I argue that women writing as Poetesses could contest the stipulations barring women from lyrical and liberal self-possession. I want to explore the possibility that Poetess poems encode public self-possession within the very exposure of those same figures' privacy.

Frances Sargent Osgood's Profession

Coppée's "gallery" of Poetesses illustrates how poetic "professions" effectively barred women writers from achieving the status of professionals. To deny these poets the protections of professionalism, the public need only cite the Poetess's accidental exposure of her interiority. To add insult to injury, the public also claimed this interiority as its property. And yet the rhetoric of professionalism did offer a means of resisting the prevailing assumptions about women writers. In order to reclaim their public names and faces, and even their signatures from editors and publishers, women writing as Poetesses would need to accomplish the seemingly impossible: namely, to signal their professionalism. As this task suggests, these women writers understood professionalism as one way to mark the absence or presence of liberal selfhood in public. To be recognized as a professional effectively signaled an author's self-possession: the professional possesses skills that denote property in the self.[11] In turn, this self-possession is publicly confirmed by compensation and name recognition. For the Poetess, professionalism would mean that her supposed profession of interiority would no longer dissolve into the public sphere. Instead, her interiority would belong to her, as proven by the fact that she was accredited and paid for her work.

The tension between public professionalism and the expression of unpolished privacy is perhaps no better depicted than in the work of Frances Sargent Osgood, a writer whom nineteenth-century critics regarded as "pure womanly" (Griswold 1850, 131).[12] But even though Osgood "personified the Poetess," her version of the figure was not all pious femininity (Richards 2004, 62). As Richards has argued, Osgood's Poetess was "a figure of Fancy, an ethereal feminine sprite with enchanting gifts of mobility, spontaneous invention, and seduction" (62). We should not underestimate the importance of such seductiveness. Indeed, Richards insists that "the hallmark of Osgood's work" was its "unlocalizable eroticism" (60). Osgood's fanciful Poetess allowed readers to eroticize glimpses of her interior; in turn, the Poetess's flightiness ensured that such moments of "sexual charm" remain fleeting and, for that reason, seem all the more accidental (72). We can see how such a reception would ensure Osgood's popularity at the same time that it suggested her accidental and amateur status.

While such flirtatiousness, accidental or otherwise, might suggest that she could not be taken as a serious professional, Osgood makes professional assertions of liberal selfhood by playing on seemingly innocent erotics. As the consummate Poetess, it is unsurprising that in her poetry Osgood points to how that figure was disadvantaged by her profession. Osgood addresses these problems in poems specifically about the "profession" of the Poetess. These poems—"To My Pen," "To a Slandered Poetess," and "To an Idea That Wouldn't 'Come'"—are not examples of autobiography as such, but of a poet's self-awareness about the Poetess's reception in the antebellum era. These poems were published separately in the late 1840s in periodicals such as the *Ladies' Repository*, *Sartains Magazine*, and *Graham's*.[13] When collected for Osgood's 1850 *Poems*, the three were printed consecutively in the order listed above. Taken together, their placement suggests that Osgood or her editors might have tried to eroticize professionalism by providing a behind-the-scenes glimpse of the Poetess's process. But Osgood is using the motif of exposure as an opportunity to display the expectations that women writers must navigate. In other words, the trade "secrets" that these poems exhibit are actually the barriers, Osgood insists, that prevent the public female poet from fashioning a circumscribed, autonomous subjectivity. Regarding this supposedly sought-after and stable subjectivity, I will also discuss Osgood's poem "Caprice." Although the poem does not explicitly address the concerns of women's writing in the same manner as the three other poems, it appeals to the rhetoric of amateurism to capture the predicament of the woman poet who would be a professional. Instructive as it may be, Osgood's response to the woman writer's predicament is, admittedly, self-defeating: her attempt to remedy it required her to deploy amateurism as a professional tool.

"To My Pen" only acknowledges the conventions of decorum associated with Poetess poetry so it can break them. The personified pen has no sense of propriety: it wanders too much, it speaks too bluntly, and sometimes it tells little lies:

Dost know, my little vagrant pen,
That wanderest lightly down the paper,
Without a thought how critic men
May carp at every careless caper,—

Dost know, twice twenty thousand eyes,
If publishers report them truly,
Each month may mark the sportive lies
That track, oh shame! thy steps unruly?
—Osgood 1850b, 169

In these opening stanzas, Osgood appears to echo Anne Bradstreet's "Prologue" in order to evoke a legacy of American women writers who were subject to the same public scrutiny.[14] The similarities start in the opening lines of

Bradstreet's poem, which also attributes agency to an inanimate object—her "mean Pen," she writes, could not possibly "sing" of "superior things" (Bradstreet 1967, 15). Likewise, Osgood's use of the word "carp" to characterize her critical reception also recalls Bradstreet, who writes, "I am obnoxious to each carping tongue / Who says my hand a needle better fits" (16).

However, Osgood is not simply rehearsing Bradstreet's techniques. Unlike Osgood, Bradstreet shifts her focus and lodges agency within herself; she, not her pen, is the "obnoxious" subject. Osgood exaggerates Bradstreet's metonymy by describing how her pen acts with a mind all its own in order to articulate the dilemmas that confront women writers. She knows that "twice twenty thousand eyes" will read the pen's antics, and she feels "shame" that "sportive lies" receive such attention. On the one hand, the Poetess is believed to profess unconscious sincerity; as Coppée demonstrated, the intentional manipulation of expression was absent from women's writing. Yet sincerity without self-awareness is invariably punished; "critic men" will "carp" about what she writes. Osgood's solution is indirect. Deflecting a more direct challenge to the root of the problem, that is, women's professional recognition, Osgood instead addresses the issue by placing agency elsewhere. It has not been Osgood talking, but her pen. She places a mediating object between herself and her audience that allows her to address the "unruly" subject of the Poetess's professionalism, but in so doing she highlights precisely her own unprofessional lack of agency.

Here we can see Osgood struggling to diagnose the problems of female public writing without having much recourse to change publishing practices. She attempts to take the tone of the skilled professional, but she dispenses contradictory advice on how to behave properly. These recommendations stem from—and are Osgood's way of self-consciously highlighting—the inconsistencies of the Poetess genre. This antithetical advice shows how she must nevertheless undermine her own status in order to point out the Poetess's predicament. For the pen's improprieties, the speaker chides, "Be never wild or false again, / But 'mind your Ps and Qs,' you rover!" (Osgood 1850b, 169). Such advice implies that, unlike her pen, the Poetess is always gentle and sincere. The expression "mind your Ps and Qs" reinforces the sense that women writers must mind their manners, but at the same time creates a parallel between their writing and a popular saying: both are clichéd, generic. Two stanzas later the speaker ignores precisely these stipulations. She advises boldness in the pursuit of originality, demanding, "I would not have my pen pursue / The 'beaten track'—a slave for ever; / No! roam as thou wert wont to do" (170). Such unladylike boldness would seem to affirm that minding "Ps and Qs" means slavishly following the "beaten track" by writing what Richards, in her reading of this poem, calls “recycled maxims” (Richards 2004, 87). In these lines, Osgood criticizes the contradictory advice that female poets must follow.[15] Yet voicing such criticism leads her to the same predicament: by scolding an inanimate, fanciful object, Osgood deflates her own artistic integrity.

This poem suggests that Osgood wants to appear unfettered, but such boldness would be unwholesome for one “mark[ed]” by tens of thousands of eyes. Professional practices dictate that she cannot enjoy such freedom. By addressing the pen, Osgood can nevertheless coyly assert her opinion while removing her own self from public scrutiny. Just as the pen “miss’d the task,” readers likewise looking for Osgood “miss’d” her and instead get her pen. This is not a solution, but a workaround to the Poetess’s privacy and propriety:

But what is this? you’ve tripp’d about,
While I the mentor grave was playing;
And here you’ve written boldly out
The very words that I was saying!

And here, as usual, on you’ve flown
From right to left—flown fast and faster,
Till even while you wrote it down.
You’ve miss’d the task you ought to master.
—Osgood 1850b, 172

This surprise is, of course, carefully planned by Osgood, and the accidental frankness testifies to the supposed unprofessionalism of the Poetess. In order to write “boldly” she must appear to write by accident. Osgood shows the bind she is in: in order to speak out about professional pressures and to write unfettered by convention, she must become a “master” of “miss[ing] the task.” Amateurism is both the professional practice and the professional undoing of the Poetess.

Following “To My Pen” is the poem “To a Slandered Poetess,” which also examines the public scrutiny that attends the Poetess’s profession. In this poem, an unnamed speaker addresses “my brilliant Blue Belle” and encourages her to rise above false public opinion (Osgood 1850b, 172). To accuse a Poetess of slander discredits the very (un)professional ethos the Poetess traffics in—the inadvertent expression of sincerity. The speaker advises the poor Poetess to ignore this indictment. In fact, she’s surprised that this Poetess would even be flustered:

My brilliant Blue Belle! droop no more;
    But let them mock, and mow, and mutter!

I marvel, though a whirlwind roar,
  Your eagle soul should deign to flutter!
—Osgood 1850b, 172

If the Poetess's pure soul has been discredited, the solution is not to confront the disrepute directly but to transcend it. This sounds like good advice, but for Osgood it is a strategy that complies with the cultural expectations that associate the Poetess with higher matters. Since she accidentally professes divine insight, the Poetess is believed to exist on some plane above the literary marketplace. However, Osgood hints that transcendence does not solve but merely diagnoses the root problem of professional recognition and the self-possession it entails. Public opinion should not bother her; yet as a public figure and as a creation of the literary marketplace, public opinion is what makes or breaks the Poetess. This speaker therefore acts as if negative publicity does not have a direct bearing on decidedly unfeminine concerns like compensation or professional reputation. Although she cannot solve these problems, by emphasizing amateurism, Osgood is able to draw attention to the issues that accompany the public woman poet.

The speaker's insistence that Blue Belle ignore the slander begins to feel like an exaggeration designed to point out the impossible position of the Poetess. Indeed, the Poetess is a figure dependent on public circulation and consumption, but must somehow simultaneously transcend common opinion. The speaker continues to remind Blue Belle of the blinders the Poetess must put on, advising her to keep writing lyrical poems because their musicality transcends the discord of everyday life: "Remember it is Music's law, / Each *pure, true* note, though low you sound it, / Is heard through Discord's wildest war" (Osgood 1850b, 173). Because the Poetess sounds the "*true* note," she is above the slanderous opinions of literary critics. Such idealized, abstract lyricality, however, contributed to the Poetess's abstraction. And indeed, this transcendence helps construct the Poetess persona but also dictates her professional compensation, or lack thereof—how do you compensate someone who is supposedly above the pettiness of pay? The last stanza of the poem explains the kind of payment the Poetess can expect:

Oh! think how poor in all the wealth
  That makes *your* frame a fairy palace—
The mind's pure light—the heart's sweet health,—
  Are they whose dearest joy is malice.
—Osgood 1850b, 174

The Poetess possesses wealth in her pure mind and her sweet heart. She is so rich in this internal goodness that her person is a "fairy palace," transcendent, yes, but still imaginary. In this poem Osgood diagnoses more of the abstractions that accompany the Poetess's publicity and professionalism. When women exist in public, they do not present full subjects but partial ones. They are disembodied as objects or transcendent abstractions. In other words, these poems demonstrate how Poetess poems strain to access liberal selfhood by presenting a public self, but are doomed to fail in the Poetess's lack of self-possession. Indeed, Blue Belle needs to be reminded that she has property in herself, yet that property is imaginary, ephemeral, fairy-like—as well as on display for readers.

In the poem that follows "To My Pen" and "To a Slandered Poetess," Osgood continues to reflect on the Poetess's public and partial presence. "To an Idea That Wouldn't 'Come'" imagines a poet begging an idea to "come" to her. Her "happy pen your host shall be"; she will "dress" the idea "in the prettiest words" and let it "sip the purest ink" (Osgood 1850b, 176). This plea has a decidedly sexy side as the poet pleads with the idea to come to her private closet or bedroom where she boasts that a "virgin page awaits thee" and no "softer," "fairer," or "nicer couch" (175). Osgood implicates all Poetesses in an inevitable promiscuity because they must circulate in public in order to exist. But because she addresses an idea and not a person, the erotic tone of this request is neutralized. This turnaround is more than just a flirtatious trick. The displacement of agency onto an object rather than her Poetess persona grants Osgood greater control over her reception, but at the same time this act ensures her partial subjectivity. She can be bold without appearing improper; she can speak sincerely without exposing her entire interior, yet these actions come at the cost of partial self-possession and accidental artistry.

The poem more explicitly turns toward professional concerns when the speaker mentions her Poetess colleagues. The poet implores the idea to abandon other Poetesses and "fly them all, and fly to me!" (Osgood 1850b, 176). Although acknowledging other female poets by name, the speaker is nevertheless reinforcing the convention that ideas visit women, which is to say, women do not create or possess ideas themselves. This amateurizing account of women's writing continues to affirm the limitations of the Poetess figure. She was "available for occupancy but also advertis[ed] [her] vacancy," both a personification of a specific name and an empty figure to be visited by poetic inspiration (Prins 2012, 1052):

Whether around the dainty tip
  Of Whitman's pen you hover,

Or rest on Greenwood's rosy lip,
To greet some poet-lover;

Or hide in glorious Hewitt's heart
Until you're robed divinely;
Or lend impassion'd Eva's line
The glow she paints so finely.
—Osgood 1850b, 176

Osgood disembodies her figured colleagues by turning them into synecdoches. The poet Sarah Helen Whitman is reduced to her pen, Grace Greenwood to a lip, and Mary E. Hewitt to a heart. The evocation of Elizabeth Oakes Smith asserts the practice of equating poet with poem; she is not even herself but her poetic character, Eva. Just as Whitman, Greenwood, Hewitt, and Oakes Smith become disembodied and depersonalized, Osgood too recognizes that her public persona will always be disabled by gendered literary expectations: the Poetess cannot circulate as a full person in public; she can only circulate as an object or body part.

In sum, then, Osgood's speakers address the Poetess's occupations, in both senses of the term: the matters that concern her, such as her pen, her friend, and an idea, as well as the business of being a professional poet. As we can see, her partial professionalism derives from women's status in the liberal public sphere. The Poetess may have to profess her unprofessionalism and disassemble her sovereign self in order to have a public presence, but, for Osgood, such feints offer a kind of strategy. Despite her failure to achieve full self-possession in public, Osgood sees this partial subjectivity as a way to protest the Poetess's absolute abstraction and consumption by her publics. The Poetess's partialness suggests that readers could never fully possess her, only parts of her. In Osgood's poem "Caprice," this attempt to resist dispossession only emphasizes the Poetess's partial subjectivity. For that reason, many critics regard the Poetess as, ultimately, a figure of failure—even if, as Lootens concludes, the Poetess failed "gloriously" (Lootens 2016, 4). Yet I would again insist that there exists the kernel of something productive in the Poetess. Perched "on the edge of dissolution," the Poetess nevertheless sketches some semblance of agency by gesturing to the woman writer's ability to harness her dissolution (4). Here, perhaps, is a small victory; after all, it is better to possess part of yourself than no part at all.

"Caprice" is the first poem in Osgood's section of Coppée's 1860 anthology. Like the poems discussed above, it was previously published in magazines before its inclusion in Osgood's collected *Poems*.[16] In the context of Coppée's collection, the articulation of gendered stereotypes in this poem is especially meaningful, as "Caprice" would seem to perfectly execute his prescriptions for reading women poets. Coppée contends that Osgood "is one of the greatest American favorites, because her large heart seemed open to the finest and most universal sentiments." Her moral purity and innocence were assured, according to Coppée, by the prevalence of children in her poetry and "in her affections" (Coppée 1860, xxii). Presumably, the portrait of Osgood that Coppée includes displays these sentiments. It was one of a few images of the poet that was circulating at the time, and similar versions of the portrait appear in the anthologies edited by May and Read, as well as in Osgood's own collected *Poems*. In the case of May's anthology, Osgood's image served as the frontispiece, a placement that "inherently called attention to Osgood as representative of the poetess" (Socarides 2018, 139). The proliferation of this portrait, or some version of it, suggests, then, that Osgood was the Poetess personified, as Socarides argues in her article "The Poetess at Work." By "the end of the 1840s," Socarides writes, "[Osgood's] portrait came to supplant that of the anonymous poetess that had circulated earlier." But as "the face of the American woman poet" she was, indeed, only a face; these images of Osgood lack "accompanying writerly paraphernalia" (139). As a result, the image also intimates an erotic appeal: the absence of professional markers suggests both a womanly and an amateur lack of self-possession. Like the other portraits and signatures in Coppée's collection, such material encourages us to "read" it alongside the literature in order to better consume the interiority of the figured poet; in the correspondence between poetic expression and facial expression, we seem to have unfettered access to the Poetess's personality.

And yet, this most idiosyncratic imagery—portrait and signature—actually worked to create a kind of generic Poetess stereotype. We know this is Osgood, but there is not much else to distinguish her from the other women pictured in Coppée's work. The majority are depicted from the neck up with pleasant expressions, large eyes, and tightly coiffed hair that displays their unfurrowed foreheads.[17] The effect suggests some kind of pseudo-physiognomy of female poets whose facial features communicate, in the context of Coppée's anthology, inherent sincerity, accidental artistry, and, as a result, feminine homogeneity. Such expectations then dictate the reading experience that should accompany poems such as "Caprice"; readers can enjoy Osgood's playful mode because her portrait denotes the "beautiful but plain, direct but deep" persona of the Poetess (Socarides 2018, 139). While the imagery would seem to override the poem's impulsivity, I argue that Coppée's visualizations

Frances Sargent Osgood

FRANCES SARGENT OSGOOD.

CAPRICE.

Reprove me not that still I change
With every changing hour,
For glorious Nature gives me leave
In wave, and cloud, and flower.

Portrait of Frances Sargent Osgood from Henry Coppée, *A Gallery of Distinguished English and American Female Poets* (Philadelphia: E. H. Butler, 1860).

help to foreground precisely the problems that Osgood attempts to solve. In this poem, Osgood launches a poetic persona who dispossesses herself in an attempt to reach beyond the social restrictions placed on women.

With "Caprice," as well as other poems that depict fanciful, feminized figures, Osgood seems to be clueing readers in to her own sunny but shifting disposition:

> Reprove me not that still I change
> With every changing hour,
> For glorious Nature gives me leave
> In wave, and cloud, and flower.

And you and all the world would do—
 If all but dared—the same.
True to myself—if false to you—
 Why should I reck your blame?

Then cease your carping, cousin mine,
 Your vain reproaches cease;
I revel in my right divine,
 I glory in Caprice!
—Qtd. in Coppée 1860, 230–31

Of course, Caprice's instability has the type of ambiguous consequences with which, by now, we have become familiar. As both asset and liability, the speaker espouses womanly feeling that makes her publicly popular. But her capriciousness disqualifies her from the self-sovereignty of liberalism, as well as from its attendant rights.

Yet capriciousness is the strategy whereby Osgood attempts to make self-possession possible. Despite the figure's apparent flakiness, I argue that Osgood uses "Caprice" to model a strategy for preserving women's self-possession in public. This approach relies on the very instability that defines capriciousness. While her poems may create fanciful figures who could be taken for Osgood, capriciousness works to undercut the sense that they could ever quite be her. The poet does offer herself, but simultaneously recedes from the poem—we learn that only part of her is available, that is, whatever mood she happens to be displaying at the moment. Osgood provides Caprice as her proxy, just as her poems about a pen, a Poetess, and an idea diverted unmediated poetic expression through an addressee. These poems frustrate any sense that we have unfettered access to Osgood. By asserting that she is just beyond the public's possession, Osgood's poems suggest that women's self-possession is perhaps possible through—and not prohibited by—public recognition and circulation. Indeed, it is a strategy for all women:

'Tis helpless woman's right divine,
 Her only right, Caprice!

And I will mount her opal car,
 And draw the rainbow reins,
And gaily go from start to start,
 Till not a ray remains.
—Qtd. in Coppée 1860, 232

The speaker takes Caprice's place as a kind of Aurora, who commands the day. By "gaily go[ing]," the speaker affirms "woman's right divine"—namely, the right to circulate without being consumed by public expectations of the profession of privacy. Inspired by Caprice, the speaker here asserts that women have the self-possession to "draw the rainbow reins" of autonomous circulation in public. Nevertheless, declaring one's inconstancy is not an ideal strategy for claiming professionalism. Osgood, in other words, helps us understand the Poetess's problematic relationship to publicity, and the problems of liberal selfhood in the nineteenth century, even if she sacrifices the possibility of achieving full subject status in the process.

Laborare Est Oblivion

Already well worn by the time that Coppée glossed them in 1860, the generic features of the antebellum Poetess persisted into the twentieth century. But, one might say, the social value of these conventions shifted, and, in what follows, I want to discuss the development of the antebellum Poetess and her profession in the early twentieth century. By the end of the nineteenth century, the Poetess occupied a complicated space in the literary public sphere. Though there were holdouts, readers and critics alike shared a general feeling of Poetess fatigue; the poems were outmoded, and the personas too old-fashioned. Whether readers enjoyed the Poetess's belatedness or yawned at her presence, both reactions attest to the persistence of the Poetess across the turn of the century. These reassessments on the part of readers and critics were not just a matter of taste, but were also made possible by changes in U.S. society, where the gradual acceptance of women as subjects with greater autonomy had begun to transform the reception of lyrical poems written by women.[18] Indeed, one of the founding premises of Poetess poetry—her domestic origins—was invalidated by women's increasing public presence, which made lip service to a feminine public/private separation seem retrograde, for better or worse.

We don't hear much about the antebellum Poetess in the era of high modernism, even though such personas and poems continue to pop up across the twentieth century.[19] Such appearances, often overlooked, write a counter-historiography that disputes later critical constructions of the Poetess as merely an ahistorical reflection of lyrical reading. Indeed, antebellum Poetess poems were taught and anthologized well into the twentieth century in publications from popular and pedagogical presses. For instance, *The Home Book of Verse*, published by Henry Holt in 1918 and regarded by the National Council for Better Homes in America as a crucial tome for the "Ideal Library," contained work by Elizabeth Akers Allen, Frances Sargent Osgood, and Lydia Howard Huntley Sigourney, along with many other women poets (Rubin 2007, 247). Osgood was also featured regularly in popular turn-of-the-century anthologies and magazines that sought to publish "representative" American poetry.[20]

The practices of elite literary publishing and criticism tell a different story. Prestigious imprints continued to disregard women as professionals; elite literary magazines like the *Atlantic* dropped women contributors to make room for high-profile male authors (Boyd 1998, 10). Even as it restricted women writers' access to professional markers such as prestige, this reevaluation of publishers' priorities had the effect of underscoring the paradoxical "professional" amateurism of Poetess poetry for the modern era. If women were published, they most likely wrote local color pieces or were expected to write domestic literature, thereby reinforcing the associations of women's poetry with a feminized private sphere.[21] While late nineteenth- and early twentieth-century critics had reached a consensus on the belatedness of Poetess practices, disagreements nevertheless persisted about the ends that belatedness served. At century's end, some critics—for instance, Helen Gray Cone, in her 1890 article "Woman in American Literature," which appeared in the *Century Illustrated Magazine*—regarded belatedness as the grounds for completely dismissing the same qualities of the Poetess that Coppée had advertised as valuable. Far from unanimous, this dismissive attitude competed with criticism—for instance, Oscar Fay Adams's 1915 remembrance of Osgood for the *Christian Register*—that emphasized the ongoing poetic relevance of the antebellum Poetess in the early twentieth century. Yet it is important to note that such broadsides against and memorials to Poetess poetry share more than belatedness as a premise. Taken together, these turn-of-the-century critical assessments also demonstrate precisely what contemporary lyric criticism would have us think impossible: namely, that the genericness and abstractness of Poetess poetry constituted its political and social significance. In other words, Cone and Adams offer readers their own accidental glimpses by insisting on the history of a genre that otherwise appears ahistorical. Whether the Poetess's antebellum work is praiseworthy or not, both critics attest to its continuing cultural relevance from the long nineteenth century into the twentieth—even if her importance is, ironically, her supposed insignificance.

Cone does not blame the antebellum Poetess for writing what she calls "Literature suited to Desolate Islands," and in a caustic passage, she argues that all Poetesses were conditioned to write such sentimental verse. While

Coppée celebrated the sincerity of the amateur, Cone seems to pity the writers and readers who perpetuate the Poetess's unprofessionalism:

> It was not their fault that their toil increased the sum of the "Literature suited to Desolate Islands." The time was out of joint. Sentimentalism infected both continents. It was natural enough that the infection should seize most strongly upon those who were weakened by an intellectual best-parlor atmosphere, with small chance of free out-of-door currents. They had their reward. Their crude constituencies were proud of them; and not all wrought without "emolument," though it need hardly be said that verse-making was not and is not, as a rule, a remunerative occupation. Some names survive, held in the memory of the public by a few small, sweet songs on simple themes, probably undervalued by their authors, but floating now like flowers above the tide that has swallowed so many pretentious, sand-based structures. (Cone 1890, 922)

Putting aside Cone's antagonistic tone, these statements reinforce how earlier convictions about the utility of the unpolished Poetess carry into the next century. Like Coppée, Cone does not recognize the Poetess's form of literary professionalism. Their concurrence about this "crude" poetry contributes to the lack of literary recognition for women writers. For Coppée, social and political customs denied professional claims at the same time that women were forced to dissimulate their skill. For Cone, the social milieu had so radically changed that she cannot acknowledge a professionalism that coheres within the public/private divide. In other words, Coppée's fantasy of the accidental poet has been taken for reality by Cone. Surprised that some Poetesses received an "emolument" for their works, Cone suggests that the women who received payment "undervalued" their poems; they were such amateurs that they could not recognize the worth of their work. "Undervalued" could also suggest that these authors considered these poems among their minor works and were unsatisfied that "sweet songs" earned them a literary legacy. But most of these women have been "swallowed" by oblivion, a telling description that implies that these figures were, indeed, consumed and then forgotten by their readers. As a result, Cone condemns these "sand-based" works to their rightful oblivion. Despite those whose "names survive," Cone's treatment suggests that even the survivors do not warrant naming.

Cone rejoiced that women writers in the late nineteenth century had finally discarded their Poetess pretentions. "As the flood of sentimentalism slowly receded," she writes, "hopeful signs began to appear" (Cone 1890, 929).

Her depiction of poetry suggests that the Poetess was a legacy that turn-of-the-century women writers would necessarily inherit—and thankfully reject. But in 1915, Adams's memorial to Osgood seems to confirm Cone's worst fears: the Poetess lived on. Ironically, Adams affirms the perseverance of antebellum Poetess poetry for the same reasons that Cone claimed it was irrelevant—its amateurism, its ephemerality, its belatedness. His memorial serves two opposing impulses: to revive a once-popular Poetess at the same time that it confirms her loss. According to Adams, Osgood "did not possess genius" (O. Adams 1915, 10). Then again, "neither did these other women who touched the lyre at the same time" (10). Adams finds this lack of skill nevertheless charming, writing that "natural, delicate, graceful" are the best terms to describe Osgood's verse (10). Such descriptors would seem to characterize Osgood's own person, as Adams rehearses the device, articulated by Coppée, that the Poetess's interiority was inadvertently on display. For Adams, Osgood had no control over what she said, or over her career path for that matter, explaining that "she wrote because the impulse to write came to her as easily as breathing" (10). As we can see, over half a century later Adams renews the attributes of women's poetry advertised by Coppée. Additionally, he understands that those attributes caused women's names to be forgotten. He is fascinated by Osgood's prior popularity compared to her current obsolescence, and, like Cone, sees them as cause and effect. "None achieved a fuller measure of popularity than did she," he writes, but Osgood "wrote too much for the best interests of her literary fame" (10). Her trendiness was the cause of her namelessness, and Adams admits that "the winnowing of sixty years and more has left few lines of hers familiar to this generation" (10).

When Cone argues that the genre has not aged well, and when Adams marvels that Osgood's works are unknown, they help demonstrate how Poetess poems are abstract *by design*. At the same time, Cone's dismissal of the antebellum Poetess and Adams's nostalgic appreciation do have one unintended benefit: they actually work to reassert the Poetess's significance. By the twentieth century, antebellum Poetesses may not have possessed the name recognition they once had, but their poems were beginning to be known for qualities other than the accidental expression of feminine interiority. For instance, Adams observes that one of Osgood's poems "keeps place in anthologies," and then reprints "Laborare Est Orare" in full (Adams 1915, 10). Indeed, this poem appeared not just in anthologies but in numerous newspapers, such as the *Christian Science Monitor*, which reprinted the poem just a year earlier.[22] Adams includes this poem not because it exhibits dusty sentiments, but due to its "high level of excellence" (10). The appearance of this poem in the early decades of the twentieth century evokes the continuing relevance of the antebellum Poetess for a new generation of readers and writers. Osgood was no longer considered a fickle, feminine figure; instead, the reception of her works implied their alignment with national narratives of liberal selfhood. In fact, in the instance that I will discuss below, it appears that the Poetess becomes a model liberal self, one with precisely the kind of agency women poets were thought incapable of possessing.

I want to conclude by examining this poem not in the context of Adams's memorial, but in that of the aforementioned *Christian Science Monitor*, which published an abridged version of "Laborare Est Orare" in January 1914 (Osgood 1914, 17). While nineteenth-century readers knew Osgood as the capricious Poetess, it appears that twentieth-century readers discerned the poem's promotion of hard work and spiritual well-being. The poem is edited down from its longer version to emphasize what sounds like rugged self-reliance:

Labor is life, 'tis the still water faileth;
Idleness ever despaireth, bewaileth;
Keep the watch wound, for the dark rust assaileth;
Labor is glory! . . .
Only the waving wing changes and brightens;
Idle hearts only the dark future frightens;
Play the sweet keys, wouldst thou keep them in tune.

Labor is rest from the sorrows that greet us;
Rest from all petty vexations that meet us,
Rest from sin-promptings that ever entreat us . . .
Work—and pure slumbers shall wait on thy pillow;
Work—thou shalt ride over care's coming billow; . . .
Work with a stout heart and resolute will. . . .

Work for some good, be it ever so slowly!
Cherish some flower, be it ever so lowly!
Labor—all labor is noble and holy;
Let thy great deed be thy prayer to thy God.
—Osgood 1914, 17

This version of the poem appears in other publications, and it is remarkable for what is not included: namely, the elements that would more directly align the poem with the femininity of the Poetess. For example, the ellipsis in the line "Labor is glory!" marks four missing words: "the flying cloud lightens." The next stanza features similar edits. Following the line "Rest from sin-

THE CHRISTIAN SCIENCE MONITOR, BOSTON, MASS., MONDAY, JANUARY 5, 1914

THE HOME FORUM

TALENT OF M. JEAN JAURES

Charm of Gentleness

GOD CREATES ALL SPIRITUALLY

WRITTEN FOR THE CHRISTIAN SCIENCE MONITOR

"THE PROSPECTOR" BY BORGLUM

Inventors in the Onward March

Value of the Bible

Research Needs Veracity

What Good Deeds Do

Class Unity at Yale

Nursery Rhymes Said to Be Founded on Fact

Florence, When Leonardo Painted the "Gioconda"

Sovereign Remedy

The Christian Science Monitor

LINCOLN A READER OF POETRY

Restoration of Habsburg

"TUNE THE VOWEL TO THE PITCH"

CHILDREN'S DEPARTMENT

Punctuation Marks

Today's Puzzle

Most Joyous Life

SPECIMENS OF BERMUDA GARDENS

Selections from "Laborare est Orare"

Labor is life, 'tis the still water faileth;
Idleness ever despaireth, bewaileth;
Keep the watch wound, or the dark rust assaileth;
Labor is glory! . . .
Only the waving wing changes and brightens;
Idle hearts only the dark future frightens;
Play the sweet keys, wouldst thou keep them in tune.

Labor is rest from the sorrows that greet us;
Rest from all petty vexations that meet us;
Rest from sin-promptings that ever entreat us. . . .
Work—and pure slumbers shall wait on thy pillow;
Work—thou shalt ride over care's coming billow; . . .
Work with stout heart and a resolute will. . .

Work for some good, be it ever so slowly!
Cherish some flower, be it ever so lowly!
Labor—all labor is noble and holy;
Let thy great deed be thy prayer to thy God.

—Frances Sargent Osgood.

"Laborare Est Orare," in Home Forum column of the *Christian Science Monitor*, January 5, 1914, 7, from Frances Sargent Osgood, "Selections from 'Laborare Est Orare.'"

promptings that ever entreat us" should be the line "Rest from world-sirens that lure us to ill." "Work—thou shalt ride over care's coming billow" should be followed by two lines: "Lie not down wearied 'neath Wo's weeping willow! / Work with a stout heart and resolute will!" In other words, self-reliance has no patience for the feminine figures of a fluffy cloud, siren singers, and a weeping willow. With the Poetess elements elided, what's left is an almost masculine liberal individualism. Indeed, the resulting poem seems to more closely evoke the inspiring work of the Schoolroom Poets—think Henry Wadsworth Longfellow's "Psalm of Life."

More important, perhaps, is how these elisions restructure the relationship between the Poetess and the very same liberal public/private divide that so vexed the figure in the nineteenth century. As a figure of literary circulation, the Poetess has always relied on the media and the materials surrounding her. The *Christian Science Monitor* endeavors to solidify this new, self-reliant Poetess by juxtaposing her with Abraham Lincoln, an exemplar of such qualities. Even the poem's placement on the Home Forum page of the newspaper speaks to the shifting significance of the Poetess. The poem is placed at the bottom of the page, below an article with the large, all-caps headline "LINCOLN A READER OF POETRY" and to the left of the "Children's Department." Given Osgood's association with children and innocence, her work's proximity to the Children's Department continues to speak to the association of these qualities with her name. But the poem's closeness to the article on Lincoln suggests some affiliation between the two. While the article mostly talks about how Lincoln read poets such as Robert Burns and Thomas Hood, as well as Shakespeare's plays, the declarative headline speaks to the poem directly below: Lincoln read poems just like this one (*Christian Science Monitor* 1914, 17).[23] "Selections from 'Laborare Est Orare'" seems to embody the values of the great man, such as hard work, humility, honor.[24] But this work and the work the poem encourages take on additional meaning in light of the Poetess tradition and the idea that the Poetess's "laborare" is unprofessional. In fact, the qualities that made her unprofessional—her purity, her familiarity, her humility—now align with qualities that would make her presidential. In other words, Osgood's legacy is linked to that of Lincoln. What has been lost is the sense that such a profession—in both senses of the term—was accidental. By the twentieth century, the antebellum Poetess's history of abstraction has become so abstract that femininity seems to have dissolved into rugged individualism. But the Poetess sticks around in what is not there, in the shadows of her verse. So much seems absent from this version of Osgood's poems—not just the elided lines, but also her portrait and signature, as well as editorial explanations of feminine purity. What she offers to these new readers is inspiration that takes its own cue from the very work the Poetess performs in the public sphere. The antebellum Poetess in the twentieth century no longer speaks from the distant domestic realm but is now unquestionably a fixture in that public world. What remains is the name Frances Sargent Osgood as a poet whose professional legacy exhorts us to work, or urges us to our own professional legacy.

CHAPTER TWO

Elizabeth Oakes Smith's Lyrical Activism

In the opening chapter of Elizabeth Oakes Smith's unpublished autobiography, "A Human Life," written while she was in her eighties, the poet describes visiting her childhood home as a forty-year-old woman. At the time of Oakes Smith's return, a young mother and her three children live there, and the mother informs Oakes Smith that "this house has an interest of itself, a Poet was born here in this very room." "I was pleased by this," recalls Oakes Smith, who then hands the woman her card. When she learned that the very Poet was standing before her, the mother, according to Oakes Smith, "grasped" her hand and exclaimed, "I must know exactly how you look." The mother then "studied [Oakes Smith's] face with pleasant scrutiny" (Oakes Smith 1994, 74). At first glance, it is tempting to read this event as a testament to Oakes Smith's lasting name as a literary figure. But the contents of "A Human Life" speak more to the anxieties Oakes Smith sought to resolve than to the life she wanted to celebrate. We can see this opening as a defensive move on her part, meant to put off what she saw as a disconcerting fate: the inevitable erasure of women writers from the public record by virtue of women's illiberal status.

The mention of this incident is also notable for its placement in Oakes Smith's autobiography, and not only because it appears in its first chapter. Just a page earlier, Oakes Smith had discussed the fragmentary, forgettable nature of a woman's existence: "We live in fragments—daughter, wife, mother, friend—no woman's life is rounded unless she fills these relations" (Oakes Smith 1994, 73). After "child-bearing," she writes with some rancor, "the books are closed and [a woman] sinks into nothingness" (73). In sum, Oakes Smith recognized in her autobiography that self-possessed autonomy was impossible for women. Even the likelihood of living a "rounded" or full life is prohibited, since women's lives were broken into prescribed "relations." And such a splintered existence, she laments, is not likely to make it on "the books," much less be celebrated. Women's lives are therefore forgotten because they lack the self-sovereignty to socially or politically establish themselves as anything beyond "daughter, wife, mother, friend." As a way to counter such expectations, Oakes Smith encouraged writing: "Women ought to write out their experiences, as by doing so the sex will be better understood." This very autobiography serves as an opportunity for Oakes Smith to assert her autonomy. Indeed, she proclaims, "I have not lived in fragments. I am sure my identity has been built up fit for the ^resurrection.^ . . . I see how piece by piece has been linked together to make an entire whole" (1994, 73).[1] No passive endeavor, the declaration of such self-possession required effort; she would have to hold herself together in order to be remembered: "Such as I am I must take hold of eternal life, and not be scattered by the elements" (73).

Coming on the heels of these musings, Oakes Smith's use of capital-P "Poet" in the subsequent anecdote about her old home is no accident. Despite her work as a lecturer, journalist, novelist, and pioneering advocate for American women's rights in the nineteenth century, the young mother knows of Oakes Smith as a "Poet."[2] Nor had the mother heard that a "Poetess" or "authoress" was born in her home. The story serves to prove Oakes Smith's status as a celebrity "Poet," or a woman who has not been forgotten. Poets, unlike women, do not sink "into nothingness"; their lives fit together to form an "entire whole." For Oakes Smith, her status as Poet signifies her possession of autonomous personhood; her autobiography, which prominently features her poetic achievements, demonstrates the sovereignty that a Poet exerts over her life and works. Oakes Smith therefore wants readers to know that she was born in this little cottage in 1806, that she returned nearly forty years later as a famous author, and that another forty years after that she "linked together" all the parts "to make an entire whole." In other words, "A Human Life" is the proof for Oakes Smith that her life was hers to control.

If "A Human Life" was meant to parry concerns about her legacy, it is unfortunate that it was never published.[3] As Leigh Kirkland argues, "Much of the poignancy of this text lies in her implicit struggle against the possibility that she will be forgotten. If she does not write, no memory of her or of the times she both was shaped by and helped shape will last" (Oakes Smith 1994, 11). Indeed, as her opening page declares, "I will now write a book in which I will figure as the principal personage. I will speak soundly of myself. I belong now to a past period, the memory of which it may be well to retain" (72).[4] To "speak soundly" and place herself in the autobiographical spotlight situated Oakes Smith as a public female figure, and in order to be this "principal personage," she must assert her self-possession, not fragmentation. These individual concerns in fact register the problems attending the reception of women writers in the literary public sphere, a reception that had roots in the larger political conditions for women in the nineteenth-century United States. As I discussed in the introduction and chapter 1, the laws and legacy of coverture prevented women from possessing full legal rights in this era. Considered the property of their husbands, women were confined to the domestic sphere and thought to lack the ability to function as autonomous individuals in public. Women poets "write without a name," as Eliza Richards argues, because the laws of coverture "disable" the "legal force" of her signature (Richards 2004, 153). With no control over the conditions of their reception, most women poets were effectively erased from public memory; their names were consumed and forgotten.[5] Oakes Smith was constantly confronted with the possibility that she could be entirely dissolved into an indistinct generic figure in the public imagination. For that reason, it is perhaps unsurprising that Oakes Smith sought to establish herself as a name in a number of ways. To distinguish herself from her husband, the popular author and humorist Seba Smith, she changed her published name from "Mrs. Seba Smith" to "Oakes Smith." She even named her children after herself; her son Appleton signified that the "apple" does not fall far from the tree.[6] Oakes Smith might attempt to establish herself as a "principal personage" with these names, but publication would nevertheless threaten to dissolve her individuality.

The problem of the female poet's fleeting fame likewise concerned Oakes Smith's audiences. For example, included among the press clippings that Oakes Smith selected for her scrapbook is Susan E. Dickinson's 1855 article "Women Writers: A Chapter on Their Ephemeral Reputations."[7] The subtitle, "Hopes and Ambitions That Have Faded in Sad Disappointments," reinforces the ephemerality of women writers' literary legacies. Dickinson muses, "I wonder to how many of my readers the name even, of Mrs. Elizabeth Oakes Smith is familiar, although she was one of America's most popular writers for a generation" (Dickinson [1855], n.p.). Perhaps this article was included in her scrapbook because it pleased Oakes Smith—or perhaps it filled her with anxiety about her literary legacy. Indeed, Dickinson's concluding words, "let us hope that her setting sun, and those of the few others of that illustrious coterie who are still among us, may linger in its going down and be beautiful and radiant to the last," could be interpreted by Oakes Smith as appropriate praise or a death sentence (n.p.). According to Dickinson, Oakes Smith cannot escape a reception that would make her a "setting sun." Oakes Smith may be a name among "American women writers" and a member of their "illustrious coterie," yet this is not enough to secure lasting fame for her (n.p.). She may have enjoyed recognition, but comments like Dickinson's tell her that this recognition will not last.

Indeed, these efforts to stake her name, it would appear, were often for naught. When it came to having a public presence as a poet, Oakes Smith's publications were read as Poetess poems composed by a Poetess persona. Her anxieties were warranted, for they map onto the conventional reception of the Poetess as a figure who inadvertently exposed her interior to readers at the cost of any semblance of self-possession. Thus dispossessed, Poetesses' names and bodies were now the property of readers. The anecdote about the young mother exemplifies this problem. As soon as Oakes Smith is recognized as a Poet, she is treated like a Poetess, which is to say, less as a person than an object to be "studied" with "scrutiny." The mother's impulse to peer into Oakes Smith's face reinforces the expectation that women poets display their interiors on their exteriors. This was assumed by laypeople as well as literary critics; for instance, in 1844 *Graham's Magazine* asserts that women "are so much the creatures of impulse that they write more from the heart than from the intellect" and that no "analysis of the female intellect can be made, therefore, without taking into consideration her [true] character" (*Graham's Magazine* 1844, 236). Because her face can be read the same way her poems are, Oakes Smith is effectively divested of her interiority—she is dispossessed and consumed by a reader. Such consequences were not lost on Oakes Smith, who herself opposed gendered terms such as Poetess. "I have from the first rejected the terminations of gender in words of an intellectual import such as poetess, authoress &c," she complained. "We say Saint Therese, Saint Elizabeth why not say poet Elizabeth Browning the Author Sarah Jane Hale?" (Oakes Smith 1994, 272). No doubt this rejection of the Poetess title stems from Oakes Smith's activism and her awareness of the connection between literary expectations and women's unequal status.

That Oakes Smith is trying to rewrite the terms of her reception—to assert that she was a celebrated Poet—is not the only point to make. Oakes Smith's motivations—her feminism, her desire to put together a complete life, and her desire to form a lasting literary name—stem from the same liberal notions of selfhood. Her writings and lectures on women's rights were steeped in the underlying ideals of liberalism: that women deserved to be treated as self-governing subjects with full legal and social rights. As Oakes Smith writes in "A Human Life," "It is time that the distinction of gender were suppressed. Now that women are taking an important share in the thoughts, and making the opinions of the age, they should be meet [*sic*] as thinkers and not as the producers of the race merely" (Oakes Smith 1994, 272). If this were the case, then she could command the same legacy as the names that she admired, such as Samuel Taylor Coleridge, Ralph Waldo Emerson, Edgar Allan Poe, even John Milton and William Shakespeare, whose busts sit in the library in which she writes her autobiography (72).

This chapter will explore the liberalizing strategies Oakes Smith developed in her poems to resist losing her name. By more closely looking at those moments in Oakes Smith's poems that seem to most exemplify the Poetess's sincere exposure of privacy, we can discern where and how Oakes Smith made the case for her status, not as a generic female writer, but as the lasting, liberal Poet. Her efforts to radically revise the expectations of the Poetess distinguish Oakes Smith from other authors who only presumed to uphold the figure and work within its productive limitations. Here a comparison to Frances Sargent Osgood is apposite. Osgood staked a claim for female autonomy *through* the Poetess persona—for instance, by encouraging women to claim partial subjectivity through the feminine flightiness of her poem "Caprice." In an effort to reach beyond the social restrictions placed on women, Osgood self-consciously exposed a feminized interior in public. Oakes Smith's poems share this endeavor to self-consciously expose a feminized interior, but with a crucial difference: these works do not equate exposure with the Poetess's transparency. She exploits the conventions regulating the Poetess's accidental exposure of interiority in order to insist on her public self-possession and, by extension, women's fitness for the full rights of liberal selfhood. As we will see, Oakes Smith's poetry revises the practices of the Poetess by displaying dark spots, which is to say, opaque moments where private thoughts are acknowledged but remain unexposed to readers. With this revised practice, which demonstrates her full control over what she sees and what she says, the Poetess figure does not reveal her dispossession but rather her self-sovereign genius.

In making this argument, I hope to draw attention to the *how* and not just the *what*: that is, to the ways in which Oakes Smith deployed lyrical strategies to claim qualities of the genius Poet for the generic Poetess. In poems that might not otherwise appear to be lyric, like the long narrative work *The Sinless Child* or the balladic poem "The Drowned Mariner," Oakes Smith employs devices associated with lyric, namely, the profession of interiority and the constitution of a speaking subject. These practices worked to parry Oakes Smith's reception as Poetess at the same time that they attempted to position her as the Poet. In other words, lyrical moments are the same moments where Oakes Smith attempts to revise the gendered expectations associated with poetry.

According to Richards, "Oakes Smith acknowledged the inevitable fall of the poetess into silence" (Richards 2004, 154). But rather than focus on Oakes Smith's "inevitable" failure, I want to concentrate on the myriad ways in which the poet nevertheless strove to combat such silence throughout her entire career. Lyrical poetry was both problem and solution for Oakes Smith's aspirations to self-fashioned and self-possessed wholeness. While she wrote in many genres, poetry offered a uniquely effective practice for proving and circulating these beliefs in a liberal age. Given the expectations accompanying poems by women, poetry allowed Oakes Smith to publicly demonstrate her command over her interiority, her fitness for autonomous selfhood, and ultimately her control over her lasting name. Her poetry is not removed from her political purposes; as this chapter will argue, the lyrical strains in her poems aspire to found a liberal subjectivity for women. Indeed, in the opening of the autobiography, Oakes Smith continues to justify the recognition of her life and women's lives, even if they are not thought to rival the careers of Coleridge, Emerson, Milton, Poe, or Shakespeare: "The struggles of a person to live . . . may present some points of interest, worth preservation, though it may not be very wonderful ^in itself,^ partaking only of that human type which none escape, and ^which^ renders us all akin" (Oakes Smith 1994, 72). Even when the Poetess's reception seems doomed to failure, Oakes Smith engaged lyric's paradoxical privacy to keep advocating for recognition of both her status as a Poet and women's "human type."

Prose Advocacy

Within her own lifetime, Oakes Smith certainly secured a place for herself in public memory, not only as a popular poet, but also as a "prominent advocate" for women's rights (Cleveland 1862, 529).[8] Because her activism is most explicit in her prose, I will start by outlining the pioneering arguments in her essays before identifying their presence in her poetry. With these elaborations on Oakes Smith's political interventions, I hope to show how her advocacy was based in liberalism's philosophy of freedom and self-development. In addition, I will introduce the salient themes that appear in her poetry, and not just her political writings. Her poems effectively imparted this struggle for equal rights. At the core of her sense of women's liberty in both poetry and prose were ideas about women's genius; the separation of spheres; women's public persona, public exposure, and private self-possession; and the fundamental right to self-sovereignty. While Oakes Smith could not control the terms of her reception, the prevalence of her work offered a means of disrupting social expectations for women.

For instance, her popular lyceum lectures, published as *Woman and Her Needs*, explicitly advocate for the equal rights of women. These ideas had a public life, both in person and on the page; the lectures were reprinted in Horace Greeley's *New York Tribune* in 1850–51 and then printed again, on their own, as a book (Kete 2000, 248). Furthermore, *Woman and Her Needs* was a timely collection, "published just as the organized women's movement forced a national public debate on the woman question" (Wayne 2005, 53). However, the work's emphasis on women's autonomous individuality was just one of many arguments that comprised the women's rights movement at the time.[9] But this variety of ideas—ideas that ranged from "equal wages to [women's own] control over their bodies to resisting racist violence"—narrowed considerably in the aftermath of the Civil War, at which point such eclecticism was deemed secondary to a central and galvanizing focus: women's suffrage (Tetrault 2015, 7). While Oakes Smith was a leader within the movement, her views were among many that were sidelined in order to promote the suffragist project. In fact, the success of this campaign depended, it would seem, on establishing a single and harmonious history of the women's movement. To that end, Elizabeth Cady Stanton and Susan B. Anthony "made an origins story" out of the famous 1848 Seneca Falls meeting in order to "unify activists and settle these disputes" (7). Oakes Smith attended this meeting but has been given only a minor part in its story because, I would argue, her views disrupted efforts to place a singular emphasis on suffrage. Despite her activity—she was even president of the Syracuse convention in 1852—Oakes Smith has been forgotten within the very history she helped to create (Wayne 2005, 53). Indeed, a glance at the multivolume *History of Woman Suffrage*, edited by Cady, Anthony, and Matilda Gage, demonstrates how the nineteenth-century women's rights movement began to efface its own diverse political imperatives. Oakes Smith is mentioned frequently in volume 1 (which covers 1848 to 1861), but is one name among many other women activists.[10] This volume has the same effect as the anthology of women poets: the effort to make distinctions becomes a blur of abstraction, and names are lost to history even as it is recorded. In volume 2 (which covers 1861–76), she is cited just once—in a footnote. Though mentioned, Oakes Smith's name is made to affirm a political platform that sidesteps the concerns made manifest in *Woman and Her Needs*.

In this collection, Oakes Smith advocates for the same freedoms that underpin liberal philosophy: that women should have the right to exist in the public sphere as autonomous, self-reliant individuals:

> The majority of women in society are suffering in the absence of wholesome, earnest, invigorating subjects of thought; expending themselves upon trifles, and fretting themselves and others for lack of employment. The routine of housekeeping, the study of the arts, or the management of children, is no more enough to fill their whole lives. . . . I wish to show that while she has been created as one part of human intelligence, she has not only a right to be heard and felt in human affairs, not by tolerance merely, but as a welcome and needed element of human

> thought; and that when she is thus recognized, the world will be the better for it, and go onward with new power.
>
> —Oakes Smith 1851, 17

When women move beyond the domestic sphere, not only will they cease suffering for lack of stimulation, but their presence will be good for the world. In other words, women deserve the right to develop their own lives and pursue their own interests. "Let her evolve her own thought, recognize her own needs, and judge of her own acts by the best lights of her own mind," argues Oakes Smith in part 2, echoing the liberal belief that every individual has the right to develop free from the encroachments of others (22). In part 3, citing constitutional guarantees "that every human being has a right to life, liberty and the pursuit of happiness—a God-guaranteed charter, which no created being may infringe," Oakes Smith protests that women are refused that same "sacred and ennobling truth" (36). In other words, women are denied the basic freedom to pursue life, which would mean a public existence beyond domestic duties, as well as control over money, marriage, and education.

Of course, Oakes Smith was not oblivious to the threat that her advocacy posed to conservative nineteenth-century ideals. She observes that for women, "genius and beauty, God's crowning gifts, are looked upon with distrust, if not with dread. . . . It is even a reproach for her to have a will of her own" (83). Indeed, this reproach came in many forms, ranging from medical "science" to public shaming.[11] When women intellectuals overstepped these boundaries or resisted this destiny, they were treated with hostility. In the periodical press, public figures such as "authors, abolitionists, lyceum speakers, and women's rights advocates" were pejoratively labeled as "hermaphrodites" (C. Patterson 2016, 514, 518). Naturally, Oakes Smith's lectures criticized those male commentators who reproached women for exceeding the narrow domestic sphere. "Read but a tithe of the twaddle written by the other sex," she quips, "and it will be seen how little we are understood. Take up a common newspaper which may be regarded as an exponent of the popular voice, and see how we are talked of, as creatures one would suppose belonging to a different race" (Oakes Smith 1851, 84).[12]

Considering the message Oakes Smith articulated in these lectures and the liberal convention of excluding women from the public sphere, her very presence on the lyceum circuit and in major periodicals was an achievement. "Praised as the first woman to speak in many lyceums in the early 1850s," Oakes Smith dismantled what she saw as an arbitrary, gendered divide between the so-called spheres (Ray 2006, 194).[13] For example, in part 2 of

Woman and Her Needs, she complains that the phrase "a 'Woman's sphere'" "has a most shallow and indefinite sense" (Oakes Smith 1851, 27). She contends that the ambiguity results from the fact that the woman's sphere is really an extension of men's lives: "It is a sphere by which every woman creature, of whatever age, appending to himself, shall circle very much within his own—see and hear through his senses, and believe according to his dogmas" (28).[14] Ironically, in this so-called woman's sphere, women cannot exist as individuals because any individuality disappears in serving men's needs: "If need be for his growth, glorification, or well-being in any way, they will instantly and uncompromisingly become extinct" (28).[15] In her description of the sphere's limitations, Oakes Smith is arguing that women were equally capable of life and labor beyond the domestic realm.

That said, critics have not conceded that the self-possessed liberal individualism I am describing was exactly the kind of selfhood that Oakes Smith was entertaining. For example, Dorri Beam explores how Oakes Smith's prose worked in fact to depict "an ecology of 'self' that extended beyond the person"; for that reason, "a notion of integral, possessive personhood, such as one now associates with individualism," is not necessarily what is "at stake" for Oakes Smith or Margaret Fuller, her literary predecessor (Beam 2013, 48). Indeed, Oakes Smith's poetic figures gloss what is an open secret in liberal philosophy and a natural state of exchange in Transcendentalist thought: that the self exceeds the boundary between private and public and relies on both internal and external forces in order to constitute autonomous personhood. Or, in the words of Beam, feminist writers such as Oakes Smith "opened the self to forces outside of it" (48).

Yet Oakes Smith advocated for women's rights in a political environment that legally defined its citizens according to liberal premises, that is, to a political environment beginning to define individualism as enclosed and self-possessed. Yes, keeping a Transcendentalist philosophy of the self in mind is important to temper the spread-eagle individualism that liberalism can foster, but not at the expense of the more fundamental liberal assumptions about selfhood that Oakes Smith's works strive to address. The depiction of an unbounded self was one strategy Oakes Smith employed to combat the liberal logic that confined women's lives to the domestic sphere. While her prose and poetry featured a Transcendentalist understanding of the exchange between self and world, I maintain that she strove to access the self-possessed individualism that defined the liberal public sphere. It was in her poetry that Oakes Smith provided this nuanced understanding of a female subject. Her poems both affirmed bounded liberal individualism and exceeded that political ideology to depict the female Poet's autonomy.

The Poet's Genius

Oakes Smith figured herself as a Poet in order to possess the self-sustaining qualities that were not afforded to women writers, such as control over her poetic talent, the ability to traverse public and private spheres without superintendence, and protection from the dissolution of her literary name into a generic mass of other writers. In other words, she desired the power of genius, the professional and discursive power associated with the Poet. As I argued in the introduction, we can locate the liberal subject of "Self-Reliance" in the lyric subject of "The Poet." Even when damning her with faint praise, Dickinson shows how this idea could afford Oakes Smith a presence in the public sphere. "Her genius, her charm of manner, her eloquence," Dickinson writes, "made her successful in winning respectful hearing" (Dickinson [1855], n.p.).

Oakes Smith also wanted a respectful hearing for her ideas on genius. But contrary to Dickinson, Oakes Smith recognized the gendered expectations associated with the subject, and that she might not receive such acknowledgment under her own name. Although "feminine receptivity was a crucial trait in delineations of male genius," genius was not often associated with women (Richards 2004, 4).[16] In addition, due to the threatening popularity of women poets, male poets were trying to "redefine ideas of creative process" (4). It seems significant, then, that Oakes Smith's 1844 essay "Genius Exempt from Ordinary Laws," published shortly after she gained fame for her long narrative poem *The Sinless Child,* was written using the pseudonym Ernest Helfenstein.[17] By adopting a masculine name, Oakes Smith confirms male authors' worst fears about the encroachment of women in the literary marketplace. But at the same time that the pseudonym allowed Oakes Smith to critique such anxieties, the credibility afforded to a male name would have also rewarded her financially. Not only does the pseudonym prevent the dilution her "brand"; it allowed Oakes Smith "to make more money by doubling her submissions" (218).[18] It also seems clear that the pseudonym reflects the opposition to women publishing on subjects such as genius.

A pseudonymous essay on genius was a savvy move by Oakes Smith because it set up the precise terms of literary genius that her poetic practices bear out. By explicitly linking genius to originality, fame, and self-sovereignty, Oakes Smith describes genius in terms of the liberal self. For instance, society's conventions do not infringe on genius's development; instead, as the title of the essay tells us, genius is "exempt from ordinary laws." If the genius must be held to other people's expectations, then he should still be afforded the liberty to flourish; Oakes Smith/Helfenstein asks, "Why may not the poet, or the prose artist employ, as the painter does, a pupil to lay colours upon his draft?" (Helfenstein 1844, 98). In this question, Oakes Smith calls attention to the quality of her ideas and not the trappings of form. Like her contemporaries, she produced a great quantity of work in order to support herself and encourages critics to recognize her genius beneath what might strike readers as conventional, generic, or forgettable. Like Emerson's Poet, genius is recognized in the poem's ideas, not the form—not meter, but a meter-making argument—or, as Oakes Smith/Helfenstein puts it, "The words of Genius may have been rugged, devoid of the graces of a set form of speech, but from thence it may be they are more impressive" (99). Oakes Smith thus sets out the salient qualities that she hopes will distinguish her from other, indistinguishable Poetesses.

Of course, in order to gain such distinction, genius must be acknowledged by others. Genius cannot be forged solely in isolation; like the liberal self, it is finally confirmed through social acknowledgment. Fortunately, Oakes Smith gains such attention due to her ability to make the common uncommon. Poe's review of *The Sinless Child* praises her originality for its "[evident discontent] with the bald routine of common-place themes" (Poe 1895, 307). Such creativity indeed exempts her from "ordinary laws." Poe concludes that Oakes Smith's genius makes up for a lack of discipline in her works, such as the imperfect rhythm of her poem "The Acorn" (312).[19] Her brilliance overrides any mistakes, and more importantly, warrants public admiration: "No work of art can embody within itself a proper *originality* without giving the plainest manifestations of the creative spirit, or, in the more common parlance, of *genius* in its author. The originality of 'The Sinless Child' would cover a multitude of greater defects than Mrs. Smith ever committed, and must forever entitle it to the admiration and respect of every competent critic" (309). As Oakes Smith suggested above, technical imperfections belie a "ruggedness" that proves the genius of the artist. These concepts of originality and freedom point to the affinity between the genius figure and the liberal self: Oakes Smith's rough originality liberates her from grosser limitations and affords her an unfettered self-expression. Indeed, this language of ruggedness shows up again years later in "A Human Life." While complaining about Longfellow's derivativeness, Oakes Smith agrees with Poe that originality is the mark of the true genius:

> There is something repugnant to me in the protracted, artistic, and scholastic toil of such writers as Longfellow; still, he has been very

> successful—his persistency has done much, and his wealth much, but, sift out what is his, from that which he has appropriated from others, and his own capital will be very much diminished. . . . And thus the author who ekes out his meager capacity by the emanations of genius, may be smooth and fine, and artistic, but can never be compared to the rugged granite of original genius, which must be ^the^ substratum of all vital literature. You may look in vain for the delicate tracery of the fern or the fine shapes of organic matter in this rugged primitive rock; so is true genius unmarked by the impress of other minds.
>
> —Oakes Smith 1994, 283

Authors such as Longfellow may be "smooth and fine, and artistic," but this is no comparison to "the rugged granite of original genius." Tellingly, Oakes Smith is adapting masculine rhetoric to explain that the liberal Poet, namely, herself, is free from the "impress" of the social world. As a result, her originality will stand the test of time.

As we can see, these comments can be read as part of Oakes Smith's anxiety about establishing a lasting legacy. If she is recognized as this "rugged" genius, then she can establish herself as an autonomous Poet, rather than become another nameless, generic Poetess. Just a paragraph earlier in the autobiography, Oakes Smith conflates generic poets with poems when she explains, "Very few persons are greater than their books. . . . They put all that is in them into their printed pages." But if a poet is a genius, then there is more individuality behind the persona presented in the poem (Oakes Smith 1994, 283). Oakes Smith explains that Poe has "much of this reserved power," but "Longfellow is deficient in it—and so is Tuckerman and most of the women writers" (283). This seems like an odd jab, but what she alludes to is the perception by the public that women writers equaled their poems, and there was nothing more to them beyond the page. They were thus dispossessed by publishing, and these comments can be understood as evidence of Oakes Smith's anxiety regarding just this—that her poems would be taken as her, and the self-possession she tried to assert beyond her works would not be recognized. However, applying the terms of genius that Oakes Smith set out would provide her with recognition as a Poet, preserving her name and fame in the public sphere.

Poetics of Activism

Although she could not avoid her reception as a Poetess, Oakes Smith did attempt to revise the persona in order to assert the Poet's self-possession. As I argued in the introduction and chapter 1, Poetesses were thought to utterly lack self-possession because they could not avoid professing their interiority; conversely, the Poet's intellectual autonomy mirrored the sovereign liberal self. Oakes Smith's work was thus laid out for her: she wanted to be a Poet in a literary public sphere predisposed to associate sovereignty and genius with men and dependence and "fancy" with women. Given her ambitious claim that she was a self-possessed Poetess, Oakes Smith relied on what appeared to be a counterintuitive strategy. In order to claim her place as a Poet, she exploited conventional lyrical devices—the constitution of a speaking subject and the expression of interiority—that were, in fact, the staples of the Poetess's generic abstraction. But with a difference, as Oakes Smith endeavored to exploit lyric's fundamental contradiction, that is, the idea that the lyrical speaker signaled her sovereignty by expressing interiority to an audience.

Oakes Smith's poetry, as one might suspect, is very different from her essays, and, for that reason, some commentators have had a hard time reconciling her progressive feminist politics and seemingly regressive sentimental poetics. Consider Ruth MacKay's surprise in White Collar Girl, a column that ran in the *Chicago Daily Tribune* in the 1940s, when she learned that "the first woman to lecture on equal rights, Elizabeth Oakes Smith, wrote a poem with the astounding title of 'The Sinless Child'" (MacKay 1944, 21). MacKay's disbelief is understandable, and one may wonder at the efficacy of Oakes Smith's activism in the first place. She was no legislator, nor could she have been, so how did Oakes Smith presume to shift the social status of women? The case for any such public efficacy depended on the special nature of lyceum lectures, which served as spaces for altering public opinion (Ray 2006, 185). But here I want to focus on how Oakes Smith's popular poetry also subtly shapes the public sphere as part of what Ray calls "the phenomenon of historical public speech that did not routinely address political policy" (185). To stake a claim for women as self-possessed liberal subjects, Oakes Smith rhetorically constitutes a self-possessed speaker who can share her interiority without being consumed. What I am arguing, then, is that her poems offered a different application of her advocacy, one that embraced the problems and solutions associated with the Poetess genre as a point of departure for accessing selfhood.

While MacKay was quick to disregard it as retrograde, Oakes Smith's most famous poem, *The Sinless Child*, challenges traditional gender roles for women. Its publication history, however, appears to confirm the opposite. From January to February 1842, *The Sinless Child* was originally serialized in the *Southern Literary Messenger*, where it was surrounded by other features.

These companion pieces suggest that the poem seemed a part of (not apart from) conventional discourse on the roles of men and women. For example, "Female Influence: In Seven Chapters" by Susan Walker has its first appearance in the January 1842 issue. In this narrative, two sisters—one modeling feminine purity and piety and the other serving as her selfish and shallow opposite—exemplify how "female influence" can, respectively, elevate or corrupt those around them (S. Walker 1842, 25–37). Walker's story is followed by H. T. Tuckerman's article "Keats," which begins by stating "a feeling has gone abroad prejudicial to the manliness of Keats," before discounting his physical weakness when compared to his "intellectual vigor" (Tuckerman 1842, 37). Later in the issue, Longfellow's poem "Maidenhood" concludes by urging the maiden "with the meek, brown eyes" to smile because it "like sunshine dart[s] / In to many a sunless heart / For a smile of God thou art" (Longfellow 1842, 57).

The apparent need for such supporting material only seemed to increase with *The Sinless Child*'s instant popularity. Just a scant eighteen months later, it was published in a stand-alone volume with other Oakes Smith poems (Oakes Smith 1843, xi). If her poems were no longer surrounded by protective articles within a magazine, then they had to be buffered by prefatory material to withstand the pressures of public circulation. This so-called need, I would posit, was fabricated by publishers so they could arrogate women's genius. In order to lay a greater claim to women's artistic ability, publishers insisted that publication risked putting women's interiority on flagrant display. Editorial superintendence, in other words, was the publishers' solution to a problem that didn't exist.

In this 1843 volume, editor John Keese supplied a number of prefaces whose ostensible function was to "claim for [Oakes Smith] a foremost rank among the writers of the country" (Oakes Smith 1843, xiv). On the one hand, the sheer amount of prefatory material here could be reasonable given the context. This was a widely popular serialized magazine poem appearing for the first time as a stand-alone work; the prefaces justify to readers why they should own *The Sinless Child* and read even more poems from Oakes Smith. But I contend that their claims to advance Oakes Smith as a "foremost" poet are essentially a marketing move: the prefatory material is intended to "sell" Oakes Smith with celebrity endorsements. In other words, these previews point to the genius of the men who knew enough to praise Oakes Smith in advance of her book-length work. Their presence rhetorically supervises the public appearance of Oakes Smith, and their contents articulate not just the expectations for the Poetess, but the expectation that women cannot exist as autonomous individuals in public—they need some power over them to oversee their public presence. The prefatory material includes Keese's own short note, "To the Reader," a sketch by John Neal that appeared in "The Family Companion," one of the "Literary Portraits" from *Graham's Magazine* by the aforementioned Tuckerman, and a short, anonymous notice originally from the *Boston Notion* when *The Sinless Child* was first published. This adds up to nearly twenty pages preceding the poem, written by reviewers who, in assessing the poem, also assess Oakes Smith's character. In sum, the prefaces are not introducing readers to Oakes Smith but are introducing readers to the Poetess.

This kind of prefatory material is not seen in the collected volumes of other established women poets. Osgood's first collection, *A Wreath of Wild Flowers from New England* (1838), presents a handful of "Notices," but includes nothing like the opening pages of *The Sinless Child*. There are, however, some similarities between Oakes Smith's book and volumes by women poets who died young. For instance, Elizabeth Margaret Chandler's and Lucretia Davidson's collected poems were published within four years of their deaths. These volumes are superintended by male editors who offer prefatory materials such as, respectively, a "Memoir" and "Biographical Sketch"; in fact, the title page of each volume advertises these extras (Lundy 1845, 7, 1; Morse 1829, v, i). Understandably, new or young artists needed some kind of backing in the public sphere to help sell an entire stand-alone volume of poetry. At the same time, the inclusion of such materials for Chandler, Davidson, and Oakes Smith suggests that the poet's work itself was not enough to entice readers. Biographical sketches provide the intimate insight necessary for readers to gain that irresistible glimpse of the Poetess's "true" nature.

Keese is gracious throughout his preface, noting that he has "availed himself of the high privilege of superintending the present volume" (Keese 1843, xii). He wants to make this highly popular work available to even more readers. But his note nevertheless sets in motion the conviction that women writers require the guidance of male editors, demonstrated by the notion that he "superintends" the poem's appearance. To justify his editorial intervention, Keese claims (in the third person) that "the act of introducing [*The Sinless Child*] to the public, under *his own name*" does not require "farther explanation or apology, with those who love pure poetry and respect womanly feeling" (xii).[20] For those who "respect womanly feeling," the fact that the editor's name "superintends" Oakes Smith's work should present no problem. After all, in order to be respected, the public expression of womanly feeling required the protection afforded by a masculine preface. Otherwise, womanly feeling could run amok, unsupervised and promiscuous. Keese had to chaperone Oakes Smith's lyricism in the public sphere, and not only that, he needed three other people to support the existence of such "pure poetry" on its own in book form.

Despite Keese's intent to place Oakes Smith among the leading authors in the United States, the prefatory material included in this edition suggests that Oakes Smith's success as a writer was inadvertent. Because other men hovered over her, Oakes Smith was not in full possession of herself or her gifts. For example, Neal's sketch from "The Family Companion" portrays Oakes Smith as a devoted wife and mother. He explains that she began writing to support her family due to her husband's financial ruin, demonstrating "her steadfast determination to do all that might become a woman" (Neal 1843, xxiv).[21] But this effort comes "years after she had begun to hazard little scraps of prose and poetry for her husband's paper, which he carefully corrected for her" (xxiv). In other words, Neal points out how her works were first superintended by and then written out of duty to her husband. Furthermore, Neal insists that Oakes Smith never expected to be considered a professional author; if you had asked her if she would be as successful as her husband, "she would have laughed in your face" (xxiv).

The anonymous review from the *Boston Notion* likewise claims that Oakes Smith's poetic success was not the act of her own agency. This time, her accomplishments are the result of divine forces acting through her. Conflating her person with her poems, the review comments that *The Sinless Child* "is an unconscious eulogy on the purity of her mind, for it is a work which demands more in its composition than mere imagination or intellect could furnish" (*Boston Notion* 1843, xxxiv). The poem is a testament to Oakes Smith's pure mind, which is itself a testament to the impress of divine forces on Oakes Smith. This sentiment is clinched when the reviewer quotes William Wordsworth's "Ode: Intimations of Immortality" and its famous lines "But trailing clouds of glory do we come, / From God, who is our home" (xxxiv). Oakes Smith's genius was divinely granted, not the product of her own individuality, and as a result she could enter the public sphere only through the protection of those possessing complete subjectivity.

The reviewers also endorse the expectation that no true woman would hazard public exposure of her gifts unless out of necessity. Like Neal, who discusses Oakes Smith's womanly duty in the face of financial ruin, Tuckerman, in his sketch from *Graham's Magazine*, has determined that "she has resorted to the pen, rather as duty than a pleasure" (Tuckerman 1843, xxxi). Unfortunately, such necessity takes a toll on artistic quality. Her works "bear the marks of haste" and could use "a higher finish." "These defects are ascribable to circumstances," Tuckerman tells us; had she not been writing for profit, "the fruits of her pen" might have been of a higher quality (xxx). Tuckerman here illustrates the paradox of the Poetess: women writers supposedly offered readers the pure profession of their souls, yet the appearance of this poetry in public always undercut the sincerity of the profession. When the work was "work," which is to say, when it was created due to necessity, it showed. To extend the logic of Tuckerman's comments, then, churning out work for readers hindered the work's genius because such poetry exhibited the inauthentic stain of commercial profit. For these reasons, Poetess poetry always risks its quality, and the woman writer was not considered equal in the literary marketplace: her poems were hasty and inauthentic, or were productions of pure womanhood and not products of her own labor.

As these prefaces demonstrate, the social expectations for the Poetess implied that her public presence required male superintendence, that her genius resulted from other powers working through her, and that her poetry's lyricism—that is, the expression of pure emotions—was marred by manipulation for profit. However, I would like to examine how *The Sinless Child* uses the transparency of the Poetess—the idea that the poem is a window into the author's interior—to deftly navigate such expectations. In so doing, Oakes Smith works to establish herself as not only a figure who possesses the Poet's genius, but one who also carves out spaces of self-possessed privacy in her poems. When read in this way, we can see how *The Sinless Child* publicly displayed women's sovereignty in a manner comparable to white, male, liberal counterparts. As the creator of Eva, a figure possessing transcendent vision, Oakes Smith points back to herself as the Poet whose genius affords her an autonomous presence in the literary public sphere.[22]

By modeling *The Sinless Child* on "romantic narrative verse," Oakes Smith asserts her poetic status alongside other established Romantic poets such as Wordsworth (Kete 2000, 249).[23] Its structure—a narrative poem in seven parts, with a prose introduction preceding each one—tells the story of Eva, a child with otherworldly insight so pure that she earns the nickname "the Sinless Child." Eva grows up with her mother in their isolated home in the woods. Then one day, as an adolescent, Eva encounters Albert Linne, the hunter. With one glance they fall in love—and Eva dies, her work on earth complete.[24] This plot would seem to confirm the expectations just articulated by Keese et al. about the Poetess's femininity, morality, and subsequent dependence. For instance, the poem's "Inscription," the five-stanza apostrophe to Eva that precedes the seven parts, appears to portray Oakes Smith as a

Undated pencil drawing of Eva captioned "Sinless Child / Eva / By H. Jenks." Elizabeth Oakes Prince Smith Papers, MssCol 2780, box 3, folder 10, Manuscripts and Archives Division, New York Public Library.

consummate Poetess. But Oakes Smith is working through these conventions, I argue, to instead symbolize the female poet's self-sovereignty.

The first stanza of the Inscription collapses the distance between poet and poem. Here the speaker frets over whether or not to send her creation, Eva, into the world. Of course, the reader is encouraged to think of the "I" here as Oakes Smith—indeed, the prefaces used Oakes Smith's poetry to investigate her person. That said, it is notable that Oakes Smith's most famous poem starts out with the image of a female figure going "forth" to circulate in public:

> SWEET EVA! shall I send thee forth,
>   To other hearts to speak?
> With all thy timidness and love
>   Companionship to seek?
> Send thee with all thy abstract ways,
>   Thy more than earthly tone—
> An exile, dearest, send thee forth, thou,
>   Who art all mine own!
>
> —Oakes Smith 1843, 37

"I," the lyrical speaker, is wary of sending part of herself—"Thou, who art all mine own"—into the world. In essence, Oakes Smith asks if she should give herself over to the reading public. This is a moot point: she already has, otherwise we would not be reading these words. But the question and the lyrical pose evoke the modesty associated with the Poetess, drawing out the assumption that she accidentally exposes her interior. This opening stanza relies on lyrical assumptions by implying that readers "overhear" or get a behind-the-scenes glimpse of the authentic Oakes Smith, who has inadvertently revealed her misgivings. And yet the inner debate is in fact printed for all to read, suggesting the performance of intimacy that is also enabled by lyrical devices. In other words, Oakes Smith's hesitancy could be sincere struggle or protective posturing. Since these possibilities contradict each other, Oakes Smith's motivations are in fact more "abstract" than transparent. By professing her ambivalence about the "exile" of her own creation, she is actually reinforcing the distance, so crucial to preserving privacy, that I propose.

Oakes Smith's use of "abstract" further complicates the relationship between poet and poem. Presumably, Eva possesses "abstract ways" because she acts and speaks with a "more than earthly tone." But rather than "abstract" in the sense that Eva is indefinite or abstruse, Eva could be also abstract in terms of clarity or purity—she is an abstraction of "I," derived from Oakes Smith. Indeed, the stanza ends by asserting that Eva "art all mine own," an essence drawn from the poet. Eva, then, is a kind of personification of the lyrical "I": she is a derivation of the speaker's own self sent out into the world. But Oakes Smith employs this seeming self-exposure to instead withdraw. By suggesting that Eva is abstracted from the poet, but that she remains too abstract for readers to fully comprehend, Oakes Smith reserves some privacy from the supposedly transparent transmission of the Poetess. In the next stanza of the Inscription, this complex notion of abstraction more clearly appears as a form of availability:

> Thou art my spirit's cherished dream,
>   Its pure ideal birth;
> And thou hast nestled in my heart,
>   With love that's not of earth.
> Alas! for I have failed, methinks,
>   Thy mystic life to trace;
> Thy holiness of thought and soul,
>   Thy wild enchanting grace.
> —Oakes Smith 1843, 38

We understand that Eva is the product of the poet-speaker, born from her spirit and residing in her heart. Here and in the previous stanza, Oakes Smith begins deploying a rhetorical strategy that will serve her throughout the rest of this long poem. The confessional quality of this stanza acknowledges the intimate emotions of its figured speaker but, crucially, refuses to excavate them for readers. Oakes Smith again emphasizes the abstract quality of Eva—and by extension, herself—by describing Eva as "mystic." The speaker gives "birth" to this "pure ideal," but if the speaker points back to Oakes Smith, then Oakes Smith is also "mystic" because she is the one who created Eva, this abstract being. Oakes Smith has therefore complicated the Poetess by pointing to that which she does not reveal; indeed, the speaker admits that she has "failed, methinks / Thy mystic life to trace." By allowing us to overhear the poet fretting about her process, the Inscription suggests transparency at the same time that the reader is denied the whole picture. In her supposed failure to "trace" all of Eva for the reader, she withholds parts of the Poetess's interiority from public consumption. Oakes Smith gestures toward but refuses to expose a private side in public, beginning to fashion for herself a lyrical, liberal subjectivity.

Oakes Smith depicts Eva as a kind of avatar but, crucially, fails to map the child's interiority. Oakes Smith also implicates herself in this conspicuous absence. To underscore that point, the final three stanzas of the Inscription repeat the failure to delineate interiority, but this time, the speaker's. By extension, Oakes Smith consciously refuses to trace her own self for audiences. In so doing, Oakes Smith stakes her claim as a female Poet who reveals her genius but not at the expense of her self-sovereignty. Indeed, these stanzas anticipate the techniques Oakes Smith will develop in the rest of the poem—techniques that do not presume to expose her interiority but the fact of her *possession* of interiority. This strategy is couched in the speaker's continued reluctance to let Eva go, a reluctance designed to offer audiences the appearance of a private confession:

With thee I've wandered, cherished one,
    At twilight's dreamy hour
To learn the language of the bird,
    The mystery of the flower;
And gloomy must that sorrow be,
    Which thou could'st not dispel.
As thoughtfully we loitered on
    By stream or sheltered dell.

Thou fond Ideal! vital made,
The trusting, earnest, true;
Who fostered, sacred, undefiled
My hearts pure, youthful dew;
Thou woman—soul, all tender, meek,
Thou wilt not leave me now
To bear alone the weary thoughts
That stamp an aching brow!

Yet go! I may not say farewell,
For thou wilt not forsake,
Thou'lt linger, Eva, wilt thou not,
All hallowed thoughts to wake?
Then go; and speak to kindred hearts
In purity and truth;
And win the spirit back again,
To Love, and Peace, and Youth
—Oakes Smith 1843, 38–39

Eva, the "cherished one," may be the product of the speaker's innermost self, but, as these stanzas demonstrate, that personification works to bar access to the speaker's interior. In fact, Eva bolsters the speaker's self-knowledge and self-circumscription; in this sense the Inscription announces that Oakes Smith's poetic project will work to foster these qualities in women. Take for instance the activities the speaker enjoys with Eva: they wander at twilight "To learn the language of the bird, / The mystery of the flower." Like Eva's "mystic" self, once again the mystery—or the language—that the speaker learns is not revealed. The speaker thereby retains this information and, in addition, her feelings of sadness. Eva cannot "dispel" the speaker's "sorrow," presumably a sorrow caused by the prospect of Eva's departure. Here Oakes Smith emphasizes a gap between Eva and the speaker. We are told that Eva is "vital made"; like the weary thoughts, she is a product of the speaker's self. Yet the speaker's complaint explains that Eva will be released to the world while the weary thoughts remain part of the speaker's interiority. Eva may be sent forth, but not all of the speaker's thoughts are likewise circulated; she bears them alone. In other words, sorrow signals sovereignty. The speaker indicates her possession of interiority, but rather than release it, Eva will go out into the world. Indeed, in the following stanza, Eva may "wake" the speaker's "hallowed thoughts," but Eva does not necessarily communicate those thoughts to others.

Here we can also see how Oakes Smith portrays the qualities of the Poetess but uses Eva as a mechanism to simultaneously distance herself from them. "Thou woman—soul, all tender, meek" suggests this femininity in Eva. Those characteristics of the true woman are on display, but lodged in Eva so that Oakes Smith may distinguish herself as Poet. In the wish for Eva's "linger[ing]" presence, Oakes Smith may seem to contradict this action, instead articulating a desire to hang onto the Poetess personification. But the command that Eva "go" communicates Oakes Smith's confidence in her poetic sovereignty. At the same time, this directive anticipates Oakes Smith's poetic project, as she attempts to help readers to discover their own liberal selfhood. Released into the world, Eva conveys to readers their ability to wake their own hallowed thoughts, to "win the spirit back again." That is, Eva will not foster self-exposing and thus self-dissolving Poetesses, but, as we will see, "kindred hearts," or women who win back their own self-sovereignty.

The Sinless Child's Sight

As I suggest above, the Inscription is Oakes Smith's attempt to affirm her self-possession through the figured Eva. Eva is ostensibly the creation of Oakes Smith's heart, a persona that seems to accidentally expose Oakes Smith's interiority to readers. But she is also the figure that Oakes Smith employs to demonstrate her sovereignty over her poetic genius. The rest of the poem continues this project—it is essentially a record of Eva's visionary powers whereby Oakes Smith underscores her own agency. In the next seven sections of *The Sinless Child*, Oakes Smith figures her artistic ingenuity by manipulating the supposedly accidental, divine insight that—so the prefaces would have us believe—true women possess. By extension, the poem becomes an exercise in which Oakes Smith tries to shift the terms of her anticipated reception in its focus on Eva. We will learn that Eva is a seer and a sayer, the picture of Emerson's Poet; as Kete argues, Eva is "the Emersonian poet imagined as a woman . . . the one who re-connects things to themselves and makes even the ugly beautiful" (Kete 2000, 249). Oakes Smith's own creation then reflects back on the genius of Oakes Smith: if Eva possesses such insight, then readers can only imagine the abilities her creator must possess. Oakes Smith thus repudiates the prefaces' picture of a poet whose womanly duty accidentally revealed her genius, and she confirms herself as the self-possessed lyrical Poet by employing the very Poetess practices prescribed to her.

In fact, Eva's sight distinguishes her from the conventional womanhood her mother represents. Oakes Smith exaggerates women's confinement to the private sphere by placing both Eva and her mother far away in the forest. For Eva, this setting enables her to develop and possess her expansive self. But it has the opposite effect on her mother, a figure whose life of apprehension and fear suggests the white, middle-class woman stunted by the illiberal effects of nineteenth-century U.S. culture (Kete 2000, 251). "Dear Eva!" she exclaims, "'tis a world of gloom, / The grave is dark and drear . . . death is standing near" (Oakes Smith 1843, 79). The mother confesses to being afraid of what Eva can show her about herself; even catching her daughter's eye fills her with dread, "As if my very soul might be / By thy pure spirit read" (73). Perhaps Oakes Smith marks the mother for limited self-development because she has been married, a state which will restrain women until both genders are equal, as Oakes Smith argues later in her career.[25] Whatever the reason, Eva and her mother sit at opposite ends of a liberal spectrum: there is Eva, the liberal subject who has the freedom to fully develop her self; and the mother, the woman whose self-development has been hindered by illiberal gender roles, namely, the state of being a wife and mother.[26]

As the mother's worries suggest, Eva's eminence stems from her powers of sight, which the poem highlights throughout its many sections. In the prose prologue to part 1, we are told that Eva "beholds a divine agency in all things" and that "she sees the world, not merely with mortal eyes, but looks within to the pure internal life" (Oakes Smith 1843, 40, 41). In part 2, Eva explains to her mother that she sees "Within this darksome veil, / That hides the spirit-land from thee," and in part 3, she tells her mother how she wishes "O, would the veil for thee were raised / That hides the spirit-land" (65, 88). As opposed to the prefaces' implication that divinity and duty inspire women's poetic vision, Eva's sight is no accident; her powers are hers and hers alone. Yet Eva's insight seemingly comes to naught when she encounters a new person for the first time, the hunter Albert Linne, who stumbles upon Eva sleeping in the forest. The narrator reports that Eva "feel[s] another soul / Is blending into thine," and Eva is, unsurprisingly, apprehensive; she "Half trembles with new fear, / And on her lip that strange, deep smile, / The handmaid of a tear" (124, 128). Eva does not understand her feelings. Contrary to every other experience, she cannot see the heavenly message written in Albert, instead sensing only that a "will of stronger growth" is "hold[ing] her own in check" (128). In other words, she knows she does not know. But Eva's inability to read Albert and understand the willpower that checks her own does not indicate the weakness of women. Instead of confirming her supposed lack of self-possession, Oakes Smith asserts her status as a self-possessed Poet in what should strike us as an odd fashion. Her Poet identifies herself as such by *not* seeing and saying. In her inversion of how liberal selfhood is formed, Oakes Smith evades the Poetess's dispossession of interiority by figuring Eva as fully sovereign over what she cannot understand and, therefore, reveal:

While doubting thus, a seraph stayed
  His radiant course awhile;
And with a heavenly sympathy,
  Looked on with beaming smile:
And thus his words of spirit-love
  Trust and assurance brought,
And bade her where the soul finds birth,
  To weakly question not.

Content to feel—care not to know,
  The sacred source whence LOVE arise—
Respect in *modesty* of *soul*,
  This mystery of mysteries:
Mere mind with all its subtle arts,
  Hath only learned when thus it gazed
The inmost veil of human hearts,
  E'en to themselves must not be raised!

—Oakes Smith 1843, 129

Eva can read beyond the veil of natural objects, but when it comes to human hearts, they remain veiled, as does her own heart to her own self. Here we can see how Oakes Smith complicates the supposed availability of the Poetess's writing and, with it, the illiberal status of women. Rather than granting Eva total insight into Albert's soul, or even her own soul, this scene conceals interiority and replaces it with trust. Couched in the terms of modesty, this trust is, admittedly, still adhering to the Poetess's conventional demureness. But Oakes Smith is also using "*modesty* of *soul*" as a cover for flatly refusing to expose Eva's soul. "Weakly question not," Oakes Smith enjoins her readers, and instead accept her reasoning, even when all is not revealed. For Oakes Smith, this lack of insight models her own poetic self-possession by accomplishing two closely related ends: it bars the reader from prying into Eva's interior and, due to the collapse of Poetess and poem, Oakes Smith's own interior. In sum, Eva is host to an opacity that she cannot fully understand but over which she can still be sovereign. Oakes Smith's version of the Poetess still adheres to lyrical devices, placing the "inmost veil of human hearts" on display—but without necessarily lifting that veil for readers. While telling us that she has the Poetess's proper soul, Oakes Smith is also reserving the right to withhold the contents of that innermost self from public view.

In her conclusion to the poem, Oakes Smith continues to exploit the expectations regulating the Poetess's dispossession in order to model feminine poetic autonomy. This scene with Albert, where Eva learns to trust great mysteries, ends with Eva kissing Albert's brow and disappearing. The next and final prose prologue, part 7, begins with the blunt statement "Eva hath fulfilled her destiny," and now, perhaps surprisingly, she is going to die (Oakes Smith 1843, 132). Albert suffers no such fate. Eva may have shown him the divine, but he "went forth to act / The better human part" (137). Yet for all this apparent inequality, Eva is not a tragic figure, and Albert is not a vampiric presence who ends Eva's existence in order to continue his own. Rather, their meeting initiates her apotheosis to the status of "the true woman," which Eva achieved by seeing, saying, and, just as importantly, circulating (133). She may forge a self free from the encroachments of others, but when it comes to achieving what the poem calls "her mission of Womanhood," Eva had to extend beyond her domestic self-enclosure, encountering both Albert and the opaque mysteries of her soul (132). Oakes Smith thereby links true womanhood to liberal selfhood, which is modeled as Eva's simultaneous self-possession and self-extension. Achieving liberal selfhood, in other words, requires recognition from other people, be it Eva or Albert or, for Oakes Smith, the readers who overhear this lesson.

While the poem itself does not define exactly what constitutes such "Womanhood" or "the true woman," it seems to associate self-sacrifice with the true woman. The significance of self-sacrifice—which is to say, intimations of Eva's death—appears in the prose introduction to part 4. We are told it is the "noon" of summer as well as the "noonday of Eva's earthly existence," and at this midpoint "cometh the mystery of womanhood." Indeed, Oakes Smith's description of womanhood is mysterious; it combines notions of communion and transcendence into a "gentle going forth of the affections seeking for that holiest of companionship, a kindred spirit, responding to all its finer essences, and yet lifting it above itself" (Oakes Smith 1843, 115). Oakes Smith pairs this mystery of true womanhood with the blunt assertion that "the mission of woman, is to the erring of man" (116). In other words, Eva's "gentle agency" is not to be used to preserve her own selfhood, but to help shape Albert Linne "for the kingdom of Heaven," sacrificing herself in the process (116). The communion, then, is for Eva, and the apotheosis is for Albert; Eva's true womanhood emphasizes women's need for a "companionship" in which they enable men's transcendence, and potentially at their own expense.

Given Oakes Smith's aspirations to the status of the Poet, the true woman's mystery should be understood in relation to Emerson's essay on the same topic. Oakes Smith seems to couch true womanhood, a concept whose emphasis on purity, transparency, and divinity necessarily divests women of autonomy, in the same terms as Emerson's "man" who "is only half himself, the other half is his expression" (Emerson 2001, 184). In other words, the same mystery that characterizes the liberal and lyrical self—that individual self-constitution ironically relies on the companionship of others—is the same "mystery" of true womanhood's "gentle going forth" of the self. Oakes Smith thereby revises true womanhood to entail the same self-possession—or productive self-dispossession—as Emerson's lyrical and liberal selfhood.

Part 7, the poem's conclusion, however, is not an unqualified victory for women's liberal selfhood, as Eva's achievement also involves her death. As we saw in the prefaces, true womanhood was ascribed to Oakes Smith. Yet the prefaces also made clear that this achievement typically entailed the death of woman's autonomy. True womanhood and liberal selfhood, it would seem, cannot coexist. Given her political activism, it seems unlikely that Oakes Smith wants readers to reach this bleak conclusion, and, as a result, she kills Eva in order to revitalize the agency associated with true womanhood. Eva's death transforms her into the aspirational lyric self—the ultimate form of an idealized, transcendent subjectivity—that, in turn, attests to the potential agency of all women. According to Kete, "To cease to be present, then, is the ultimate sign of Eva's transcendence, for to 'cease to be present' is to continue to be ideal" (Kete 2000, 255).

Death confers other benefits on Eva, whose transcendent form also grants her sovereignty in her self-knowledge. For example, in the prose prologue to part 7, the narrator continues to describe Eva's ability to perceive what others cannot. Eva may be gone, "the lost pleiad in the sky of womanhood," but in her ideal, celestial form she continues to display "noble aspirations and spiritual discernments." As a progression of rhetorical questions makes clear, her wisdom lives on in women, which is to say, all women possess the agency of the liberal self: "Has her spirit ceased to be upon the earth? Does it not still brood over our woman hearts?—and doth not her voice blend ever with the sweet voices of Nature! Eva, mine own, my beautiful, I may not say—farewell" (Oakes Smith 1843, 133). We are to understand that yes, Eva is still on the earth, found inside all women's hearts and blended with their nature. The speaker need not say farewell because Eva is there, "brooding" over women, incubating the values associated with her spirit. Eva's dissolution does not indicate her dispossession; rather, she blocks readers' possession of her by willingly dissolving into them—and empowering them through her genius. With this transcendence, she encourages their self-sovereignty by demonstrating the little Eva that broods over and in them. We could even say that a "strain" of Eva's lyricism has infected female readers. Oakes Smith shifts the position of her female readers from consumers of female interiority to Poet-like figures who are gifted with Eva's insight.

In Eva's seemingly triumphant death, the conclusion of *The Sinless Child* leaves us with contradictions that prove productive for the construction of a liberal female self. As we have seen, Oakes Smith revises the assumptions associated with the Poetess genre in order to model women's liberal autonomy: a lack of insight indicates poetic power, and liberal self-possession is only possible through self-dissolution. Eva thus serves double ends. She models a form of transcendent individualism that is positively unbounded at the same time that she shows Oakes Smith's self-possession in the literary public sphere as a Poet, not Poetess. In the words of Adam Tuchinsky, Eva presents the model and making of a woman who is insulated "from the ravages of individualism" (Tuchinsky 2016, 56).[27] It is through such self-dissolution that Eva's ideal form of transcendence opens the self beyond the boundaries of circumscribed individualism. Furthermore, the women over whom Eva broods are unified by sharing this part of their individual interiority with each other. The self is made up of other selves, and the shared existence that Eva fosters aligns with what Elizabeth Duquette calls Emerson's "liberal ideal—the dissolution of particularistic identity as a way to ground universal justice and equality" (Duquette 2015, 652).[28] Here is further proof of lyric's open secret, in that woman is only half herself, and the other half is her reception. In death, Eva blends with Nature and extends into women's hearts, and these are actions that refute the need for male superintendence by replacing it with shared female autonomy.

The Poet's Sight

Oakes Smith navigates the seemingly contradictory impulses of transcendental self-dissolution and liberal self-circumscription in figures like Eva, whose insight asserts the Poet's sovereignty even as she invites readers to look into her "sinless" self. To avoid implying that she is just a Poetess inadvertently gifted with divine sight and ideal transcendence, Oakes Smith shifts readers' expectation from what they could see *in* her—a glimpse inside her pure mind or soul—to what readers could see *through* her own powerful sight. To put it another way, rather than letting readers look into the Poetess's interior, Oakes Smith instead offered to readers the opportunity to see through the Poet's gaze. In so doing, Oakes Smith also presumes to transform her readers' roles by shifting them from agents in the Poetess's dispossession to subjects of the Poet's revelation.

In Oakes Smith's poetry, this revision of the reader's position is not limited to *The Sinless Child*. The similar use of omniscient, poetic insight occurs in "The Drowned Mariner," which first appeared in Rufus Griswold's *Gems from American Female Poets* (1842) and was later collected in *The Poetical Writings of Elizabeth Oakes Smith* (1845). The poem begins with a mariner "on the shrouds" watching the whales below, only to end as a revenge tale. The mariner has broken his vow to his betrothed, and she is dead, presumably of heartbreak. In the moments before a storm sinks his ship, the mariner sees her face in the waves.

While the poem may appear to develop as a straightforward narrative about retribution, the speaker seems to know details beyond the telling of this story. In the sixth stanza, the speaker demonstrates her knowledge of the events preceding the ship's sinking. Pausing in her telling of the tale, she scolds the mariner: "Bethink thee, mariner, well of the past . . . Bethink thee of oaths, that were lightly spoken; / Bethink thee of vows, that were lightly broken" (Oakes Smith 1845, 188). With these warnings, Oakes Smith suggests the self-sovereignty of the female poet: exceptional moral knowledge comes not from forces working through her, but from her own omniscience. Readers are no longer encouraged to sense that they benefit from the Poetess's inadvertent exposure; instead the narrator has power over what the reader can and should know.

Another way to assert the Poet's command over what is revealed to readers is to stop telling this tale altogether. While it continues to emphasize the speaker's insight, the last stanza takes an unexpected turn away from the drowned mariner's story to a final, quiet, and everlasting scene:

A peopled home is the ocean bed;
    The mother and child are there;
The fervent youth and the hoary head,
The maid, with her floating locks outspread,
    The babe with its silken hair;
As the water moveth they lightly sway,
And the tranquil lights on their features play;
And there is each cherished and beautiful form,
Away from decay, and away from the storm.
—Oakes Smith 1845, 189

This last stanza is a departure from the Poetess's availability in several ways. First, this voice is one of vision, not the personal, transparent Poetess. Furthermore, the stanza refuses to provide a moral that readers might associate with women's writing. Contrary to the reviewers who presumed to assess Oakes Smith's person by evaluating her poetry, this last stanza blocks knowledge of our poet—except to suggest that she knows all. In so doing, Oakes Smith casts herself in the role of the poetic seer whose gaze falls equally on all people. While this stanza does not profess emotion, one of the key devices of the antebellum lyric, I argue that it nonetheless employs lyrical devices in its figuration of an all-knowing speaker. The very description of this quiet scene suggests an omnipotent speaking subject who, in place of some moral reckoning, offers an alternate lesson. Like Eva, whose insight pointed back to the Poet who tells her tale, this ending denotes Oakes Smith as the Poet-seer. These powers are further confirmed as Oakes Smith continues to associate the dead with transcendence. The drowned have ceased to be present and yet are still present in the poem as inaccessible and self-contained figures. Though each "cherished and beautiful form" is exhibited, the reader is not granted full access to their minds, hearts, or souls. In this final stanza's shift away from "the storm" on the surface to the "home" of the ocean floor, Oakes Smith creates a quasi-family of the dead that shows but does not tell. They may be dead, but they are "away from decay" and have achieved the ideal, timeless transcendence of Eva, self-enclosed and ever-present.

This poem features characteristics—a plot-driven narrative, dramatic conclusion, and alternating lines of four and three stressed beats—associated with the ballad in nineteenth-century literature. Furthermore, the ballad presents challenges for the application of lyric theory. For example, ballads were not necessarily understood as being "spoken" by a lyric subject, as I am proposing. Indeed, the ballad form militates against any such notion of the unitary speaker; as Michael Cohen argues, "The socio-political value of ballads derived from their association with the idealized oral cultures of imagined folk communities, rather than from qualities inherent in the individual objects themselves" (M. Cohen 2008, 4). But reading this poem for its lyrical strains brings Oakes Smith's liberal project into focus. Oakes Smith had lyric's transcendental selfhood in mind given the uncharacteristic last stanza of the poem; furthermore, the narrator's lyrical insight suggests the constitution of a figured speaking subject.

In "The Drowned Mariner," Oakes Smith confirms her vast vision. She possesses an imagination that can depict the isolated domesticity of *The Sinless Child* as well as the wild seas. I think it is no accident that Oakes Smith and other female poets picture exotic locations and adventures in their works as a way to project their own selves beyond the expectations of the domestic, transparent Poetess. Due to the popularity of her poetry, we can even say that Oakes Smith's name traverses the world, public and private spheres alike, through her poems. In the poem "The Acorn," she again deploys nautical adventure in order to reframe the Poetess's autonomy. Published in Keese's 1843 edition, this poem is the story of an acorn that turns into an oak tree that, in turn, becomes a ship—only to have the ship sink. The poem continues to exhibit the restrictions on the physical circulation of women, as Oakes Smith must displace this adventurous spirit onto an inanimate object. Nevertheless, a little thing, descended from a mighty legacy, grows to greatness and circles the globe—the acorn even travels to the Indian sea with its "spicy breeze" (Oakes Smith 1843, 156). With the acorn's transformations, Oakes Smith once again attempts to merge Poetess with Poet. By describing the acorn, tree, and ship with masculine language such as "mighty," "regally," "gallant," and "stout," Oakes Smith tries to adjust the terms associated with the Poetess persona (150, 149, 152, 145). The Poetess, she is suggesting, comes from an arboreal and masculine literary tradition, not separate from but part of the legacy of prominent male writers (Richards 2004, 152). But the poem does not allow readers to forget the fanciful femininity associated with the Poetess—the acorn only grows into a tree because "woodland Fays" and sprites plant it in the ground; eventually the ship "sits like an ocean-sprite" (142, 155). The association with woodland Fays stems from the conventions of women's writing in the nineteenth century, and the need for women to be somehow fanciful or disembodied in order to have a public, unerotic presence.[29] Like the acorn, the Poetess had to manage a contradictory poetic public persona that was both gallant and sprite-like—in other words, an impossible set of standards.

Like Eva in *The Sinless Child*, the fate of the acorn offers a metaphor for the fate of the Poetess in the literary marketplace and in literary history: the figure eventually ceases to be. Although "The Acorn" suggests success—the acorn descends from great forebears and is fated to circulate all around the world—Oakes Smith shifts away from the optimistic transcendence she depicted in *The Sinless Child*. "The Acorn" appears to say that her version of the Poetess is an impossible achievement for women, and the goal of gaining the Poet's legacy is doomed to failure. As Richards argues, Oakes Smith's writings imply that "though the poetess cannot write her way out of her problems of reception, she can identify and diagnose the terms under which she labors" (Richards 2004, 157). I would add that Oakes Smith diagnosed and drew attention to the liberal subjectivity that she was denied, even though she met the requirements and was destined, like the acorn, for this greatness. Given such premises, "The Acorn" becomes legible as Oakes Smith's attempt to navigate between the reputation she desires and the gendered expectations that invariably shape the reception of her poetry. In short, the poem presumes to capture the Poetess's illiberal public status. To these ends, "The Acorn" is already outlining its reception. From the start, even fanciful and fairy-like Fays cannot but admit that the acorn's future is "fraught" with "destruction" (Oakes Smith 1843, 142). By the poem's close, the pretense to the strong individualism associated with trees, ships, and masculinity ultimately fails—the tree is cut, the ship sinks:

Helmless, but on before the gale,
She ploughs the deep-troughed wave:
A gurgling sound—a phrenzied wail—
And the ship hath found a grave.
And thus is the fate of the acorn told,
That fell from the old oak tree,
And the woodland Fays in the frosty mould
Preserved for its destiny.
—Oakes Smith 1843, 157

Oakes Smith asserts that external conditions make female poetic self-possession impossible. Circumstances, and not merit, determine the fate of the Poetess—consider the fate of the ship, which sinks because she is struck by lightning. Women poets are not afforded the self-possession that would keep their names alive in the literary public sphere. Indeed, the dispossessed ship becomes "helmless," losing parts of itself to the bigger world. No less than the acorn, the Poetess thought she was meant for greater things, but her "destiny" is to "f[ind] a grave."

But for all this talk of impossibility, Oakes Smith does imagine a brief moment of success in "The Acorn." To discern it, we must entertain the possibility that the poem does not figure liberal selfhood through the acorn, but through the lyrical speaker of the poem. This "I" persists as the indigestible kernel of a poetic presence, a bulwark against the dispossession of the Poetess. In the fifth stanza of the poem, the speaker refers to herself as she watches a little sprite struggling to plant the acorn:

I laughed outright at the small thing's toil,
As he bow'd beneath the spade,

And he balanced his gossamer wings the while
To look in the pit he made.
—Oakes Smith 1843, 143

Yes, the acorn is destined to be forgotten, but Oakes Smith tells us that she might not be the acorn. Instead, "I" knows and tells—like Emerson's Poet—at the same time that she superintends the decision to preserve the acorn for its destiny.[30] Oakes Smith thereby elevates the Poetess figure to a position of literary genius, one that oversees the creation of an American literary tradition.

Gendered Expectations

As this chapter has argued, Oakes Smith employed different lyrical strategies in order to approach the liberal self that was denied to women. By changing the terms on which the Poetess claimed genius, these strategies allowed Oakes Smith to align herself with the Poet figure and the subjectivity it promised. Rather than the double-edged transparency of the Poetess—celebrity at the price of exposure to and consumption by readers—Oakes Smith made such exposure work to her advantage. She alluded to opaque spots of privacy to demonstrate how women could be in full possession of a private and public self, and crafted models of female autonomy in transcendent poetic figures. The lyrical subjects of these poems point back to the presence of its poetic creator—hence the "I" who narrates the tale of the acorn from its initial planting, or the "I" who frets over sending Eva into the world. "The Drowned Mariner" may lack an "I" speaker, but the narrator's control over the story and concluding omniscience constitutes a "speaking" subject who asserts the power of the Poet-seer. Her figurations of circulation—ships that sail exotic seas, for example—combine with the actual wide circulation of her poems to suggest that Oakes Smith turned the Poetess's public availability into evidence of her autonomy. She may not have been able to write her way out of her reception, as Richards notes, but she could at least publicly assert herself as a self-possessed literary presence.

Yet these poems share more than just a preoccupation with liberal and poetic self-possession. Each poem also ends in failure: Eva dies, the mariner joins an ocean floor full of dead bodies, the acorn's ship sinks. This is a telling pattern for a woman poet who was concerned with achieving access to the self-possession that liberal selfhood represents. Eva had to die before she could "brood over" women, that is, become a transcendent, Poet-like figure who can imbue other women with universal, divine knowledge (Oakes Smith 1843,

133). Likewise, "The Drowned Mariner" also dwells on figures whose demise preserves them in ideal forms. The doomed destiny of the eponymous nut in "The Acorn" implies that the female poet's public presence comes at the price of her eventual erasure. As these poems suggest, it was precisely this failure that made transcendence possible. Thus for Oakes Smith, poetic transcendence emerges as a rhetorical strategy, but it did not entirely solve the problem of the female poet's self-possession or self-perpetuation. The lesson to be derived, it would seem, is that female poets must cease to be if they are to achieve the autonomy of the Poet. The trouble, then, is with transcendence, and Oakes Smith's versions of transcendence diagnose the failure that issues from trying to achieve that perfect state of self. As I argued in the introduction, the lyrical and liberal self always hovered beyond the grasp of readers and writers because it was an aspirational ideal.

By confronting failure in her writing, Oakes Smith hoped to avoid or at least assuage a reception that would undermine her efforts to position herself as the liberal Poet. Recall that in her autobiography, Oakes Smith asserted that she would not be forgotten, perhaps because she suspected she could be. Such concerns seem to be on Oakes Smith's mind in the poem "Man and Woman," which appears to have been written shortly after she completed "A Human Life," that is, late in her life. It develops the same anxieties about fragmentation and dissolution in women's lives that she articulated there:

Warrior and statesmen have their meed of praise,
    And what they do or suffer men record;
But the long sacrifice of woman's days
    Passes without a thought, without a word,
And many a lofty struggle for the sake
    Of duties sternly, faithfully fulfilled,
For which the anxious mind must watch and wake,
    And the strong feelings of the heart be stilled,
Goes by unheeded as the summer wind,
    And leaves no memory and no trace behind;
Yet, it may be, more lofty courage dwells
    In one meek heart which braves an adverse fate
Than his whose ardent soul indignant swells,
    Warmed by the fight or cheered through high debate.
The soldier dies surrounded; could he live
Alone to suffer and alone to strive?
—Oakes Smith 1887, 2

While poetic transcendence offered a way, albeit flawed, to access the mutual recognition and public self-possession that accompanied liberal selfhood, here Oakes Smith looks at mundane realities. In this poem, no woman is transcendent; her work is grounded in the toil of everyday life. Rather than ceasing to be and achieving the status of the ideal, women in real life must disappear from the public realm. The separate spheres philosophy appears to still be in place at the end of the nineteenth century, with women's work associated with the silent, invisible realm of the domestic, and manly action receiving public praise. Like the "warrior and statesmen," women sacrifice themselves to their sense of duty. Yet for all these similarities, women's actions are forgotten "without a word." Oakes Smith implies that the greater courage resides in the woman who meekly "braves an adverse fate," rather than the man who is publicly "warmed" or "cheered" through his tasks. Can man live "alone to suffer and alone to strive" like woman? No, Oakes Smith would suggest, but neither should woman remain helplessly alone and silent. Merely fulfilling the divine obligations of true womanhood is not enough compensation for the labor that women perform.

We can see that at the end of her life the legacy of the Poetess's reception may still render Oakes Smith's career "unheeded as the summer wind." Yet there is distinction in a woman poet who publishes her thoughts as, at the minimum, she separates herself from the women who go on "without a word." Whether Oakes Smith is remembered or not, her poems' very public existence enacts a self-sovereignty in which, she hopes, equality knows no gender. Oakes Smith's contemporaries were grappling with and making manifest for readers the professional problems facing women writers. But Oakes Smith's work instead offers radical solutions that attempt to abolish gender by obliterating the imaginative boundaries associated with the Poetess.

To conclude, let's consider a text in which Oakes Smith's desire for gender equality is asserted through the rhetoric of gender fluidity. Sometime in the 1840s, Oakes Smith delivered a speech in verse to a woman's convention in Boston at which Emerson was present. Roughly forty years later, the text of this speech, "Thoughts on Woman. By Elizabeth Oakes Smith," was published for the very first time. The text is among the clippings in Oakes Smith's scrapbook, but date and source are not clear—no date is printed, and the text reads "For the Home Journal" above the title (Oakes Smith, n.d.). The reprint serves to acknowledge "the inspiring influence of [Oakes Smith's] genius," and the editors offer this unpublished material as a "tribute of esteem" in her "declining years" (Oakes Smith, n.d.). They did not ask for Oakes Smith's permission, "knowing well that the permission would not be granted"

(Oakes Smith, n.d.). This publication suggests that her identity—as a genius no less—was to be preserved. And yet these comments are perhaps too ambiguous in their praise to assuage Oakes Smith's anxieties about losing her literary legacy. She may be in her eighties, but the editors' mention of her "advanced" age, their lack of effort to gain her consent, and their composition of what is essentially a eulogy may have exacerbated such worries by treating her as if she was already gone (Oakes Smith, n.d.).

Yet the republication of her works does more to solidify Oakes Smith's lasting legacy than doom her to the Poetess's nameless fate. The printed, public appearance of "Thoughts on Woman" suggests that the appropriate tribute to Oakes Smith's genius is not prose, but poetry. Furthermore, this text confirms that Oakes Smith's version of liberal advocacy lent itself to poetic forms. According to the editors, Oakes Smith deserved to be remembered through the work that explicitly combined liberal thought with poetic practices. In reprinting it without Oakes Smith's permission, the editors have highlighted the lyricism of the piece by taking her personal profession and sharing it with an audience of overhearers. Such lyrical qualities foreground the supposed sincerity of the utterance and make Oakes Smith's liberal argument more forceful:

> The very God who made us gave to each
> The right to own himself; the he or she
> Who his own selfhood sells for any gaud,
> For station or for pelf, deserves to wear
> The shackles of a slave . . .
> —Oakes Smith, n.d.

Oakes Smith promotes the equality of women because they, like men, are self-sovereign and self-possessed. The God-given "right to own himself" is possibly the most private, intimate attribute of liberal selfhood, and the lyrical exposure of privacy asserts this equal sovereignty within public view.

And so, at the end of her life, the legacy of the Poet allows Oakes Smith to be remembered for defending the liberal subjectivity of those to whom it had been denied. Oakes Smith positions herself, and is publicly recognized, as a Poet who will not fade away without a word. Her anxieties would seem to be allayed: here is proof that her genius has made her recognizable as a literary figure, not a generic type to be forgotten. In fact, this document shows us that the Poet, formerly figured as a masculine literary tradition, nullifies perceived gender differences by her transcendence. Oakes Smith more explicitly breaks down the boundaries between men and women by creating a transcendentalist female subject:[31]

True man and woman true but represent
A soul, where sex is not. All fairest forms
Will take the woman shape; the finer sense
Take hers. Poets are women in disguise—
And such was Christ, and Abel, martyr made
Unto brute force, as woman has been made.
The resurrection light will show that men,
The truest, noblest types of manly worth,
Have all been women.
—Oakes Smith, n.d.

According to Oakes Smith, Poets are women; in fact, the "true," equal form of the soul is gendered female. Thus Oakes Smith's idea of a truly lyrical self—a Poet who speaks her interiority and is not consumed but self-possessed enough to circulate and interact with others—is transcendently female. Indeed, as Kete argues, "the endpoint of transcendental metamorphosis is not 'manhood' but 'womanhood'" (Kete 2000, 251–52). The earthly Poetess necessarily fails, but the Poet surpasses the bounds of self-possessed individualism to "take the woman shape." With this we can understand that while the Poetess tradition may dictate the terms of her reception, Oakes Smith's message and quite possibly her name will live on. Oakes Smith transcended literary practices to prove that women are self-possessed Poetic subjects. In a text that explicitly combines advocacy and poetry, lyrical expression and liberal ideology, the transcendent female subject is not a failure, but the final form for all liberal subjectivity.

CHAPTER THREE

Frances Ellen Watkins Harper's Two-Body Problem

Frances Ellen Watkins Harper's body was a problem.[1] Indeed, Watkins Harper was doubly disadvantaged in the nineteenth-century public sphere, where her presence on the antislavery lecture circuit and her antislavery writings could not help but draw attention to her own black, female body. The resulting public "scrutiny and abuse" often struck chords that were especially sexual and proprietary in nature (Sorisio 2010, 80). A public woman was, after all, already suspected of promiscuity; in Watkins Harper's case, these suspicions were only amplified by "scientific" arguments about the lasciviousness of women of color (80). Race further complicated this public gaze, as there was the sense—before and after emancipation, and even though she was never enslaved—that Watkins Harper's body was not her own property but "part of the public domain" due to the influence of slavery on how African Americans, "free" or enslaved, were perceived (79).[2] Finally, this scrutiny even extended beyond Watkins Harper's physical presence to include her print persona; as Mary Loeffelholz argues, "Print authorship was throughout her career inseparable from encountering the public gaze" (Loeffelholz 2004, 99).

It is no surprise, then, that a vein of scholarship on Watkins Harper attends to the interanimation between Watkins Harper's body and the body politic, and that such work concludes that Watkins Harper responded to racist and misogynistic public scrutiny in her poetry by figuring the black female body according to a rhetoric of restraint and discipline.[3] This rhetoric in Watkins Harper's antislavery poetry is most evident, it is argued, in two closely connected tendencies in her work. First, Watkins Harper's poetry evinces diversionary tactics designed to minimize sexualized attention to such a body. According to critics in this vein, her second tactic replaces any sexual associations with modest assertions of rational self-possession. Carolyn Sorisio aptly captures the interplay of these tendencies when she argues that Watkins Harper's poetic restraint enabled her "to represent corporeality while figuratively avoiding the public's inappropriate gaze" (Sorisio 2010, 81). Taken together, these tactics enabled Watkins Harper to maintain some semblance of a public body, as Carla Peterson writes, in order to call "attention to the plight of the weak and the oppressed while refusing to scrutinize their bodily form"

(Peterson 1995, 128). In sum, critics agree that in poems about enslaved women, such as "The Slave Mother" and "The Slave Auction," Watkins Harper exhibits a rational restraint that downplays the public presence of black bodies, especially her own. And she was successful—according to Peterson, her reviewers "emphasiz[ed] the quietness of her body, the chastity of her language, and the purity of her voice" (122).

Here it is worth noting that the public scrutiny with which Watkins Harper grappled was only one expression of widespread white anxieties about the threat that freely circulating black bodies posed to the nation. Such anxieties testified to the bounds of nineteenth-century liberalism, which could be considered "powerful in the United States," Judith Shklar argues, "only if black people are not counted as members of its society" (Shklar 1989, 22). In other words, there has never been liberalism in the United States, but only "racial liberalism," a term Charles W. Mills uses to designate the regime of constitutive exceptions and carve-outs that show just how far this philosophy has fallen short of its universalist pretensions (Mills 2008, 1381). Liberalism in the United States was founded on racial injustice, and the very notion of the American liberal subject, Mills makes plain, is based on implicit principles of racial inclusion and exclusion, wherein "conceptions of personhood and resulting schedules of rights, duties, and government responsibilities have all been racialized" (1381).[4] Consider, for example, how the racial liberal imagination envisioned the fundamental differences between white liberal subjects and black people. Though the white liberal subject was "driven by desire," "reason and rationality" acted as a crucial counterbalance to temper those desires before they became too impulsive or destructive (Connolly 2014, 7). Conversely, this racial imagination, and the U.S. policies it underscored, presumed that black people lacked those same mechanisms of self-control. Black people were creatures who were "devoid of 'higher' human qualities, such as tenderness, intelligence, aesthetic sensitivity, and spirituality"; in the absence of those traits, blacks only "existed on the plane of physical passions" (Sanborn 2005, 696). This conclusion animated the political arguments of those white political and economic stakeholders most invested in preserving slavery and upholding institutionalized white supremacy.

Given such a context, Watkins Harper's politics of the black female body, as critics such as Sorisio and Peterson understand it, effaced or avoided that body to instead emphasize the liberal self-governance black people possessed. This liberal discretion, they argue, permeates Watkins Harper's poetic forms, which enable the body to be erased or obstructed. But this obstruction is generative. According to Sorisio, "The ballad also provides a literary shield for the poem's presenter," one that allows Watkins Harper "to speak the stories of slaves without calling attention to herself; her voice eclipses her body" (Sorisio 2010, 84). Peterson turns this basic metaphor of eclipse or erasure into a figure for self-discipline, arguing that "the conventionality and formal limitations of the ballad stanza further served [Watkins Harper's] imperative of emotional restraint" (Peterson 1995, 129). Watkins Harper avoided lyric's overflow of emotion, so the story goes, because such emotional spontaneity would affirm African Americans' lack of self-discipline. With its emphasis on rational restraint, this approach risks implying that Watkins Harper's works cannot help but work within and thereby accommodate the very racial liberalism that grounded the institution of slavery. While I agree that Watkins Harper attempts to avoid impropriety and assert the rationality of African Americans, restraint exists in Watkins Harper's poetry as a permeable boundary she self-consciously crosses through the strategic use of lyrical conventions.

Working from the fundamental premise that Watkins Harper essayed to "shield the black female body from undue public scrutiny," these critical approaches overlook how Watkins Harper revised conventional depictions of black bodies in order to elaborate new forms of black liberal subjectivity—or what I am terming a form of black liberalism—to counter those more prominent racial liberal forms (M. Bennett 2005, 50). Ultimately, her project is concerned not with condemning but with revising the liberal political philosophy that supported the disenfranchisement of black Americans in the nineteenth century. Contrary to the critical consensus, I argue that Watkins Harper's apparent efforts to back away from the body instead suggest its centrality to her work, and such body-abnegating practices actually serve to reaffirm its presence. Watkins Harper's poetry dwells on the bodies of those who are enslaved, I argue, and she does so by developing a poetics of disassembly. Her poems, in other words, dissect black bodies and depict their component parts. By presenting pieces of a body rather than the embodied whole, Watkins Harper rhetorically affirmed her restraint as well as avoided cultural expectations about the promiscuous black female body. Indeed, Watkins Harper could be said to "rationalize" the body in the sense that she breaks it down and reorganizes it. For Watkins Harper, such disassembly does not abet slavery or its racial logics but instead recognizes how, in the words of Saidiya Hartman, "liberal narratives of individuality idealize mechanisms of domination and discipline" (Hartman 1997, 116). From the standpoint of racial liberalism, the circumscribed, singular subject offers no resistance to slavery's violence but creates a focal point for slavery to exert more control. In lieu of such racial liberal subjects, what Watkins Harper *does* create are differently embodied selves that avoid the problematic encumbrances of proprietorial selfhood in the context of slavery. She fashions a solution in which the sum of body parts exceeds notions of the circumscribed liberal self.

For Watkins Harper, no figure better captures this poetics of disassembly—and the issues of gender, race, and politics that accompany it—than the enslaved mother. Rather than focusing on the institution of slavery and its denial of self-possession to African American women, this chapter will linger with Watkins Harper on the connection between disassembled bodies and mothers who exceed the boundaries of the singular liberal subject. For Watkins Harper, motherhood complicates liberalism's autonomous self-circumscription by reminding us that no person is entirely separate from others—every individual once shared a mother's body. Hence the "two-body problem" of the enslaved mother, in which slavery renders motherhood doubly devastating by denying women rights over their own bodies and over the bodies of their children.[5] Through this maternal figure, Watkins Harper can address another type of two-body problem, that is, the double barriers to liberal selfhood presented by black women's bodies. First, slaves were considered private possessions, not people, and as "private property," slaves were "decisively excluded from public, political participation" (Dillon 2004, 17). Second, encumbered or extended by their children's bodies, mothers were forbidden the self-circumscription synonymous with liberal selfhood. As Elizabeth Dillon argues, "Women's bodies have been described as insufficiently bounded; the penetrable female body is understood to be inherently lacking in autonomy, conjoined to children and dependent upon men" (12). In the context of racial liberalism, these two conditions combined into a devastating consequence: motherhood as a means for perpetuating profit. I argue that Watkins Harper's poetry contravenes liberalism's notions of individual circumscription by reflecting on how enslaved mothers' bodies and the enslaved children attached to those bodies were broken down into publicly saleable parts. Yet this poetics of disassembly was not without its affirmative aspects. Aspirants to the rights and freedoms associated with a black liberal subject, Watkins Harper's enslaved mothers did not seek to merely achieve individuality but to exceed it.

Rather than breaking with cultural norms, Watkins Harper achieved what Derrick Spires calls "pedagogies of revolutionary citizenship" by working through the tradition of the Poetess (Spires 2019, 211). We can better understand Watkins Harper's invocation of the Poetess when we consider that much of her poetry was performed and delivered on the antislavery lecture circuit.

Indeed, Tricia Lootens argues that Watkins Harper's "performance" of the Poetess allowed her to "take a 'deep hold' on the 'popular heart'" (Lootens 2016, 192). With its recognizable and acceptable conventions, Poetess poetry enabled Watkins Harper to align the protective tropes of true womanhood with the vulnerable enslaved mother. But as I have argued elsewhere in this book, the figure and its associated poetic practices offered a means of political intervention for those who were denied recognition in the nineteenth-century public sphere. Watkins Harper was no different. Her use of the Poetess persona sought to claim feminine morality for black women and, perhaps more importantly, to apply the lyrical devices comprising Poetess poetics toward liberal ends. By performing in public, Watkins Harper also complicated lyric's supposed disregard for an audience, and, in so doing, she was able to speak what was, for black women in public, unspeakable: she condemned the violence enabled by racial liberalism and expanded liberal selfhood to the very people who had been denied its freedoms.

Indeed, lyrical strains in Watkins Harper's poetry worked to reverse the dispossession enacted upon women's bodies by slavery. As we have seen, liberalism's politics impacted Poetess poetics; while the lyrical expression of emotion signaled liberal self-possession for men, this same device signaled the female poet's inadvertent and un-liberal self-dispossession. But this very problem allowed Watkins Harper to draw meaningful parallels to slavery. Far from equating the position of the Poetess with the enslaved, I argue that Watkins Harper's poetry aligns expectations of the Poetess's dispossession in public with the enslaved woman's loss of power over her physical and intimate capacities.[6] Identifying such disassembly allows Watkins Harper to claim a revised liberal selfhood for the enslaved mother, and she exchanges the Poetess's problems for the black woman's property in being.

Through this maternal figure, Watkins Harper offers a revised, expansive liberalism based in notions of community, not individuality, from which the black, free, and female self emerges. This chapter likewise demonstrates an expansion in its reading of Watkins Harper's poems, progressing from mothers to families and then to community. First, I explore how Watkins Harper's enslaved mothers demonstrate that their selfhood enabled expansion via their children. I then examine the relations surrounding the enslaved mother by discussing Watkins Harper's poems that depict the enslaved family. Finally, I discuss Watkins Harper's "single" women, whose individuality actually serves to foreground community. Singleness offers Watkins Harper an opportunity to assert collectivity, and I argue that, for Watkins Harper, individual self-possession grows out of black community. This progression—from enslaved mothers, to the families of the enslaved, to seemingly single women—shows how kinship in its many forms resists the domination that racial liberalism enforces upon the individual. Ultimately, these readings are pieces of the black liberalism puzzle, which serves as a rejoinder to racial liberalism and its premises.

Liberal Motherhood

Watkins Harper's poetics advocates for abolition by closely attending to the myriad violent ways in which slavery disassembled the black body. For instance, in her poems on slave auctions, she breaks down black bodies in order to duplicate the violent objectifications enacted by the marketplace of slavery. Buyers and sellers in the U.S. slave trade commodified black subjects by assigning monetary value to their parts with complete indifference to humanity. As Walter Johnson explains, "[Prices] could be used to make even the most counter-intuitive comparisons—between the body of an old man and a little girl . . . or between the muscular arm of a field hand and the sharp eye of a seamstress" (W. Johnson 1999, 58). This objectification shifted from a matter of monetary calculation to physical violence in the plantation field or manor, where parts of black bodies were overworked and abused. Here slavery created a rhetorical problem for abolitionists who needed to criticize its violence without reinforcing images of black suffering; accounts of violence would erode—not affirm—the black subject's humanity. As Hartman argues, "The endeavor to bring pain close exploits the spectacle of the body in pain and oddly confirms the spectral character of suffering and the inability to witness the captive's pain" (Hartman 1997, 20). Using Hartman's argument as a point of departure, I investigate how Watkins Harper breaks down the body to avoid describing the explicit violence that spectacularizes the black body and effaces the suffering of the enslaved person.

This is not to say that violence is absent from Watkins Harper's poetry. Rather, the violent events of slavery become the underlying premise or preconditions from which her poems emerge. In that way, Watkins Harper's focus on enslaved mothers serves to symbolize what cannot be spoken in the public sphere: many enslaved women were mothers because they were raped. Given what Hartman calls the "indirection of polite discourse," Watkins Harper could not be explicit about sexual violence, even though it "exists as an unspoken but normative condition fully within the purview of everyday sexual practices" (Hartman 1996, 543). Watkins Harper implies rape because fathers are very much left out of these poems. In other words, Watkins Harper combats the elision of sexual violence with elisions of her own. She refuses to duplicate explicit violence and refuses to create a circumscribed black body.

To assert the violence of slavery, Watkins Harper's poetry dismantles and differently assembles the individual. Watkins Harper's enslaved figures depict how black subjectivity develops with a difference—under extreme duress, or what Shklar calls a "liberalism of fear" (Shklar 1989, 23). Whereas liberalism as a philosophy, such as the kind depicted by John Stuart Mill, insists that "every adult . . . be able to make as many effective decisions without fear or favor," a liberalism of fear recognizes that liberalism is a "political doctrine" in which "fear and favor" "have always inhibited freedom [and] are overwhelmingly generated by governments" (21). Shklar's discussion is meant to broadly clarify liberal philosophy from its lived experiences, but I employ her distinction specifically within the political-philosophical framework underpinning American chattel slavery. Liberalism's supposed liberties were undercut by the institutionalized cruelty of slavery, and enslaved selfhood could only develop from a fear of white violence. In turn, Watkins Harper's poetry was developing what I am calling a black liberalism, a political and social environment that neither limits liberty to mere protection from fear nor excuses domination. Through the enslaved mother, a figure whose race, gender, and encumbrances mark her as especially defenseless, Watkins Harper hopes to examine the racist underpinnings of American liberalism.

At the same time, Watkins Harper's enslaved mothers demonstrate the conceptual and practical chasms that push forms of black liberalism to incorporate, as Michael Dawson has argued, "decidedly antiliberal" elements (Dawson 2001, 13).[7] As we will see, Watkins Harper's enslaved mothers clearly suggest illiberality when they contemplate infanticide. By discussing such a shocking act, Watkins Harper's most obvious point is to emphasize how slavery ruined the freedom upon which the nation was supposedly staked. As her poetry shows, the resulting nation belies its claims to "positive" liberty; rather, it is a nation whose very political foundations rely on a liberalism of fear, and these mothers are so *fearful* for their children that they consider killing them.[8] Notably, such talk of fear, as well as the concepts of domination that accompany it, motivates a shift in political registers from liberalism to republicanism—which is to say, to a form of illiberalism. Indeed, scholars most often understand Watkins Harper's black maternal figures as attempts to complicate the project of republican motherhood.[9] For instance, Stephanie Farrar argues that Watkins Harper "aim[ed] to extend the very real privileges associated with Republican Motherhood to black women" by "challeng[ing] black women's exclusion from citizenship" (Farrar 2015, 53). The institution of slavery disrupted republican motherhood's nationalist ambitions by excluding black mothers from "ideal maternity" (56). Children born into slavery had to follow the condition of their mother, and, for that reason, enslaved mothers could not raise sons with capacities for civic virtue (53). Under such dire circumstances, infanticide is an act of kindness, as "Harper presents the willingness to kill as a rational extension of maternal love, potentially the only parental decision a slave mother may make" (57). Indeed, in poems such as "Eliza Harris" and "The Slave Mother: A Tale of the Ohio," Watkins Harper's characters contemplate and carry out, respectively, infanticide because they fear the life of violent domination that their children would experience as slaves.

As we can see, a republican concept of liberty clarifies how Watkins Harper understands her maternal figures. But what could be construed as republican motherhood in Watkins Harper's poetry is, I argue, a reaction to and a refinement of more fundamental liberal political practices. This is not to deny that Watkins Harper engaged in ideas of republican motherhood to configure a self that accorded with and posed a challenge to the prevailing currents of liberal political thought.[10] Indeed, Watkins Harper's poetry balances notions of liberal self-sovereignty with republican community, of individual self-possession with civic responsibility. In other words, Watkins Harper bears out Dawson's conclusion that "the advancement of the self, the liberation of the self, is a meaningless concept outside the context of one's community" (Dawson 2001, 255). Through the figure of the enslaved mother, Watkins Harper endorsed the liberty, self-sovereignty, and self-ownership of liberalism while revising its boundaries so that these rights extended to excluded others. Watkins Harper's hope for a free, liberal black subject could only be recognized through collectivity; her maternal figures asserted their dependence on others in order to achieve individual self-sovereignty.

To articulate her form of black liberalism, Watkins Harper sought to reconfigure the standard liberal subject—a subject who was implicitly conceived as white, male, and circumscribed—into one who is black, female, and expansive. For Watkins Harper, this reconfiguration required a reconsideration of poetic form; to amplify the permeable individual/collective distinction that defines her maternal figures, she uses hybrid poetic forms and formats. Sometimes lyrical, sometimes balladic, and with shifting, multiple speakers and focalizations, her poetic forms model the idea that the sum—which is to say, the individual subject—is more than the parts.[11]

Indeed, even the "format" for her public poetry exceeded traditional boundaries, blurring the line between fiction and fact, aesthetics and advocacy, poetics and politics (McGill 2012, 55).[12] These poems were delivered within Watkins Harper's antislavery speeches (Ammons 1985, 64). Speaking for up to two hours at a time and with no notes, Watkins Harper's lectures were as numerous as they were long (Ammons 1985, 62). For instance, Eric Gardner has identified "over 200 individual lecture dates representing at least 20 distinct lecture texts given between 1864 and 1870 alone" (Gardner 2018, 447). The poems I will discuss in this section were delivered in lectures and collected in *Poems on Miscellaneous Subjects* (1854), which began as a chapbook intended for circulation at abolitionist meetings (McGill 2012, 57). Late nineteenth-century editions of this collection "with their floral-image, illustrated cloth covers, three-quarter-length author photo, facsimile signature, and copyright registration" can, as McGill argues, create a misleading sense of their social purpose (57). But Watkins Harper's poems were not meant for "parlor display"; they were written for "activist uses" and should be recognized as disparate pieces presented in an ephemeral medium to mobilize a specific audience (57).

But activist uses certainly do not preclude the practices of Poetess. The fact that much of Watkins Harper's literary production and presence involved public performance reiterates the importance of the Poetess persona for Watkins Harper. Crucially, Watkins Harper could "mobilize" the Poetess "to expose the racist violence of slavery" precisely because the persona was the "[embodiment] of the very femininity . . . that stood charged with defending the heart of the nation itself" (Lootens 2016, 192). She could, in other words, call upon feminized tropes—hearts, children, motherhood, to name a few—to serve activist, and not conservative, political ends. Indeed, Watkins Harper's own words help to clarify how her use of Poetess conventions aspired to a new form of liberalism. In an 1861 letter to the editor of the *Anglo-African*, Watkins Harper wrote, "If our talents are to be recognized we must write less of issues that are particular and more of feelings that are general" (qtd. in Wilson 2001, 64). Watkins Harper is implicitly responding to the dilemma that faces women poets: the individual expression of emotion associated with the lyric taps into universal human feelings, but in the hands of women poets, such lyrical devices dissolved specific biographical authors into the abstract Poetess. Watkins Harper's innovation is to recast the abstract and generic quality of the figure as an asset for promoting her message.[13] In his recent discussion of this letter, Ivy Wilson captures something of this innovation. Watkins Harper, he writes, "accentuated the generic identity of the mother figure" in her attempt "to suspend the particularity of her enslaved condition" (Wilson 2001, 64). With this abstracted "generic identity," Watkins Harper is working to make stereotypical and mainstream those women who exist on the margins of public life. We can now recognize the activist uses of the Poetess. Through the performance of the Poetess, the enslaved mother became a generic trope who kept literary and literal slave mothers, such as Eliza Harris and Margaret Garner, in the nation's consciousness.

Take, for instance, "The Slave Mother," one of Watkins Harper's most famous poems, whose Poetess-activist format revises lyrical conventions in order to critique notions of liberal individualism. In this poem, Watkins Harper begins such revisions by drawing on the open secret of lyric, namely, that disregard for the listener is a self-conscious effort to draw her closer. In the opening line, the address to a fictional "you" positions historical audiences and readers as overhearers:

> Heard you that shriek? It rose
> So wildly on the air,
> It seem'd as if a burden'd heart
> Was breaking in despair.
> —Foster 1990, 58–59[14]

While this thinly veiled address to an imaginary other presumes to situate audiences as eavesdroppers, Watkins Harper's critique of liberalism was quick to trouble notions of individual circumscription. In the direct address to "you," the poem exposes lyric's pretense of turning away from the reader as just that—a pretense. But exposing the pretense does not necessarily mean its rejection; instead Watkins Harper calls on lyrical devices in order to revise the liberal selfhood they help imagine. This trick of lyric address works to implicate audiences in the slave auction; they overhear not the utterance of the speaker but the "shriek" of the slave mother. And the result, for Watkins Harper, is a poetic foray into black liberal expansiveness: we cannot tell where a fictional "you" ends and the audience begins. Watkins Harper underscores this precariousness by using the phrase "it seem'd"; audiences are not sure of what they hear, and this uncertainty allows Watkins Harper to place audiences in the position of both lyrical eavesdroppers and witnesses to slavery's trauma.

Recent criticism disagrees with my contention that Watkins Harper's poems are in any way lyrical. McGill unequivocally insists that Watkins Harper's poems "were not intended to be read as lyrics"; instead, they were "instruments of exhortation, nodes for the condensation and transfer of oral authority, and vehicles for collective assent" (McGill 2012, 62). McGill seems to suggest that lyric reading opposes these qualities: in other words, lyric is not persuasive, not oral, not collective. For example, McGill claims that "The Slave Mother" resists lyrical conventions. She argues that the opening question, "Heard you that shriek?," constitutes "a hyperconscious attempt to recast readers as listeners," not "the lyric's palpable disregard of an audience" (62). But McGill's generic purity overlooks how lyrical strains are a major part of Watkins Harper's appeal. Watkins Harper's poetry contained lyrical elements because they were effective means of accomplishing the goals that McGill lists above. In fact, the depiction of emotional interiority was one of the rhetorical strategies that Watkins Harper used to advocate for the liberation of enslaved African Americans. Poems printed in ephemeral pamphlets and poems read at public lectures still contained strains of nineteenth-century lyrical aspirations because they figured the emotions associated with an imaginary subject. By giving voice to the feelings of the enslaved through lyrical poetry, Watkins Harper was working to demonstrate a humanity deserving of political freedom and its attendant rights. I argue that lyric's rhetorical pose—the supposed "disregard of an audience"—works to explicitly engage "readers as listeners."[15]

The confusion over address and over what is meant to be "heard" at the end of this first stanza suggests that Watkins Harper's efforts to articulate a form of black liberalism also involve revising the supposedly inadvertent and lyrical expression of the Poetess. Indeed, this project creates contrary effects for the audience and the maternal speaker—whereas the former experiences a provisional sense of expansion, the latter is subject to processes of disassembly. Consider the remarkable lack of interior insight on display in the poem. We do not overhear the emotional expression of either the speaker or the enslaved mother. Instead, readers only get the shriek: an emotional utterance, but a decidedly nonverbal one. In lieu of lyrical verbalization or the Poetess's transparency, Watkins Harper is substituting discrete physical attributes and actions—the anguished shriek, "a burden'd heart" that "break[s] in despair." Here we can identify Watkins Harper's ambivalence toward lyric as it is conventionally understood. As I argued in the introduction, lyric relies on the exposure of interiority to help constitute the self-possession and circumscription of its speaker. But for women poets, especially black women poets, such exposure was thought to signal a lack of possession. In a liberalism of fear, these expectations meant that lyrical insight worked to exacerbate the vulnerability of the enslaved to exposure and dispossession. As a result, Watkins Harper's poetry presents a counterintuitive solution, one that disassembles the mother's body to thereby protect her emotional interior. In the second and third stanzas of "The Slave Mother," this poetics of disassembly enables Watkins Harper to demarcate the fact of the mother's emotional interiority while barring us from accessing it:

Saw you those hands so sadly clasped—
  The bowed and feeble head—

The shuddering of that fragile form—
That look of grief and dread?

Saw you the sad, imploring eye?
Its every glance was pain,
As if a storm of agony
Were sweeping through the brain.
—Foster 1990, 59

The syntax of these questions emphasizes disassembly. None of these parts are circumscribed in a body; instead, the parts are kept distinct through the use of the definite article "the." Though the phrase "that fragile form" does sketch the outline of an entire female body, Watkins Harper's countervailing emphasis on frailty and "shuddering" suggests that this body might fall apart at any moment. Indeed, any such embodiment is undercut in the next line, which returns the reader to the dreadful, maternal "look," and the next stanza, which catalogues the agonized "eye" and "brain."

Watkins Harper condemns an American liberalism of fear by exposing the duress slavery inflicts upon black subjects. Here we must also note that Watkins Harper's poetic disassembly advances her claims about black liberalism by striking a complex analogy with the slave market. Her poem inventories the slave mother in much the same way that potential buyers would size up the attributes of the enslaved. Of course, Watkins Harper is not singling out these features to condone or duplicate the appraisal of physical attributes that occurs in a slave auction. She duplicates the rationalization of a slave auction in order to reverse its value system: she inventories the components that constitute a human subject, not a commodity. These isolated parts communicate the emotional integrity and human depths of the enslaved but, importantly, without further exploiting already vulnerable figures.

Besides guarding the sovereignty of the enslaved mother, Watkins Harper models a vision of black liberalism whose differently configured bodies exceed the sums of their parts. In the fourth stanza, she continues to reconfigure the mother, not by breaking her apart this time, but by adding to her:

She is a mother pale with fear,
Her boy clings to her side,
And in her kyrtle vainly tries
His trembling form to hide.
—Foster 1990, 59

No sooner than Watkins Harper finally presents the embodied whole—"a mother, pale with fear"—do we learn that there is actually more to this body. The mother is not single; she is physically connected to other bodies. Here Watkins Harper incarnates the attachments of motherhood in the boy who "clings to her side." Such extensions of the mother's self are also moments where Watkins Harper addresses—but does not exploit—the physical duress of slavery. In lieu of describing the ubiquitous physical violence of the slave auction, Watkins Harper instead concentrates on other signifiers to communicate slavery's harm. For instance, mother and son are becoming unenlivened, as she loses her color and as he tries to erase himself by hiding in her skirts.[16] Like the mother's "shuddering . . . fragile form" in the second stanza, the son is a "trembling form." These bodies can barely hold themselves together.

With this trembling and the fragility it represents, Watkins Harper introduces the underlying issue of the poem: self-possession. According to racial liberalism, the enslaved mother is not self-possessed, and for several reasons. First, she was already the "property" of someone besides herself. Furthermore, attachment to children signaled a lack of self-possession, not its overabundance. In short, racial liberalism regards liberal self-possession as impossible for the slave mother because her self extends to other selves. But Watkins Harper uses the next stanzas to focus on the inner workings of the mother's body and to thereby consider the possibility of an extra-bodied liberal subject:

> He is not hers, although she bore
> For him a mother's pains;
> He is not hers, although her blood
> Is coursing through his veins!
>
> He is not hers, for cruel hands
> May rudely tear apart
> The only wreath of household love
> That binds her breaking heart.
>
> —Foster 1990, 59

By exploring the idea that mother and son are separate but joined, the poem complicates liberalism's idea of singular self-enclosure. The mother "bore" her son through the pain of childbirth; her blood "is coursing" through his body. These physical actions suggest that he should in fact *be* hers, an assertion thrown into relief by the anaphora's denial of ownership—"he is not hers." Maternal self-possession, Watkins Harper insists, is not restricted to an individual mother's body but extends to other bodies. The anaphora exaggerates to the point of absurdity the logic that would deny such expansive self-possession to an enslaved mother. Indeed, the repetition rhetorically enhances the primary cruelty of this poem—how slavery's destruction of the mother-child bond is tantamount to the destruction of individual selves. The poem further emphasizes this point through the action of encircling or wreathing. Only a band of "household" love secures the mother's broken heart. Without her son, the slave mother's emotional core cannot "hold." A fundamental assumption of liberalism is denied, as individual self-circumscription is accomplished not by the recession but by the extension of the individual.

Watkins Harper is confirming yet another open secret, one made explicit in black liberalism—namely, the notion that others are necessary for the constitution of individuality. The boy is integral to the mother's interiority; though a separate entity, he is nevertheless caught up in her very being. Through such a relationship, Watkins Harper encourages readers to acknowledge that the individual self is a fiction, and that individuality is found in union. In the seventh and eighth stanzas, Watkins Harper describes their love and its centrality to the mother's life, which serves to anticipate the anguish of their parting:

> His love has been a joyous light
> That o'er her pathway smiled,
> A fountain gushing ever new,
> Amid life's desert wild.
>
> His lightest word has been a tone
> Of music round her heart,
> Their lives a streamlet blent in one—
> Oh, Father! must they part?
>
> —Foster 1990, 59

These lines seem to rehearse the conventions of the Poetess. In her description of the boy's ever-gushing love, Watkins Harper echoes the understanding that Poetesses acted as "fonts of unmediated emotion" (Richards 2004, 16). At the same time, Watkins Harper recognizes the consequences—positive and negative—of applying these associations to black women. The lyrical elements characterizing Poetess poetry—the unstoppable or "ever new" expression of emotion—align the black mother's interiority with the true womanhood of the Poetess persona. But such expressions are usually problematic for the Poetess because they dissolve her sovereign interiority into public poetic profession. However, Watkins Harper uses the lyrical exposure of interiority to criticize racial liberalism's individualism. Indeed, this glimpse of the enslaved mother's "heart" sketches the components of an expansive and multiple black liberal subject. Consider how the description of the boy shifts between the individual and the collective. In one line, the boy is a separate fountain of love, and in another, the son's and mother's lives are one "streamlet." His "tone" echoes the household wreath—it is "music round her heart." The plaintive question ("must they part?") implies that more than one body comprises the mother's self. Once again, the challenges to elaborating black liberalism persist, as Watkins Harper must balance questions of lyrical exposure and self-sovereignty. To outmaneuver the risk of exploitation, Watkins Harper packs these stanzas with physical symbols of emotional interiority. Even the final stanzas, which enact the traumatic separation, code the anguish of Watkins Harper's maternal figure in physical parts, as the poet returns us to the shriek and disassembled pieces. Ultimately, Watkins Harper's poem can only gesture to new possibilities for the black liberal self because of the ongoing realities of slavery; she closes by depicting slavery's violent shattering of that self:

> They tear him from her circling arms,
> Her last and fond embrace.
> Oh! never more may her sad eyes
> Gaze on his mournful face.
>
> No marvel, then, these bitter shrieks
> Disturb the listening air:
> She is a mother, and her heart
> Is breaking in despair.
>
> —Foster 1990, 59

While Watkins Harper's poem insists that self-possessed singularity hinges on multiplicity, slavery's violence ruptures these life-sustaining bonds. Two bodies merged to create the mother's self, evidenced in the devastation of that self as the boy is torn from his mother's "circling arms." The poem underscores the severing of mother and son with severed body parts—arms, eyes, face, heart. The poem also returns to the lyrical premises of its opening stanza by subtly re-invoking the figure of its readers and audiences. Such figures return to the position of lyrical eavesdroppers, but with a difference. Given what they have witnessed, audiences no longer "marvel" at the shriek: even if the poem does not divulge the mother's explicit emotions, it endeavors that the figured "you" understands the pain communicated by this nonverbal address.

With its emphasis on the bond between mother and child, "The Slave Mother" offers, one might say, a straightforward formulation of Watkins Harper's black liberalism: the component parts that constitute individual selfhood also point to commitments that exceed the individual. Watkins Harper is keen to continue describing those larger commitments that produce autonomous individualism. Whereas "The Slave Mother" focused on mother and son, "The Slave Auction" expands the range of connections that create the self to include extended and fictive families. Indeed, Watkins Harper's poetry depicts the enslaved as a family—a family linked by a liberalism of fear. In slavery's destruction of blood relationships, Watkins Harper suggests that families are reconstituted in a kind of kinship of trauma. The slave auction undoes family bonds, but in their place Watkins Harper finds some solace in the possibility of a greater, extended family that replaces these ruined relations. Like the enslaved mother, these families resist the logic of racial liberalism by showing how fear perverts the liberty—in this case, the very freedom to have a family—that liberalism supposedly promises. At the same time, these families articulate Watkins Harper's hopes for a black liberalism in which blood has no impact on kinship and in which the individual is situated within and created by this expansive community.

Like "The Slave Mother," "The Slave Auction" depicts the destruction of families. Rather than focusing on a specific family, Watkins Harper renders individual relationships ambiguous in order to emphasize the larger symbolic family to which all enslaved peoples belong:

> The sale began—young girls were there,
>   Defenseless in their wretchedness,
> Whose stifled sobs of deep despair
>   Revealed their anguish and distress.
>
> And mothers stood, with streaming eyes,
>   And saw their dearest children sold;
> Unheeded rose their bitter cries,
>   While tyrants bartered them for gold.
>
> —Foster 1990, 64

Watkins Harper undermines the primacy of the liberal individual by dissolving it within the plural forms of girls, mothers, and children. She still carefully navigates the cultural conventions about black women and withholds any description of either the girls' or mothers' bodies. Once again, the poem substitutes physical acts or signs thereof—"stifled sobs of deep despair" and "bitter cries"—for specific emotional detail. This substitution continues into the second stanza, where the young girls' tears connect to the mothers' "streaming eyes." In a liberalism of fear, families are connected not by blood but by tears.

To convey this expansive notion of family, but one formed by the violence of slavery, Watkins Harper modifies the typical family genealogy. She replaces the familiar linear form of social development—from child to girl to wife to mother—with one that instead gestures toward a collective, shared existence—girls, mothers, then children. The third and fourth stanzas incorporate men, and in these lines young women turn into mothers who turn into wives, who look to husbands, who are in the same situation as children:

And woman, with her love and truth—
  For these in sable forms may dwell—
Gazed on the husband of her youth,
  With anguish none may paint or tell.

And men, whose sole crime was their hue,
  The impress of their Maker's hand,
And frail and shrinking children too,
  Were gathered in that mournful band.
—Foster 1990, 64

As the progression of people in this poem shows, the liberalism of fear affords the enslaved a collective circumscription. To constitute such collectivity, blood and marital relations between these figures remain ambiguous: we understand that "woman" is married to "husband," but this figure dissolves into the collective "men" who are paired with "children." Watkins Harper poses this extrafamilial sense of kinship against slavery's violent insistence on black individuals as saleable units of property. To emphasize this common humanity, Watkins Harper returns to imagery of circling, of beneficial codependence between family members. The enslaved are a "band" even if they are described as "mournful."

Though "The Slave Auction" affirms the powerful bonds of expanded kinship, it is a foregone conclusion that the poem—written in 1854, more than a decade prior to the abolition of slavery—stakes its abolitionist politics on the destruction of those same powerful bonds. For that reason, the final stanzas shift the focus from the binding relationships of the "band" to the traumatic dismantling of families. This move is articulated by a change in the speaker's focus from an omniscient narrator to lyrical address:

Ye who have laid your loved to rest,
And wept above their lifeless clay,
Know not the anguish of that breast,
Whose loved are rudely torn away.

Ye may not know how desolate
Are bosoms rudely forced to part,
And how a dull and heavy weight
Will press the life-drops from the heart.
—Foster 1990, 64

As with the opening question in "The Slave Mother," Watkins Harper again draws on lyrical strains in order to revise their pretenses. Here the feint that lyrical poems supposedly ignore their readers is revisited or "remixed"; Watkins Harper deliberately blurs the line between a fictional "you" and the audience to begin sketching the expansive subjectivity necessary to combat the violence enabled by racial liberalism's individualism.[17] The canny use of direct address builds a relationship with the reader, only to highlight the relationships that slavery destroys. Loved ones may have died, but death is not the same as the kind of death-in-life created by slavery, as the sale of "your loved" presses the life from your heart. By calling attention to this life-sustaining connection, the final stanzas suggest that all people are in the position of mothers. A mother brings into existence another person who depends upon her for life, but, as we saw in "The Slave Mother," the reverse is equally true. In the family of the enslaved, Watkins Harper reconfigures liberal individualism to assert that no one self is ever truly individual.

Liberty in Death

In Watkins Harper's telling, the slave auction stresses how the self needs other selves in order to live, and that wrecking these connections between people is tantamount to death. Watkins Harper's poems on infanticide elaborate on this death-in-life produced by slavery by looking to its converse—namely, that there is a life in death. For Watkins Harper's enslaved mothers, freedom is impossible in this life, but available in the next. This hope applies most forcefully to their children, and Watkins Harper depicts maternal figures that must consider the possibility that if life was freedom for white children, then death was freedom for black children. Watkins Harper explores this disturbing hypothesis in the poems "Eliza Harris" and "The Slave Mother: A Tale of the Ohio," which describe enslaved mothers contemplating and committing infanticide in order to free their children from slavery. Watkins Harper's audiences would have been familiar with the fictional and historical women discussed in these poems. Eliza Harris is one of the heroines of Harriet Beecher Stowe's novel *Uncle Tom's Cabin*; pursued by slaver hunters, Eliza heroically crosses the semi-frozen Ohio River to save her child from slavery. "The Slave Mother: A Tale of the Ohio" is based on the enslaved woman Margaret Garner and her notorious act of infanticide. Garner, her four children, her husband, and her husband's parents attempted to escape slavery in 1856. Cornered by slave hunters, Garner killed one of her children and intended to kill the rest and then herself before she was stopped (Threadcraft 2016, 35). In these poems, Watkins Harper uses infanticide to uncover what American liberalism tries to obscure: that the experience of slavery dismantles the sanctity of the private sphere and the rational restraint of the liberal subject. Watkins Harper condemns racial liberalism for its moral bankruptcy: liberalism's ideals are bankrupt when the choice is between slavery in life or liberty in death.

These poems on infanticide are Watkins Harper's most dramatic assertion that racial liberalism's protections are incomplete. She more narrowly uses infanticide to single out a pillar of racial liberalism for critique: the notion of a productive public/private divide. For Watkins Harper, the existence of slavery will always confuse distinctions between private and public, distinctions that are crucial to determining the liberal subject. Liberalism's fundamental concept of liberty valorized freedom from the influence and infraction of others—meaning that the home or private sphere became the realm of true liberty, a refuge from the social, political, and economic pressures of the public world. However, Watkins Harper's depiction of infanticide removes any pretense to "the home as liberty's precinct" (Dillon 2004, 200). The pernicious effects that racial liberalism has on the sanctity of privacy are particularly obvious in Watkins Harper's depiction of enslaved children. In the sentimental culture of the nineteenth century, Dillon argues, children are free by virtue of their "nonutilitarian status," that is, they are "dissociated from wage-earning labor and the cash nexus of the marketplace" (205, 199). Childhood may mean exemption from the "exigencies of market competition," but the child born into slavery never enjoys a state of nonutiliarian freedom (202). For enslaved children, childhood could never be "the source of freedom and moral truth" because it was subject to the vagaries of the marketplace (205).

Translated into the logic of liberalism, these murderous mothers lament that liberalism's guarantees—freedom from life-limiting fears and the separation of the home from the marketplace—do not apply to them and their children. For instance, in the opening stanzas of "The Slave Mother: A Tale of the Ohio," the mother's description of her children suggests her vain attempts to uphold the child's nonutilitarian remove:

I have but four, the treasures of my soul,
They lay like doves around my heart;
I tremble lest some cruel hand
Should tear my household wreaths apart.

My baby girl with childish glance;
Looks curious in my anxious eye,
She little knows that for her sake
Deep shadows round my spirit lie.

My playful boys could I forget,
My home might seem a joyous spot,
But with their sunshine mirth I blend
The darkness of their future lot.

And thou my babe, my darling one,
My last, my loved, my precious child
Oh! when I think upon thy doom
My heart grows faint and then throbs wild.
—Foster 1990, 84

These stanzas generate their emotional weight from the inevitable cruelty of the slave market by insisting on a family where one is about to be torn asunder. To that end, the mother takes a nonutilitarian tack by regarding her children as the "treasures of [her] soul" and peaceful "doves" whose worth cannot be translated into market value. The phrase "household wreaths" recurs—a phrase, as we have seen, that Watkins Harper associates with a child's ability to cohere the mother's sense of self. Yet the enslaved mother simultaneously recognizes that her status as slave revokes her property in her self or her children. The stanzas describing her four children place them in the home, a potentially "joyous spot," but the mother pairs the joy each child brings with the despair of slavery. Their every joy serves to remind her that her private life is subject to the marketplace's manipulations. Without the protections of liberal subjectivity, the nonutility of the sentimental family is nullified. These children always risk being "torn" from the private into the public, their sentimental value suddenly transformed into market value.

Only by gaining their freedom can the mother and her children attain the nonutilitarian joy of a truly private family life. As the mother explains in the fifth stanza, she will "take the nestlings of my heart" and cross the frozen Ohio River. But once the mother has made her momentous decision, the poem suddenly switches speakers from the mother's first-person voice to an omniscient narrator:

> She fled, and with her children all,
> She reached the stream and crossed it o'er.
> Bright visions of deliverance came
> Like dreams of plenty to the poor.
> —Foster 1990, 85

The isolated lyrical speaker is not enough to tell this whole tale, so Watkins Harper shifts subjects mid-poem. Indeed, the expansive narratorial focus suggests that individual lyrical subjects cannot solely bear witness to slavery's violence for the simple reason that the individual enslaved speaker is not the only victim of its trauma.

Perhaps this turn is meant to preemptively protect the mother's privacy and avoid making a spectacle of the impending violent act. Regardless, the switch is disorienting because it complicates the narrator's omniscient role: she starts as an impartial observer of the action, but then she adopts qualities of the lyrical, expressive speaker, only to conclude by ventriloquizing the slave mother's voice.[18] This confusion of the poem's speakers and their respective function reflects, I argue, the confusion between private and public wrought by the existence of slavery. By constantly wrenching the private into the public, and vice versa, slavery renders such distinctions meaningless—which is why the narrator is neither strictly a public observer nor an intimate lyrical speaker.

What is arguably the most forceful evidence of how slavery dissolves public/private distinctions comes when, at a crucial moment in the poem, the narrator assumes the mother's voice. The merging of narrator and mother attests to how the violence of slavery dismantles individual circumscription:

> Then, said the mournful mother,
> If Ohio cannot save,
> I will do a deed for freedom,
> She shall find each child a grave.
>
> I will save my precious children
> From their darkly threatened doom,
> I will hew their path to freedom
> Through the portals of the tomb.
> —Foster 1990, 85

The fugitive mother and children occupy an ambiguous space, one that blurs the distinctions on which liberalism stakes itself: they are between slavery and freedom, the domestic sphere and the public sphere, and nonutility and labor. Indeed, the mother phrases her contemplation of infanticide in a language that combines love and labor: to save her children, she must "do a deed" and "hew their path to freedom." This "deed" is Watkins Harper's most forceful illustration of how slavery had desecrated the intimate realm with utilitarian, exploitative, and violent forces. Margaret Garner had been raped by her owner and bore his children, and, for that reason, Shatema Threadcraft argues that we can understand her infanticide as "a pivotal act of resistance within the black feminist political project" (Threadcraft 2016, 55, 38). Indeed, it is an act of resistance that draws its force from the intimate realm. As Threadcraft suggests, "The sexual, reproductive, and caretaking coercion and exploitation within the slave system was a burden that fell almost exclusively on enslaved women" (38). The disturbing stanzas depicting the infanticide recall the intimate and thus invisible injustices enacted upon enslaved women. Here Watkins Harper produces figures who disrupt the neat boundaries of liberalism's sphere separation and, subsequently, self-circumscription:

> They snatched away the fatal knife,
> Her voice shrieked wild with dread;
> The baby girl was pale and cold,
> They raised it up, the child was dead.
> —Foster 1990, 85

The blurring of figural boundaries starts with ambiguous references. For example, the speaker's reference to "they" is unclear—are "they" the surviving children or perhaps a group of onlookers? Furthermore, this scene disrupts any coherence in the speaker's role; she is not part of the group who wrests the knife from the mother, but despite her previous insight, she no longer appears to operate as an omniscient narrator or a lyrical speaker given that all she can do is describe the scene. Finally, Watkins Harper asserts the self's breakdown in her description of the mother who, in her gruesome act, acts without reason.[19] She "shriek[s] wild," suggesting that she has become unhinged by this action. She is no longer a self-governing subject, as she has just killed what was her own.[20]

After the confusion of this stanza, the last two stanzas of the poem reinstate the omniscient perspective of the speaker. But the return to such a reasonable perspective insists on the moral integrity of American sentimental culture. Watkins Harper concludes the poem with a nationwide plea for "moral action," "a sense of the significance of social virtue as a response to the trauma of slavery" (Fisher 2008, 64). The speaker laments that this horrifying act makes no difference in the country's attitude toward slavery:

Sends this deed of fearful daring
Through my country's heart no thrill,
Do the icy hands of slavery
Every pure emotion chill?

Oh! If there is any honor,
Truth or justice in the land,
Will you not us men and Christians,
On the side of freedom stand?
—Foster 1990, 86

In the last stanza's plea for civic responsibility, Watkins Harper uses the rhetoric of republican motherhood to advocate for liberal reform. While she directly addresses "us men," Watkins Harper invokes republican motherhood's goal to raise sons who would become good citizens. She uses the figure of the enslaved mother to foster good citizenship in "us," admonishing audiences to stand "on the side of freedom." Conversely, this conclusion suggests that slavery could effectively ruin the nation if an act this horrible causes no civic response. The "deed" sends no emotion or "thrill" through the country, and as a result the speaker concludes that slavery has the ability to "chill" or suspend human feelings. The ideals that a liberal political system supposedly ensures, like "honor," "truth," and "justice," hinge on social participation, but slavery suspends that activity.

Whereas "The Slave Mother: A Tale of the Ohio River" testifies to the hypocrisy of American liberalism and the necessity of reform, "Eliza Harris" uses infanticide to affirm Watkins Harper's vision for black liberalism, a vision that recognizes a new selfhood and the reality of the racial liberalism that conditions it. In "Eliza Harris," Watkins Harper makes this appeal by reimagining one of the most the famous scenes from Harriet Beecher Stowe's *Uncle Tom's Cabin,* in which Eliza and her son successfully cross the frozen Ohio River to escape slavery.[21] In Watkins Harper's retelling, Eliza declares that if she cannot free her son, then she will kill him. It might be hard to imagine that infanticide could represent anything productive, but in Eliza's freedom, Watkins Harper recognizes a new black selfhood and the reality of the racial liberalism that conditions it. In "Eliza Harris," the process of affirming a black, liberal subject has a familiar start, as Watkins Harper returns to a poetics of disassembly in order to complicate liberal individualism. But this repetition of techniques from Watkins Harper serves a different end, that is, the creation of a free black subject, a figure we have not yet seen in this chapter.[22]

For an eponymous poem, we never glimpse Eliza as a whole. Instead, Watkins Harper focuses on her fading face and provides pieces of Eliza's body at the same time that she adds other bodies—more specifically, her son's—to it:

> Like a fawn from the arrow, startled and wild,
> A woman swept by us, bearing a child;
> In her eye was the night of a settled despair,
> And her brow was o'ershaded with anguish and care.
>
> She was nearing the river—in reaching the brink,
> She heeded no danger, she paused not to think!
> For she is a mother—her child is a slave—
> And she'll give him his freedom, or find him a grave!
>
> —Foster 1990, 60–61

Once Eliza is declared free after crossing the Ohio, as we will see, her face and body belong to her and her alone. But in these opening stanzas, the still-enslaved Eliza is, like her son, connected to but not in full possession of her body. Because she is depicting the familiar figure of the enslaved mother, Watkins Harper describes outcomes already familiar to us. She describes Eliza as an "eye" and a "brow." Both features are dark, and the opacity creates a sense that Eliza cannot "read" her own self. Indeed, Eliza's "wild[ness]" suggests that she is out of sorts or not fully autonomous. In Watkins Harper's telling, the enslaved mother does appear to possess autonomy over another body, her child's body—but as long as she is enslaved, such autonomy can only be exercised in his death. The act of "bearing" her son, much as she bore him in pregnancy and childbirth, reiterates the peculiar relationship motherhood presents to the logic of liberalism: How is individual circumscription possible when mothers and children are conjoined? Eliza's threat of infanticide emphasizes the multiplicity of motherhood. Eliza can choose to kill her son because he is in a perverse sense "hers," and his life hers to determine. Mothers are not singular subjects, but in the context of slavery, such multiplicity is self-defeating.

Once Eliza is free, Watkins Harper offers a new vision of motherhood in which self-ownership recognizes and, in fact, relies on life-affirming bonds with others. In other words, circumscribed individualism does not necessarily attend liberty in Watkins Harper's version of black liberalism. Consider the stanzas where Eliza makes her escape and gains freedom:

In agony close to her bosom she press'd
The life of her heart, the child of her breast:—
Oh! love from its tenderness gathering might,
Had strengthen'd her soul for the dangers of flight.

But she's free—yes, free from the land where the slave
From the hand of oppression must rest in the grave;
Where bondage and torture, where scourges and chains,
Have plac'd on our banner indelible stains.
—Foster 1990, 61

With this strength gained from contact with her child, Eliza makes her harrowing leaps across the river's ice chunks. When the next stanza declares that she is free, a multi-bodied mother—a mother who gathers her power from her child—has complicated the circumscribed, self-possessed individual associated with liberty and liberalism in the United States. Her child is "the life of her heart," and in this poem Watkins Harper incarnates this sentiment: the child is the life force that sent blood through her heart, giving her the energy to move and ensuring their freedom. Eliza therefore relied on others—her freedom is neither individual nor autonomous. This expansive self models Watkins Harper's hopes for a liberated black subject. In Watkins Harper's version of black liberalism, the individual self must exceed its boundaries, both physically and politically:

With the rapture of love and fullness of bliss,
She plac'd on his brow a mother's fond kiss:—
Oh! poverty, danger and death she can brave,
For the child of her love is no longer a slave!
—Foster 1990, 62

The mother experiences "fullness," suggesting that the black liberal self exceeds the boundaries of normative liberal selfhood. The last line affirms that the edges of this self have been exceeded because "the child of her love" is free—the child who augments Eliza's body, heart, soul, and life. In this blissful state, Eliza and her son are free from "poverty, danger and death," the life-limiting fears that accompany racial liberalism. The qualities that previously signaled defenselessness—race and gender—now combine to make an abundant, multi-bodied self.

"Free" Mothers

During the Reconstruction era, Watkins Harper's hopes for a black liberalism were not borne out. In the words of Gardner, the "Civil War, in many ways, raged on well after 1865," as the Reconstruction Amendments did not do enough to ensure protection or liberties for African American people (Gardner 2018, 435). The practices of racial liberalism continued to restrain black subjects, who remained, in fact, "burdened" and "encumbered" (Hartman 1997, 117).[23] Newly freed people had to navigate a contradictory political and social landscape in which they were considered "self-determining" liberal subjects at the same time that their race rendered them "members of a population whose productivity, procreation, and sexual practices were fiercely regulated and policed" (117). In other words, freedom, and the self-sovereignty it conferred, were undermined at every turn by political, social, and economic practices meant to actually evacuate liberalism of its liberties. Watkins Harper's task in the post-emancipation era, then, was to address old problems that now appeared in a new light. She must continue to fulfill the promise of collectivity depicted in her antebellum poems while serving to remind readers of the ongoing consequences of slavery.

In light of these injustices, Watkins Harper continued to advocate for the rights of African American people.[24] From the end of the Civil War until 1871, "[her] primary occupation was lecturing in Southern cities, towns, and rural areas to black audiences as well as to white ones" (Foster 1990, 135). Her experiences meeting freed people during these tours are reflected in her 1872 poetry collection, *Sketches of Southern Life*. As Rebecka Rutledge Fisher points out, *Sketches* is "an undeclared collective memoir, the composite testimony of freed African Americans Watkins Harper met in the course of her postbellum travels" (Fisher 2008, 57).[25] That testimony includes a set of six poems about Mrs. Chloe Fleet, a nearly sixty-year-old former slave whose children were sold away years earlier. Dismayed by the political practices of the Reconstruction South, this remarkable "no-nonsense woman," Foster writes, is "probably the first black female protagonist, outside the tragic mulatto tradition, to be presented as a model for life" (Foster 1990, 137).

In Chloe, for whom the title of "Aunt" emphasizes kinship rather than maternity, Watkins Harper's poetry finds a figure to symbolize the enslaved mother and to testify to how Reconstruction-era policies perpetuate slavery's injustices. In other words, the Aunt Chloe sequence is examining the legacy of slavery as it emerges. Fisher argues that these poems "serve as Harper's articulation of alternative subjectivity and her testimonial archive of the slaves' experience" (Fisher 2008, 61). Spanning slavery, abolition, and Reconstruction, the Aunt Chloe poems assert that the trauma of slavery cannot just be forgotten, because it persists into the present moment. For that reason, Watkins Harper redeploys familiar poetic practices in *Sketches* because they maintain much of their social purpose in the Reconstruction era by serving as reminders of the continuing violence that differently assembled the black subject. Emancipation offered no corrective to racial liberalism, and Watkins Harper's postbellum poems continue to offer a revision of liberal selfhood through the figured Chloe, who expands individualism to exist within and emerge out of collectivity.[26]

On first glance, Chloe is a counterintuitive point of departure for more expansive notions of black liberal subjectivity. Her seemingly spinster title of "Aunt" reinforces her singleness inasmuch as she seems to lack the bonds of kinship that more clearly attend a wife or mother.[27] But this singleness serves to emphasize a sense of "domestic and civil engagement"—not isolation—"that individuals offered apart from marriage" (Williams 2014, 101). Indeed, the figured Chloe can be read according to what Williams calls a nineteenth-century "rhetoric of single blessedness": "From the kind aunt who aids her overwhelmed married sister to the unwed churchgoer who masters fund-raising, 'singly blessed' women could aspire to ideals of womanhood outside marriage, including in the public domain" (101).[28] "Aunt" suggests the fictive kinship of African American communities in which enslaved individuals unrelated by blood or marriage fulfilled the roles of extended family members for each other because, as we have seen in Watkins Harper's poems, slavery ruined the bonds of blood kinship. Chloe's singleness continues to foreground the lasting impact of slavery: the freed individual was situated within a family that existed beyond the relations of marriage and bloodline. Her singleness is, in other words, a trace of slavery.

With Chloe, then, Watkins Harper crafts a poetic persona whose defining features invoke what American policy and society wanted to overlook: a singleness designed to evoke community and a liberty designed to evoke the legacy of slavery. These features are necessary checks, Watkins Harper suggests, because liberalism in the United States always risks revoking the rights of others. The way to assuage this risk is through the protection of community, as demonstrated in the poems' emphasis on extended family. The first poem of the sequence, "Aunt Chloe," begins to parse these protections. Despite the title "Aunt Chloe," the poem immediately turns to enslaved motherhood as Chloe recalls the sale of her children. Watkins Harper wants readers to remember, as Chloe remembers, that the enslaved mother is an enduring figure behind the emancipation of black Americans:

I remember, well remember,
  That dark and dreadful day,
When they whispered to me, "Chloe,
  Your children's sold away!"

It seemed as if a bullet
  Had shot me through and through,
And I felt as if my heart-strings
  Was breaking right in two.

And I says to cousin Milly,
  "There must be some mistake;
Where's Mistus?" "In the great house crying—
  Crying like her heart would break.

"And the lawyer's there with Mistus;
  Says he's come to 'ministrate,
'Cause when master died he just left
  Heap of debt on the estate.

—Foster 1990, 196–97

Here Watkins Harper condenses two of the conventions we have seen so far in her writing about enslaved mothers. In the breaking "heart-strings," she reiterates the idea that children create the mother's innermost self, at the same time that children help hold the mother's sense of self together. In the absence of her children, the mother breaks. Through Chloe's memory, Watkins Harper points to the newly freed mothers who might have liberty but not self-possession due to the loss of their children.

Yet Chloe's life is not one of unmitigated loss. She still had family in her enslaved community even if no blood relations existed. "They," which is to say, other plantation slaves, warn Chloe of her impending trauma; the familial nature of such bonds is explicitly referenced in the third stanza, where Chloe addresses a "cousin Milly." Watkins Harper uses Chloe's confusion—"there must be some mistake"—to remind readers about how slavery allowed marketplace concerns to impact the supposedly nonutiliarian sphere of the domestic. The influence of slavery breaks hearts and homes: Chloe, the "Mistus" of the plantation, and Milly (who later confides, "I thought my poor old heart would break, / When master sold my Saul") cry to show their heartbreak, and the plantation itself breaks up under a "heap of debt" (Foster 1990, 197). Watkins Harper isn't telling us anything new about slavery; what is new are the forms that the legacy of slavery takes in the Reconstruction era.

To remind readers of this legacy, Watkins Harper continues to disassemble the black body. When Chloe mourns the absence of her children, Watkins Harper signifies emotion in physical parts:

> Then I had a mighty sorrow,
> Though I nursed it all alone;
> But I wasted to a shadow,
> And turned to skin and bone.
> . . . .
> . . . I began to pray,
> And I felt my heavy burden
> Rolling like a stone away.
> —Foster 1990, 197, 198

In "The Slave Auction," the sale of loved ones pressed "life-drops" out of the heart; here Watkins Harper figures loss as a "heavy burden" that crushes Chloe. Watkins Harper repeats conventions associated with the enslaved mother in this poem—encircled hearts, body parts, the absence of explicit violence. But repetition is not the same as stagnancy. Watkins Harper's return to this poetics reflects the incontrovertible fact that freed black people still carry with them the memories of slavery. What they "well remember" Watkins Harper does not want readers to soon forget. And because this memory is not something that can be ignored, it has shaped the selfhood of freedpeople. She wants audiences to recognize this new selfhood and the reality of the racial liberalism that conditions it. This free self bears the impress of slavery, and as a result, it revises how selfhood should be understood in the Reconstruction era.

The poetic sequence ends with "The Reunion," which depicts Chloe's eventual reunion with her sons after emancipation. In this poem, Chloe unexpectedly runs into her son Jakey on the street. She has not seen him since he and his brother were sold away as children. Jakey reports that his brother, Ben, is alive and well in Tennessee with a wife and son. However, Watkins Harper is careful not to overwrite the enduring trauma of slavery with this happy turn of events. The poem shows that the lasting effects of slavery's violence ensure a differently individuated self for freedpeople, one that only guarantees self-circumscription through expansion. In the last four stanzas of the poem, Chloe explains her hopes for the future, which, in turn, illustrate Watkins Harper's hopes for black liberalism:

> "Then, Jakey, you will stay with me,
> And comfort my poor heart;
> Old Mistus got no power now
> To tear us both apart.
>
> "I'm richer now than Mistus,
> Because I have got my son;
> And Mister Thomas he is dead,
> And she's got nary one.
>
> "You must write to brother Benny
> That he must come this fall,
> And we'll make the cabin bigger,
> And that will hold us all.
>
> "Tell him I want to see 'em all
> Before my life do cease:
> And then, like good old Simeon,
> I hope to die in peace."
>
> —Foster 1990, 208

Chloe is "richer" than her mistress because, she suggests, she has property in her son. In fact, she has two, and no one can "tear" this newly protected property from Chloe. Chloe's comment about her old mistress could be mere observation or ironic commentary. But the acknowledgment brings up the fundamental property rights protected by liberalism: Chloe now has property in her children, her home, and her self. Chloe's ownership speaks to precisely the kinds of ownership that slavery denied—and the kind of ownership possible in a black liberalism. Of course, social and political practices continued to replicate slavery's disenfranchisement.[29] Watkins Harper therefore asserts the fact that freedpeople have a right to their property that no one has the "power" to change. This idea of property is reiterated in Chloe's mention of personal wealth, and now that she is "richer" it seems that she can afford to expand her home. Chloe's plans for the future are characterized by ownership; she will find "peace" once all her possessions are collected under the roof of *her* loving ownership.

Indeed, the poems in this sequence reverse lyric's potential to exploit those not afforded liberalism's protections. Instead of exposing the formerly enslaved mother's interior, Watkins Harper uses lyric to preserve Chloe's self-ownership as a liberal subject. Such revisions symbolize for Watkins Harper how lyric can be harnessed to enable black women's dominion, not their dispossession. Gone are Watkins Harper's shifting narrators, and in their place is the fully realized "I" of Aunt Chloe. But such an "I" is not the individual of liberal and lyrical isolation—isolation that, for the enslaved mother, meant vulnerability. Instead the "I" insists on an identity created by compassing others, evidenced by the cabin Chloe plans to expand. Watkins Harper amplifies such encircling—or perhaps we could say "household wreathing"—in her positioning of her audiences. When it invokes the lyrical pretense of a speaker ignorant of any audience, the poem now does so to suggest an expansive constellation of audiences contained within audiences: Chloe recounts her experience to fictional interlocutors, and Watkins Harper recounts these conditions to contemporary readers.

We can see that Watkins Harper continues to deploy lyrical techniques but for her own ends. She shows how ownership of one's own labor, life, and love is claimed through lyrical forms. In fact, this attention to property that closes out the Aunt Chloe sequence suggests the significance of property to Watkins Harper's project as a whole. Watkins Harper has insisted that slavery entangles the fundamental property rights that underline notions of the liberal subject. In fact, we could say that Watkins Harper rewrites liberalism in order to create a new individuality for a newly freed people. Freedpeople possess property in themselves by "owning" the bonds that connect them to other people; for that reason, Chloe claims property in people, that is, in her own children. This nonviolent, life-affirming possession asserts that the boundaries of the individual self expand to include and incorporate others. In Watkins Harper's revision, people are no longer detachable from each other and subject to sale, but connected to each other because their sense of self-possession is lodged in someone else. In these poems that strive to make a record of how the legacy of slavery endures in the post-emancipation period, Watkins Harper does not let slavery merely persist in all its perniciousness. Through this revised figure of the enslaved mother, Watkins Harper likewise revises the liberal property rights that allowed slavery to exist. This black liberal subject has property in herself and is even "richer" because she has shared property in a family that extends to encompass entire communities.

CHAPTER FOUR

Making the Modernist Poetess

Edna St. Vincent Millay

Turning from the 1870s, where the previous chapter left off, to the poetry of Edna St. Vincent Millay and of the early twentieth century constitutes a sizeable historical jump. Despite these intervening decades, the antebellum Poetess's legacy had not disappeared, but, in fact, remained very visible. The rest of this book will trace the historical continuities from antebellum Poetess poetry to late nineteenth- and early twentieth-century works by women. The Poetess tradition, I argue, persisted across this period in its performance. While the first three chapters elaborated the Poetess's lyrical interventions in a liberal public sphere, the next two chapters employ the Poetess tradition to critique the very premises of a liberal self. These chapters expose the liberal fantasy of private self-possession by explicitly "performing" the Poetess in public. For instance, chapter 5 will discuss poems that E. Pauline Johnson wrote in the 1880s and performed for audiences on the Chautauqua circuit in the early 1900s.

In this chapter, I discuss Millay (1892–1950), who was born just before Elizabeth Oakes Smith's death, and whose first major publication appeared just one year after Frances Ellen Watkins Harper's death in 1911. That said, the late stages of these women's careers are not so far from the beginning of Millay's: Oakes Smith was working on her autobiography in the 1880s, and Watkins Harper published *Iola Leroy* in 1892. In order to further illustrate the Poetess's legacy, I would like to briefly address the developments in women's poetry across the turn of the nineteenth to the twentieth century. The year 1890 offers a convenient midpoint in which literary critics are themselves reflecting on the past, present, and future of women's poetry.

Recall Helen Cone's essay "Woman in American Literature" from 1890, discussed in chapter 1. With great relief, Cone explained that the time of the Poetess had passed. For instance, she noted, Lydia Sigourney's books were "undisturbed and dirty in the libraries now, and likely to remain so," for readers were no longer interested in the "quantity, dilution, diffusiveness" that constituted the Poetess's persona (Cone 1890, 923). In her essay, Cone is looking forward to a new vanguard of women writers. Over the last twenty years, she writes, "the flood of sentimentalism slowly receded" from women's writing, which now "gives no general evidence of limitation" (928, 929). In other words, since roughly 1870, women poets have shed the sentimental and abstract pretentions of the Poetess. Indeed, the year 1890 seems to mark a turning point. Any number of women poets—Cone's list includes Rose Terry Cooke, Sarah Piatt, Emma Lazarus, and Louise Imogen Guiney—write on the brink of genius. Indeed, an "individual genius for literature is sure, sooner or later, to appear" (930). Of course, this sentiment is not universal among critics. A response to Cone in *Poet-Lore* by Helen Clarke cites the example of an already accomplished woman poet to claim that a genius comparable to male counterparts has already appeared. "As to the paucity of literary achievement imputed to woman," Clarke asserts, "we have already had an Emma Lazarus to put with Emerson and Whitman in the front rank of genuinely original American writers" (Clarke 1890, 668). According to Clarke, "We need not feel any disappointment whatever about manifestations of womanly power in literature" (668). With the example of Emerson and Whitman, Clarke seems to be suggesting that Lazarus writes innovative and "genuinely original" works—that is, works unlike the abstract, generic, and "diffus[e]" poems of Cone's antebellum female poet (668; Cone 1890, 923).

But these disagreements are minor. The general critical consensus in the 1890s heaped praise on iconoclastic women writers by explicitly (Cone) or tacitly (Clarke) rejecting those who participated in feminine poetic traditions. Such praise continues a trend visible in the antebellum anthology inasmuch as it reaffirms the notion that the Poetess and the Poet are mutually exclusive figures. Regardless of women's recent accomplishments in poetry, both critics equate innovation with genius—and, it would seem, tradition with the Poetess. This general wariness regarding feminine poetic traditions seems to perennially stalk women poets. Indeed, recent criticism concerning the chronology of women poets from the late nineteenth century into the modernist era displays a similar logic. Cristanne Miller writes that female poets of the 1890s such as Ella Wheeler Wilcox, E. Pauline Johnson, and Alice Dunbar-Nelson are among "the first Western women to write not just accomplished or powerful poems but in distinctly innovative forms, thereby helping to shape one of the most significant shifts in literary aesthetics and cultural attitudes since the days of Shakespeare" (C. Miller 2016, 43). Thanks to their inventive "forms, genres, and modes," these writers "redefine the possibilities of imagining the poem for the following generations" (43).

In other words, critical assessments (both then and now) suggest that women writers of the late nineteenth century were freeing themselves from the cultural and conventional limitations that had made their predecessors' works generic. Such innovations placed them on the same artistic and intellectual plane as the male poets—especially Whitman, who was long credited with creating a new American poetry. But what these critics neglect, I argue, is the continuing use of the practices and persona of the Poetess by women poets who were otherwise considered innovative. Indeed, the Poetess tradition continues to be a formative influence on turn-of-the-century literature—the persona and its practices inform the works of the very poets whom critics praise for ushering in a new era of poetry. Thus, this chapter discusses the legacy of the Poetess from the late nineteenth century to the twentieth century, from an era in which the figure was disappearing (Cone) to a time in which she will no longer need to exist (Clarke).

If we are to believe the magazine the *Smart Set*, the twentieth-century Poetess had not disappeared, nor was her obsolescence imminent; rather, she was a force to be reckoned with. Consider Theodosia Garrison's short dramatic piece "The Literati" in 1904. Abandoned by his wife at a literary party, a character called "the Husband" is hiding behind a screen from the other guests. "Three Poetesses" are also in attendance, and, much to the Husband's dismay, they spot him. "Oh, how terrible they are!" he exclaims. It is their self-centeredness that is so awful. "One would think," he says, "to see them, that he was looking into three convex mirrors" (Garrison 1904, 149). With this oblique comparison, the piece suggests the distorting effects of the Poetesses' self-absorption; their focus on their own selves warps everything else. One of the Husband's other complaints also conveys just how clichéd the Poetess's obliviousness had become; he gripes, "She writes purple verse for pale people" (149). In a sense, the Husband affirms what Cone, Clarke, and Cristanne Miller have tacitly claimed: in light of the innovations by women writers, the Poetess still traffics in old-fashioned and out-of-touch conventions. "Purple verse for pale people" suggests that these writers retained their flowery sentimentalism to appeal to the tastes of the intellectually weak.

Despite her ridicule, the Garrison piece suggests what makes the persona and its practices into a source of innovation for twentieth-century women poets. This sketch emphasizes how the Poetess becomes more performative as the century progresses, suggesting a shift from earlier attempts to embody and thereby speak through the Poetess to a self-conscious performance that makes room for critical insights. The Poetesses' costumes bear this point out; for instance, one is wearing "a kimono" accessorized with an "ox-chain" (Garrison 1904, 149). By 1904, the Poetess was in on the joke and apt to signal her self-absorption by performing in absurd ensembles. It is an ironic twist for a figure so closely associated with tradition, as the outfits suggest her self-inspiration and indifference to convention. The sketch even contains a scene of Poetess performance. Another Poetess, still wearing her rubbers and an "Alpine hat," stands on a divan to recite. The first Poetess (the one in the kimono) chides the Husband to "listen! She is telling when she wrote this poem; she is telling why; she is telling on what paper she wrote it; she is telling the color of the ink. She is very wonderful! She writes only of the dead" (150). This description lays out the elements of antebellum Poetess performance in the twentieth century: one must retain the collapse between biographical poet and Poetess persona, hence the pedantic explanation of when, where, and why the poem was written (and on what kind of paper). And, of course, Poetess performance retains the sentimental tropes associated with women's poetry, now grotesquely exaggerated; the Poetess in this sketch recites poems about "a little, burned child" and "a mildewed moon" (150). As the nineteenth century came to its close, the Poetess becomes more performative and less "real." This is not to say that the Poetess devolved into fantasy. At the very least, the emergence of a performative persona demonstrates the ongoing viability of Poetess poetics in twentieth-century literary culture. More specifically, this chapter, as well as the chapter that follows, demonstrates how this performative Poetess allowed women writers to address modern problems. In short, I would like to call attention to the performance of the Poetess as an overlooked but active strain in women's poetry, one that extends from the late nineteenth to the early twentieth century.

Millay and Modernism

Proof of such modern Poetess performance is perhaps best exemplified by Millay. Millay's work was conservative in the sense that it conserved past poetic traditions. While the work of her female contemporaries, such as H. D. (Hilda Doolittle) and Marianne Moore, distanced itself from the conventions of nineteenth-century poetry, the majority of Millay's poems evoked them. For that reason, she has been excluded from the modernist canon for not only expressing the emotional unruliness and vulnerability of the modern woman but containing these responses within traditional forms.[1] Concerned to preserve individual agency against the invasiveness of political, economic, and cultural changes—such as welfare state policies, a growing corporate economy, and the rise of mass and middlebrow culture—modernist artists questioned both the personified expression of private emotion and the traditional forms that typically expressed such emotion. For that reason, innovative approaches and objective exteriors seemed to offer modernist poets the best means to sustain individual agency. Millay appeared to practice a poetics uninformed by these concerns.

Because Millay has not been read through canons and criticism shaped by modernist influence, critics turn to other features of her poetry to signify her modernity. Recent literary scholarship therefore attends to how her works reflect the sexual and social liberation of the modern woman. But doing so appears to create its own set of problems, given what critics see as the opposition between her subversive ethos and her traditional forms. A number of scholars have tried to make sense of this opposition by concluding that Millay exercises a healthy poetic restraint. Her poetry, so the argument goes, curbs emotional excess within self-imposed and protective formal limitations.[2] In sum, Millay's poetic self-discipline assuaged a conflict between innovative content and conventional form.

I want to suggest that this critical consensus insists upon conflicts—between form and content, innovation and tradition, emotion and impersonality—where none exist. While it has been stigmatized, Millay's use of seemingly conservative forms communicates, rather than confines, an appropriately modernist affect and intuition. In what follows, I argue that Millay developed an alternative modernist practice that was geared to tackle the most fundamental problems of modern and modernist selves. Millay was uniquely positioned to confront such problems because her poetic practice was derived from the Poetess tradition, a tradition that has always expressed emotional insight through seemingly conservative poetic conventions. Over the course of the nineteenth century and into the twentieth, the Poetess tradition investigated the problems that faced the woman poet: the self-diminishing, if not nearly impossible, practice of professing privacy. Although the woman poet's problems with privacy were dissolved within the larger investigations of the modernist movement, Millay's poetry helps to demonstrate the ways in which American modernism emerged from the Poetess's poetics. This demonstration would belie the typical story of American modernism. Rather than a radical break, modernist practice signified a continuation or modulation of existing nineteenth-century trends, as modernists also undertook to examine the authenticity and feasibility of interiority. After all, nineteenth-century poetic traditions were preoccupied with a similar question, and one nearly synonymous with women's poetry: the question of how to render privacy in public.[3]

As my description of modernist inquiry suggests, both modernist and Poetess poetry are informed by liberalism's privacy/personhood relationship, that is, the idea that sovereign interiority is necessary to create individual agency. What Millay's poetry exposes is the open secret that conjoins liberal and lyrical thought: namely, that the self was never entirely private and was equally forged by public influence. Where other modernists employed innovative or experimental practices to investigate the line between the inner self and the external world, Millay's poetry elaborated a mode of modernist inquiry that engaged with a tradition based on public figurations of interiority. The critical legacy of high modernist American literature tends to obscure the social relevance of contemporaneous literatures, but in this chapter I will consider what connects the Poetess to a literary movement that explicitly rejected its very premises.

The Poetess's Persistence

In no small part, critical neglect of Millay's relationship with the Poetess tradition owes to her deserved reputation as a "new woman." Ever one to flout social conventions, Millay was a literary celebrity by the time she graduated from college. She was recognized from a very young age as possessing remarkable talent, and, unlike the Poetess, she did not need either a husband or male superintendence to establish her literary reputation—in fact, Millay married in 1923, more than a decade after her poem "Renascence" was published to much acclaim.[4] Even then, hers was an open marriage, and Millay a cosmopolitan bohemian. In turn, her poetic subjects seem to only reinforce this figure of the flighty, free young woman. Of course, Millay's new woman also experienced a much different public sphere than her Poetess precursors. Millay's "popularity," Cheryl Walker argues, "reflected a genuine loosening of restrictions on female behavior. Unlike her nineteenth-century sisters, she could and did travel alone, control her own money, smoke and drink without apology, attend lesbian and interracial parties, and sleep with a number of partners" (C. Walker 1991, 143).

But the freedoms Millay enjoyed also sparked a backlash, and conservative cultural pressures emerged in response to women's newfound opportunities. Millay came of age during what historians have described as the Gilded Age or the Progressive Era, and which extends from the 1870s to the close of World War I. No doubt these were tumultuous years, but the changes that perhaps had the biggest impact on Millay were shifting and contradictory attitudes toward gender.[5] On the one hand, women now had greater access to opportunities in the public sphere—for instance, they could attend college and hold jobs.[6] On the other hand, a countervailing retrenchment of traditional gender roles added "gendered standards to previously ungendered aspects of life" (Hamlin 2017, 87). Indeed, such gendering extended beyond popular culture to include science, which standardized supposedly "appropriate gender presentation and often classified these boundaries as 'natural'" (Hamlin 2017, 89).[7] The new (but utterly familiar) norms were externalized in "the idea that men should look as masculine as possible and women as feminine as possible" (94). In other words, these gender norms underscore notions of gender presentation or, for Millay, gender as performance. By adopting the most feminine of poetic personas in both her poetry and public appearances, Millay was making the most of an era in which "mass culture widely popularized acceptable appearances" (89).

Given this tension between traditional gender roles and the "new woman," Millay's relationship to the Poetess tradition is, in so many respects, no surprise. Indeed, Millay's celebrity depended on her close association with the Poetess. As Suzanne Clark has remarked, "Millay had a popular and sweeping success as a 'poetess.' Her sentimental readers were in the majority, and they recognized her immediately" (Clark 1996, 144). Millay's fans demonstrate how the influence of the Poetess extended beyond her antebellum heyday: women poets continued to write as Poetesses, and Poetess poetry was taught and anthologized well into the era of high modernism. The names of antebellum authors may not be as prevalent, but the numerous poetry anthologies of the early twentieth century attest to how the Poetess's practices still possessed value. In these works, we can see strains of the Poetess in a number of women poets from the second half of the nineteenth century, such as Elizabeth Akers Allen, Rose Terry Cooke, Julia Ward Howe, Sophie Jewett, Emma Lazarus, Louise Chandler Moulton, Josephine Preston Peabody, Sarah Piatt, Lizette Woodworth Reese, Harriet Prescott Spofford, Celia Thaxter, and Ella Wheeler Wilcox. Indeed, the work of these writers, as well as that of antebellum American and eighteenth-century British Poetesses, can be found in the numerous poetry anthologies of the early twentieth century, such as Bliss Carman's *The World's Best Poetry* (1904), Thomas R. Lounsbury's *Yale Book of American Verse* (1912), or Sara Teasdale's *The Answering Voice* (1917), which contains only works by women. Citing some of these names, Cristanne Miller sees the prevalence of "female poets in the 1890s and first decade of the twentieth century" as "pav[ing] the way" for modernist women writers to "contribute to the elite field of poetry on an equal basis with men" (C. Miller 2016, 41). This may be the case, but I would add that "the popularity and critical success" of these turn-of-the-century writers are related to their retention and revision of Poetess practices (41). This is not to suggest that if a woman was not writing innovative, proto-modernist verse, she was a Poetess. Rather, I am suggesting that traces of antebellum Poetess performance persist in poetry by the authors named above, and these works have a public life in the early twentieth century—critically evaluated, included in anthologies, and published in magazines big and little.

Besides the popularity of such poetry, Millay could not help but be aware of the Poetess tradition through her mother.[8] Throughout her daughter's youth, Cora Buzzell Millay clipped Poetess poetry from newspapers, pasted Poetess poems into scrapbooks, and filled bookcases with collected works by Poetess poets such as Felicia Hemans and Jean Ingelow (Milford 2002, 41).[9] Starting in the 1890s, Buzzell Millay even published her own feminine, sentimental, didactic poetry in northeastern newspapers.[10] In the years surrounding Millay's birth, Cora was an active contributor to the *Maine Farmer*.[11] From at least 1889 to 1894, the paper published a number of Buzzell Millay's poems that, I argue, engage with Poetess devices. For instance, the poem "Good-night" from October 1889 displays the Poetess's feminine piety at the same time that it explicitly references Elizabeth Akers Allen's "Rock Me to Sleep"—the speaker longs for her childhood and for "the mother-love holy—too holy to last" (C. Millay 1889, 4). While I am not certain how many poems Cora contributed to the *Maine Farmer* or for how long, it is evident that poetry was a passion she pursued during Millay's lifetime. Years later, in 1928, Cora even published a collection of children's poems, *Little Otis*, with W. W. Norton. Reviewers were quick to suggest that Millay inherited her mother's poetic practices; in a reference that includes Edna's sister, Norma, a review from the *Independent* comments that "behaviorists may now have a good time explaining the effect of the stimulus of Little Otis upon Mrs. Cora Millay's two famous daughters. These were the verses that may have delighted them in youth" (*Independent* 1928, 333). Even though Little Otis is not given to "whimsical sentimentality," the childish speaker is a feature of Millay's poems, and one that links both mother and daughter to the performed innocence of the Poetess (333).

Reviews of Millay's work also demonstrate how the Poetess tradition continued to exert pressure on the reception of women's poetry. Even as she was recognized as the model of a modern female artist, her reviewers latched onto Millay's youthfulness to resurrect expectations about the Poetess—first, her unprofessionalism, and, second, ideas about how female poetic privacy perpetuates the figure's genericness.[12] But these reviews do more than affirm the ongoing presence of the Poetess in the larger twentieth-century literary public sphere. The expectations on display in these same reviews also help us understand how Millay's poems figured a radical poetic publicity that deflated fantasies of women's perfect privacy.

For instance, Harriet Monroe's 1918 review of *Renascence,* Millay's first volume, echoes nineteenth-century assumptions about the Poetess's exuberant inability to contain emotion. In the title poem, "Renascence," Monroe writes that "the surprise of youth over the universe, the emotion of youth at encountering inexplicable infinities—that is expressed in this poem, and it is a big thing to express. Moreover, it is expressed with a certain triumphant joy, the very mood of exultant youth" (Monroe 1918, 167). In Monroe's description, Millay becomes a young thing who inadvertently possesses otherworldly vision, similar to Eva in *The Sinless Child.* Monroe celebrates Millay's youth for giving her remarkable insight into "the universe"; like the Poetess, in other words, Millay possesses an accidental naïveté that allows access to universal truth. In turn, this callow amateurism becomes the basis for reasserting claims about authorial genericness. As we saw in chapter 1, the Poetess was rendered abstract and forgettable because her supposed profession of privacy tapped into universal—but generic—feminine feeling. Monroe appears to repeat such conclusions. Millay, she worries, is at risk of losing her originality, or becoming generic: "Life, closing in on this poet as on so many others, may narrow her scope and vision" (Monroe 1918, 167). But Monroe's own praise implicates Millay in a generic cliché. Monroe seems to be reaffirming that feminine poetic vision is found in its most pure form only when removed from life or the workings of the public, adult world. It's best, she implies, that Millay should remain eternally an "exultant youth," which is to say, an idealized innocent who inadvertently exposes her interiority (167).[13]

More than a decade later, reviewers still kept expecting Millay to exhibit the Poetess's immature interiority. In his review of Millay's 1928 collection, *The Buck in the Snow,* Edd Winfield Parks upholds a reception history that conflates femininity, lyrical intimacy, and immaturity. As he explains it, "until she reached the age of thirty-five," Millay's poetry was "intimate rather than conventional, emotional rather than intellectual, realistic rather than philosophical, and inconstant to an extreme. In brief, feminine" (Parks 1930, 42). Parks draws a bright line between immature and mature Millay (a line apparently crossed at the age of thirty-five). This simplistic distinction confirms the convention that "feminine" poetry expresses emotional intimacy. In fact, with the publication of *The Buck in the Snow,* Parks can contend that "her mind can no longer be called feminine, in the derogatory sense"—Millay finally sheds a feminine poetic tradition for a more modern and masculine practice (49).

These reviews are correct, I argue, to notice Millay's youthful invocation of a pure feminine privacy. But they also overlook how Millay explicitly manipulates this privacy. In fact, her poetry demonstrates how this commonplace association of women poets with the exposure of interiority—an association that these reviews take as a given—is the condition that enables the public female self even as it drastically circumscribes the possibilities of such a self. Millay revises the reception of the Poetess by making this sense of limitation palpable. Such female privacy, her poetry insists, is a fantasy. Innocent or immature, the intimacy supposedly discovered by her reviewers was always already public, a point that Millay underscores by self-consciously presenting privacy as the stuff of public consumption. In turn, this revision of female privacy ultimately levels the distinctions promoted by liberal selfhood. Because her poetry asserts that the public/private divide was an imaginary one, Millay deflates the sovereign interiority that constitutes liberal self-possession.

Consider Millay's poem "The Penitent," which uses the terms of traditional propriety to characterize a freewheeling femme's failed attempt at self-revision. The speaker in this poem performs as a Poetess, professing personal conflict in terms of ideal feminine morality, which she resolves to uphold in the privacy of her room. However, the poem undercuts the ethical soul-baring associated with women's public poetry; the speaker seeks seclusion in order to trouble the relationship between privacy and ideal womanhood:

> I had a little Sorrow,
> Born of a little Sin,
> I found a room all damp with gloom
> And shut us all within;
> And, "Little Sorrow, weep," said I,
> "And, Little Sin, pray God to die,
> And I upon the floor will lie
> And think how bad I've been!"
> —E. Millay 1956, 139

The speaker mandates that she, along with Sorrow and Sin, will atone for being "bad." By shutting herself away, the speaker admits that she could not muster the requisite propriety to function in the public sphere—so back to seclusion she goes. This opening premise builds on the conjoined traditions of liberalism and the Poetess: interior spaces, removed from publicity, are where the work of selfhood is completed. Of course, for women, this selfhood must be morally correct. Therefore, in that gloomy room, the trio is supposed to work on devotedly fulfilling the terms of feminine propriety:

Alas for pious planning—
It mattered not a whit!
As far as gloom went in that room,
The lamp might have been lit!
My Little Sorrow would not weep,
My Little Sin would go to sleep—
To save my soul I could not keep
My graceless mind on it!
—E. Millay 1965, 139

Vindication appears to come easy, as the speaker simply commands Sorrow, Sin, and herself to atone. But Sorrow will "not weep," Sin simply "go[es] to sleep," and the speaker cannot keep her "graceless mind" on the task of saving her "soul." In the final stanza, she surrenders to wickedness:

So up I got in anger,
And took a book I had,
And put a ribbon on my hair
To please a passing lad,
And, "One thing there's no getting by—
I've been a wicked girl," said I;
"But if I can't be sorry, why,
I might as well be glad!"
—E. Millay 1965, 140

Notably, the tiny tantrum at the poem's end demonstrates that this exercise in seclusion does not purge impropriety. Instead, seclusion is what renders the speaker a "wicked girl," a shifting, fickle female. Nor does any sustaining "soul" ameliorate the conflict between the speaker's inherited ideals about moral femininity—the expectation that privacy will rectify the components of her self—and the reality of her public, provocative persona. Such a problem of inner moral integrity emerges because the speaker, performing as a Poetess, was invariably public: she was subject to and constructed by the expectations of observers and readers. The poetic speaker shows that a sincere, sustaining spirit is bound to fail when constituted by cultural fantasies of feminine privacy and propriety. Millay exploits the expectations already associated with public women poets in order to depict the Poetess as the public creature she had always been. In other words, she disputes any notion of an authentic self forged in private.

Millay's Alternative Approach

Using a poetic tradition founded on privacy's utter publicity, Millay staged a direct confrontation with the fraught privacy that defined the public female poet in the modern era. Although her means were perhaps the most direct, Millay was not the only poet to stage such a confrontation. While Millay specifically engaged the Poetess's conservative forms in order to target publicity, privacy, and possession in the modern era, other women poets, such as Marianne Moore and H. D., used modernism's innovative forms to indirectly grapple with such problems. "Like Moore," writes Cristanne Miller, "H.D. repeatedly represented aesthetic and gender conventions as interwoven" (C. Miller 2016, 47). And like Millay, Moore and H. D. grapple with the individual autonomy that characterized the concerns of Poetess and modernist practices. Their poems contended with gendered privacy in a modern context, but by departing from and experimenting with traditional verse. For example, in the poem "The Fish," Moore extends strict metrical rhythms into original poetic forms. The result echoes the Poetess's self-abnegation in order to explore the objective surface of life. The last lines transform the absent or deflated physicality of the Poetess into unenlivened biological imagery: "it can live / on what can not revive / its youth. The sea grows old in it" (Moore 1994, 38–40). A sense of stagnation, used to explore objective existence, replaces and revokes the living self. To make sense of the world, this poetic subject withdraws or sacrifices herself, reflecting the Poetess's performance in the place of embodied, sovereign subjectivity. Similarly, H. D.'s poetry explores the female poet's lack of autonomy. In the poem "Helen," the ideal woman is culturally acceptable only in generic, objectified form. "All Greece hates" Helen because she "remember[s] past enchantments / and past ills" (H. D. 1986, 1, 10–11). When the public female figure, be it Helen or the Poetess, reserves some part of her self, she is "revile[d]" (6). But if she were dead, "laid / white ash amid funereal cypresses," Helen would be accessible, beautiful, and beloved (17–18). H. D. is expressing concern that culture was "unmoved" by the autonomous public woman (12). If Helen were to be cremated—literally objectified—Greece "could love [this woman] indeed" (16).

As I have already suggested, privacy and its attendant issues of interiority, intimacy, and vulnerability were major concerns of the modernist movement. Indeed, early twentieth-century poetry probed questions about the relationship between personhood and personal utterance; such poetry constituted an arena, J. Hillis Miller argues, "in which things, the mind, and words coincide in closest intimacy" (J. Miller 1965, 8). To protect this intimacy, modernist poetry cordoned off a space free from outside threats by emphasizing depersonalized, innovative poetic utterance. More specifically, such poetry sought to "foreground the fact that [modernist works] are constructed by an individual consciousness," by "call[ing] attention to the ways that we have been habituated to seeing the world" and exposing these ways of seeing as "simply conventions" (Barnhisel 2015, 30). In other words, modernist innovation can be understood as an effort to prevent the encroachment of conventional forms—which is to say, the encroachment of much of what constitutes nineteenth-century verse—on individual agency.

But what circumstances made notions of individual agency so valuable or, put the other way, what made the individual seem so embattled to the modernists? We can answer these questions by first attending to the echoes of the circumscribed liberal subject evident in modernist concerns over authentic selfhood. As I have already suggested, this confrontation was spurred by the emergence of welfare-state liberalism and mass culture, themselves threats, or so it seemed, to the liberal circumscribed self. Modernists' concerns presume what Andrew Hoberek describes as "a degraded, deindividualizing social realm" (Hoberek 2016, 119). Their distrust of "the collective, rather than individual, agency," was exhibited in "hostility to bourgeois society" and "attacks on mass culture" (Barnhisel 2015, 35). Indeed, modernism sought to preserve the circumscribed self in the face of political and social encroachments by drawing a line between the "so-called middlebrow" and modernist exclusivity (35). Modernist inquiry therefore produced an analog to liberalism's public/private divide, symbolized in the modernist tension between culture's "deindividualizing" conventionality and individual innovation. According to a modernist standard, Millay's poetry would seem to evince the supposedly pernicious effects of modern society on the circumscribed self inasmuch as her private, personal "sensibility" has been so spectacularly given over to the public sphere.

As we can see, the modernist discourse of innovation effectively set the terms of Millay's reception. Modernist critics saw her accessible poetry as exactly the problem with mass culture. For middlebrow critics, she was a palliative for modernist difficulty. Allen Tate's 1931 *New Republic* review articulates this divide between modernist estrangement and Millay's genteel accessibility. Tate suggests that Millay's facile feeling was not the mark of the modern: "Her poetry does not define the break with the nineteenth century" (Tate 1993, 62). Whereas "Eliot penetrated to the fundamental structure of the nineteenth-century mind and showed its breakdown," Tate writes that "Miss Millay assumed no such profound alteration of the intelligence because, I suppose, not being an intellect but a sensibility, she was not aware of it" (62). Millay is old-fashioned, Tate argues: she does not break down nineteenth-century sensibility for the modern age but maintains it. Here Tate is prototypically modernist, as his desire to separate modern intellect from nineteenth-century sentiment derives from the modernist compulsion to separate innovative literature from middle-class mass consumption. With her familiar poetic forms, Millay appears to confirm Tate's opinions, and indeed, Millay's reception within the popular press strongly suggests that she purposefully made herself accessible to mass and middlebrow tastes. For example, in 1923, *Life* magazine comments that Millay's poetry is, colloquially, "simply swell," and the fact that "that popular lay figure known as the man in the street" would "grasp" her works is commendable (Warwick 1923, 20). In the 1921 *Poetry* magazine review of *Second April,* Marion Strobel fantasizes about gathering her friends whose "brows which have knitted at the mention of poetry," and "read[ing] to them—or get Edna St. Vincent Millay to read to them, if it were only possible!" (Strobel 1921, 152).[14]

As middlebrow publications celebrate Millay, it becomes clear that modernist critics like Tate are correct, I think, to contend that her works privileged the very traditions with which modernism conflicted: availability, emotional transparency, and formal verse. However, these critics only saw Millay's conservation of tradition—they did not see how it attempted to answer their own concerns. Millay understood that the Poetess offered a strategy for expanding critical understandings of modernist poetry, and for engaging in modernist inquiry via an alternate approach: as a radically public, accessible poet who nevertheless shared modernism's concern over individual agency.[15] To her, modernism's signal preoccupations—preoccupations with form and freedom, the private and public, the subjective interior and objective exterior—were permutations of the Poetess's problem of a private poetic self created for public consumption. By turning the profession of interiority inside out, so to speak, Millay's poems dissolved the line between personal and public. In such a state, personal privacy is so fickle and ephemeral that it confirms modernism's worst nightmare: individual agency was never formed by the individual herself. In other words, individual consciousness is created not through estrangement from public convention, but by familiarity with it.

Millay's poems about travel (or the lack thereof) are predicated on the Poetesses' understanding of the radically public nature of privacy. These works exaggerate personal privacy in order to dismantle modernist anxiety over surfaces and interiors. For example, "To the Not Impossible Him," a poem in *A Few Figs from Thistles,* depicts a female speaker confessing her inner turmoil.[16]

To question the value of the domestic, the speaker in this poem contemplates roaming. In so doing, the poem intensifies the Poetess's techniques by taking idealized insularity to its most hyperbolic extreme:

How shall I know, unless I go
　To Cairo and Cathay,
Whether or not this blessèd spot
　Is blest in every way?

Now it may be, the flower for me
　Is this beneath my nose;
How shall I tell, unless I smell
　The Carthaginian rose?

The fabric of my faithful love
　No power shall dim or ravel
Whilst I stay here,—but oh, my dear,
　If I should ever travel!

—E. Millay 1965, 130

In order to determine the sincerity of her love, the speaker considers travel and experience. Unless she actually goes to "Cairo and Cathay," how will she know "Whether or not this blessèd spot / Is blest in every way?" While the speaker's candor makes the question seem innocuous, not promiscuous, Millay is reversing the cliché that associates sincerity with the home. The sanctity of the home does not promise stability but the feebleness of feeling. Here it is travel, or the possibility of travel, that will determine honesty, and this poem demonstrates just how "impossible" privacy and authenticity are. Thus, its final ironic apostrophe—"but oh, my dear, / If I should ever travel!"—points to the contingency of the speaker's feelings in the first place. This conditional reasoning implies the ironic flimsiness of her love—merely traveling will put an end to her "faithful love."

The poem's metric repetitions and rhymes also question the sincerity of private feelings. In the first and third line of each stanza, the repeated rhyme on the second and fourth stresses lends the poem its bubbly, playful quality. But this exaggerated repetition also suggests a forced cheeriness, a point the poem reinforces when the tone shifts in the final stanza. The drawn-out "o" vowels ("of," "love," "power") suggest a turn to solemnity by lowering the poem's prior energy and volume. The speaker seems to be confessing a sober moment of sincerity, and this moment of intimacy disrupts the poem. Indeed, it is as if the speaker forgot her character and let another, more authentic self break through. Although the entire poetic utterance is ostensibly sincere, this profession of privacy actually renders sincerity questionable. Indeed, Millay has executed a clever reversal, as the use of sincerity now troubles our very notions of sincerity. But the point isn't to trade one version of sincerity for another, more authentic, version. As quickly as it came along, this sober interlude is swept away by the comical apostrophe of the last two lines. This glimpse, then, was as much a part of the performance as the rest of the poem. Millay uses these final, confessional lines to highlight the impossibility of privacy. Since even private moments are inadvertently offered to the public, sincerity is always dubious. In sum, Millay suggests there was nothing to overcome, no struggle between staying home or traveling, because there was no point: ideal female sincerity was a fantasy of privacy offered to the public.

This exposure of feminine flakiness would also seem to confirm that the sanctity of the private sphere has no impact on sincerity. Whereas domestic ideology would have associated "this blessèd spot" with authenticity and self-knowledge, Millay shows there is nothing inherently sincere in domestic stasis. In this conclusion, Millay may appear to validate nineteenth-century liberal ideals about women lacking the self-possession necessary to withstand public exposure. But this reading, I argue, is incomplete. It misunderstands the significance of her speaker's changing mind, which Millay uses to exaggerate modernist anxieties. Because the speaker's fickleness evacuates any sense of sincerity or self-sovereignty, the poem depicts individual agency as utterly constructed by deindividualizing social conventions. Autonomous selfhood might be "not impossible," but Millay tells us that the tools for creating it—privacy and sincerity—are impossible.

Whereas liberal ideology associates the home with the authenticity and self-knowledge needed to ground sovereign selfhood, Millay divorces the private sphere from seemingly sincere self-development. Another poem from *A Few Figs from Thistles* likewise questions travel and domestic stasis. But this poem is notable for the parallels it strikes with modernist practices—in "The Unexplorer," the very exposure of interiority has the protective effect of depersonalizing interiority. Only six lines long, this poem describes a figure confined to the domestic space. Her innocence—her naïveté and her ostensible honesty—is the by-product of a lack of worldly experience:

There was a road ran past our house
Too lovely to explore.
I asked my mother once—she said

That if you followed where it led
It brought you to the milk-man's door.
(That's why I have not travelled more.)
—E. Millay 1965, 138

The speaker's ignorance suggests that she is a child, if not strictly in years, then in experience. The speaker only has one resource beyond her self—the mother, an idealized woman who serves in a domestic-tutelary role. Innocence has traditionally translated to accidental interiority, as we saw with the Poetess. Here, the speaker's simplicity suggests that she lacks the ability to craft both public and private sides. There is no more to this figure; there is no public, performed persona because, in her innocence, she does not have the guile to be anything but transparent. What the poem presumes to present is an open, unadulterated soul whose innocence collapses the line between interior and exterior.

Too innocent to understand that what was private has become completely public, Millay's speaker is an exaggeration of the Poetess. But even such radical publicity has crucial limits in Millay's poem, as the speaker's transparency does not necessarily entail the full disclosure of her interiority. Indeed, "The Unexplorer" foregrounds this refusal to fully disclose with a parenthetical final line: "(That's why I have not travelled more.)." The line appears to be an aside that would presumably contain a more direct form of address from speaker to audience—which is to say, readers expect it to offer a more substantial reason for unexploring. But the line instead gestures toward what is not revealed about the speaker's reasoning: the road is too beautiful, the road leads to the milkman, hence I have not traveled. The elliptical explanation has the makings of a scandalous tale—perhaps the road once led the mother to the milk-man and the speaker is his child, but she must never meet him. But even without firm details, this is the outline of a confession. While compelling her to reveal her interior, the speaker's innocence also inadvertently obscures it at the same time. The speaker may profess privacy, but what she reveals remains inaccessible to readers. This is to say that Millay manages to protect the privacy of the poet by depicting a supposedly transparent figure whose interiority stays obscure.

By flattening the distinctions associated with Poetess poetry, "The Unexplorer" places sincerity on the same level with publicity. In her exaggeration of the Poetess's privacy, Millay actually re-creates modernism's unavailability: even though the utterly open speaker publicly offers an oversimplified, inconclusive, childlike logic, she remains a self that cannot be penetrated or fully ascertained. This practice, I argue, signals Millay's participation in a modernist project. She redeploys traditional poetic conventions in order to make a modernist claim for the impersonality and opacity of the poetic utterance.

Modern Media

While the abandonment of tradition might qualify as the telltale characteristic of modernism, nineteenth-century practices were evident in modernist poetics: indeed, the specter of tradition hovers as a presence that Millay and other modernists choose to invoke or revoke, and in ways that need not imply retrograde aesthetic or political practices. In other words, Millay and the high modernists shared a common lineage, but differed in how they envisioned and reacted to their inheritance. As I argue above, Millay draws on the Poetess tradition in order to problematize the privacy associated with women's lyrical legacy. She does this not to demonstrate the irrelevance of the Poetess to the modern era, but to show that the Poetess's confrontation with sovereign selfhood, publicity, and interiority provided a productive model for addressing modern issues. In poems that perform feminized personas whose privacy is radically public, Millay destabilizes, as I have argued, the ideal intimacy associated with women's poetry. Now I want to call attention to how Millay deployed this public profession of privacy in her media presence, which enhanced the fantasy of privacy-rendered-public that was already encouraged in her poetry.

Millay uses the various forms of her media presence—in print, performance, and radio—to demonstrate the constructedness of a supposedly essential poetic persona. To do so, she animates a tension between the promise of perfect lyrical availability and the utter absence of the figure such media purport to produce. Across these forms, Millay fashioned herself such that she appeared to pinpoint, package, and present one identity to readers at the same time that this single fixed identity gestured to other flexible personas. Indeed, as Catherine Keyser argues, "Millay's private writing suggests her self-awareness about the role of the mass media industry in producing attractive (and hence consumable) feminine roles" (Keyser 2010, 24). With her popular media presence, Millay showed that modernism's concern for the loss of individual agency in the face of deindividualizing culture was a foregone conclusion: an essential, stable selfhood was always already impossible.

Millay's positioning of her printed works and her public persona drew upon traditions of circulating the female poet in the public sphere. Across her career, Millay published her works in a number of literary and popular periodicals: *Poetry*, the *Dial*, *Harper's*, the *Nation*, the *Saturday Evening Post*, the *New York Times,* and *Ladies' Home Journal,* to name a few.[17] In the 1920s she was a regular contributor to *Vanity Fair*. There she published prose under the pseudonym "Nancy Boyd" and poems such as "To the Not Impossible Him" and "The Ballad of the Harp Weaver." *Vanity Fair* also published the earliest image of Millay in 1920; thereafter, her photographed image became a commonplace device for promoting her works (Parker 2016, 385). "Millay was not simply a celebrated poet; she was a mass media celebrity," writes Sarah Parker; that fame was "due to the circulation of her photographic image" (380).[18]

Millay's clever, sexy, and emotionally wry writing was well suited to *Vanity Fair,* a magazine that, as Keyser explains, "praised 'smartness' as an attitude, an acquisition, an image, and an aspect of New York daily life" (Keyser 2010, 27). For *Vanity Fair,* such praise was part of broader commercial strategies, as the magazine sought to establish "its modernity and smartness" in opposition to nineteenth-century traditions (69). For instance, a *Vanity Fair* columnist claimed that the magazine was "invariably up on the latest thing in fashion, art or literature," whereas "all the contributors to *Harper's Magazine* are women with three names" (qtd. in Keyser 2007, 69). Yet for all its claims to banish sentimental "sob sisters" from its pages, *Vanity Fair* nevertheless duplicated nineteenth-century strategies for circulating the Poetess (69). The magazine promoted the Poetess's supposed sincerity, as it put on display Millay's exemplary interior and exterior—her poems and her image—for public consumption. For instance, a full-page spread about Millay's poetry from the November 1920 *Vanity Fair* names Millay "the Most Distinguished American Poet of the Younger Generation." But at no point does the write-up suggest the qualities of a modern female poet. Instead, it reproduces the fantasy of sincerity associated with the Poetess. The page features eight poems and the first printed photograph of Millay. Under her image, the editors describe Millay's sincerity—not the charm, wit, or cynicism that would seem to distinguish her as "the latest thing": "Millay is one of the very few first-rate figures in modern American poetry. Her work, by the extraordinary vigor of its language and the sincerity of its emotion, achieves a lyric intensity scarcely to be found in the work of her contemporaries. Her best poems—and those printed here for the first time are some of her very best—have much more than the felicity of the artist contriving a literary form; they speak with the arresting naturalness and passion of a living human voice" (*Vanity Fair* 1920, 49). Millay's "arresting naturalness" echoes expectations that women poets lack professional guile; she could never "contriv[e] a literary form." Likewise, the accompanying photograph of Millay bolsters these editorial comments; her

Poems by Edna St. Vincent Millay

A New Set of Lyrics by the Most Distinguished American Poet of the Younger Generation

WILD SWANS

I LOOKED in my heart while the wild swans went over;—
And what did I see I had not seen before?
Only a question less or a question more;
Nothing to match the flight of wild birds flying.
Tiresome heart, forever living and dying!
House without air! I leave you and lock your door!
Wild swans, come over the town, come over
The town again, trailing your legs and crying!

THE SINGIN' WOMAN FROM THE WOOD'S EDGE

WHAT should I be but a prophet and a liar
Whose mother was a leprechaun, whose father was a friar?
Teethed on a crucifix and cradled under water,
What should I be but the fiend's god-daughter?

And who should be my playmates but the adder and the frog,
That was got beneath a furze-brush and born in a bog?
And what should be my singin', that was christened at an altar,
But *Aves* and *Credos* and psalms out of the psalter?

You will see such webs on the wet grass, maybe,
As a pixie-mother weaves for her baby;
You will find such flames at the wave's weedy ebb
As flashes in the meshes of a mermother's web.

But there comes to birth no common spawn
From the love of a priest for a leprechaun,
And you never have seen and you never will see
Such things as the things that swaddled me!

After all's said and after all's done,
What should I be but a harlot and a nun?

In through the bushes on any foggy day
My da would come a-swishin' of the drops away,
With a prayer for my death and a groan for my birth,
A-mumblin' of his beads for all that he was worth;

And there'd sit my ma with her knees beneath her chin,
A-lookin' in his face and a-drinkin' of it in,
And a-markin' in the moss some funny little sayin'
That would mean just the opposite of all that he was prayin'.

Oh, the things I haven't seen and the things I haven't known,
What with hedges and ditches till after I was grown,
And yanked both ways by my mother and my father,
With a *Which-would-you-better?* and a *Which-would-you-rather?*

He taught me the holy talk of vesper and of matin,
He heard me my Greek and he heard me my Latin;
He blessed me and crossed me to keep my soul from evil,
And we watched him out of sight and we conjured up the devil!

With him for a sire and her for a dam,
What should I be but just what I am?

EDNA ST. VINCENT MILLAY

Edna St. Vincent Millay is one of the very few first-rate figures in modern American poetry. Her work, by the extraordinary vigor of its language and the sincerity of its emotion achieves a lyric intensity scarcely to be found in the work of her contemporaries. Her best poems—and those printed here for the first time are some of her very best—have much more than the felicity of the artist contriving a literary form; they speak with the arresting naturalness and passion of a living human voice

FOUR SONNETS

I

WHEN you, that at this moment are to me
Dearer than words on paper, shall depart,
And be no more the warder of my heart,
Whereof again myself shall hold the key;
And be no more—what now you seem to be—
The sun, from which all excellencies start
In a round nimbus, nor a broken dart
Of moonlight, even, splintered on the sea;

I shall remember only of this hour—
And weep somewhat, as now you see me weep—
The pathos of your love, that, like a flower,
Fearful of death yet amorous of sleep,
Droops for a moment and beholds, dismayed,
The wind whereon its petals shall be laid.

II

HERE is a wound that never will heal, I know,
Being wrought not of a dearness and a death,
But of a love turned ashes and the breath
Gone out of beauty; never again will grow
The grass on that scarred acre; though I sow
Young seed there yearly and the sky bequeath
Its friendly weathers down, far underneath
Shall be such bitterness of an old woe.

That April should be shattered by a gust,
That August should be levelled by a rain,
I can endure, and that the lifted dust
Of man should settle to the earth again;
But that a dream can die, will be a thrust
Between my ribs forever of hot pain.

III

PITY me not because the light of day
At close of day no longer walks the sky;
Pity me not for beauties passed away
From field and thicket as the year goes by;
Pity me not the waning of the moon,
Nor that the ebbing tide goes out to sea,
Nor that a man's desire is hushed so soon,
And you no longer look with love on me.

This have I known always: love is no more
Than the wide blossom which the wind assails,
Than the great tide that treads the shifting shore,
Strewing fresh wreckage gathered in the gales;
Pity me that the heart is slow to learn
What the swift mind beholds at every turn.

IV

WHAT lips my lips have kissed, and where, and why,
I have forgotten, and what arms have lain
Under my head till morning; but the rain
Is full of ghosts tonight, that tap and sigh
Upon the glass and listen for reply,
And in my heart there stirs a quiet pain
For unremembered lads that not again
Will turn to me at midnight with a cry.

Thus in the winter stands the lonely tree,
Nor knows what birds have vanished one by one,
Yet knows its boughs more silent than before:
I cannot say what loves have come and gone,
I only know that summer sang in me
A little while, that in me sings no more.

SPRING

TO what purpose, April, do you return again?
Beauty is not enough.
You can no longer quiet me with the redness
Of little leaves opening stickily.
I know what I know.
The sun is hot on my neck as I observe
The spikes of the crocus.
The smell of the earth is good.
It is apparent that there is no death.
But what does that signify?
Not only under ground are the brains of men
Eaten by maggots.
Life in itself
Is nothing,
An empty cup, a flight of uncarpeted stairs.
It is not enough that yearly down this hill
April
Comes like an idiot, babbling and strewing flowers!

WEEDS

WHITE with daisies and red with sorrel
And empty, empty under the sky!
Life is a quest and love a quarrel;
Here is a place for me to lie.

Daisies spring from damnèd seeds,
And this red fire that here I see
Is a worthless crop of crimson weeds,
Cursed by farmers thriftily.

But here, unhated for an hour,
The sorrel runs in ragged flame;
The daisy stands, a bastard flower,
Like flowers that bear an honest name.

And here awhile, where no wind brings
The baying of a pack athirst,
May sleep the sleep of blessed things
The blood too bright, the brow accurst.

Photograph of Edna St. Vincent Millay from "Poems by Edna St. Vincent Millay," *Vanity Fair*, November 1920, 49.

half-shadowed face suggests a "lyric intensity." Perhaps *Vanity Fair* is trying to declare that Millay's poetry was the most sincere expression of cleverness. Nevertheless, the magazine's efforts to ditch nineteenth-century traditions invariably lead back to them.

As *Vanity Fair* inadvertently recalls the reception of the Poetess, it also recalls the problems of the Poetess's publicity. Millay could become another feminine cliché, especially as her cleverness lost its edginess and was considered, in the words of Louis Untermeyer, merely a "pretty talent" (Untermeyer 1993, 118).[19] As we saw in Henry Coppée's *Gallery of Distinguished English and American Female Poets,* this combination of words and image suggested that the female poet was specifically a product for public consumption (Coppée 1860). The availability of Millay's image would seem to support such sentiments. Since it was as widely circulated and "read" as her poems, her picture offered yet another layer of possessable, public intimacy. Her picture also posed a risk to her presence as an active, self-directing author because it threatened to "enshrin[e]" Millay "as an object" (Parker 2016, 382). The beautiful face of Millay, no less than that of the Poetess, could be conflated with the beauty of her poems.[20]

However, Millay was more closely attuned to the impossible dilemma that this media dependency posed to the female public poet. As the example of innumerable Poetesses attested, such a poet was memorable only inasmuch as she established the conditions for her dissolution. For her part, Millay anticipated the "smartness" or "cleverness" that accompanied her print reception and, in so doing, was able to undermine the fixed identity her readers were so eager to consume. Clever women were associated with a natural charm and wit to the exclusion of masculine, philosophical thought—an assumption that has held over since the heyday of the Poetess (Keyser 2007, 67). The clever woman's intellectual inattention enabled a certain nimble inconstancy; like Frances Sargent Osgood's "Caprice," cleverness necessarily suggests variability. Millay capitalizes on the shallow inconstancy of cleverness as a print persona in a self-portrait poem that she wrote for her friends Edmund Wilson and John Peale Bishop. The poem, Parker argues, "is incredibly revealing of [Millay's] attitude toward her physical appearance" (Parker 2016, 385). According to Millay's assessment of her own image, she finds herself not at all clever—in fact, she is a little obnoxious, vulnerable, and unremarkable. In scrutinizing her appearance, Millay thwarts the readerly expectation that focusing on her image provides insight into interiority:

Hair which she still devoutly trusts is red.
Colorless eyes, employing

A childish wonder
To which they have no statistic
Title.
A large mouth,
Lascivious,
Aceticized by blasphemies.
A long throat,
Which will someday
Be strangled.
Thin arms,
In the summer-time leopard
With freckles.
A small body,
Unexclamatory,
But which,
Were it the fashion to wear no clothes,
Would be as well-dressed
As any.
—E. Millay 1952, 99–100

Critics have typically regarded this poem as Millay's commentary on how she uses poetry and photography for self-promotion. For instance, Parker sees this poem as evidence of Millay's "complicit[y] in marketing her various parts," which was "further intensified by the location of her work and image in fashion magazines such as *Vanity Fair*" (Parker 2016, 387). Cheryl Walker places Millay in the position of a consumer who scrutinizes a marketed object, "as though her body were part of a department store inventory" (C. Walker 1991, 139). But this poem, I argue, asserts more drastic consequences for publicity. It demonstrates what happens to women poets in print: they are symbolically disembodied and "strangled." Putting herself in the position of her readers as they look at her image, Millay concentrates on what viewers do to the displayed body of the supposedly clever woman. In describing her hair, eyes, and mouth, we see how the body is "read" for hints about the subject's self. A far cry from innocuousness, this reading is an act of violence against the female poet. Her strangled throat suggests a kind of muting of the public female voice. While this may be the punishment for a "lascivious" mouth that speaks "blasphemies," the silencing also suggests the fate that befalls the poet once her image and her texts are consumed by the literary marketplace. The body no longer speaks—it is "unexclamatory"—and, finally, is stripped bare. In this process, we see that the female poet is utterly reduced to speechless, naked parts. Appropriately, the poem ends on a clever note: if it were fashionable to be naked, then she would be fashionable. But this conclusion also suggests that if the terms of reception were reversed—if her supposed cleverness was stripped away to concentrate on, almost literally, bare bones—then she would be unremarkable. Millay echoes the paradox of the Poetess, who, in all her memorable specificity, offered another generic product to be consumed; from her hair to her freckled arms, the public display of specific attributes actually works to erase Millay's identity. However, the Poetess's problematic genericness is what allowed Millay to make a larger criticism about modern selfhood: underneath it all, there was no essential cleverness to Millay, no essential identity. When readers attempt to possess her, they will find she is the same "as any."

Complementing the print presence of the clever woman were live readings, which further demonstrated the fantasy of the modern private subject. According to Derek Furr, Millay began giving readings across the country in January 1924 to promote "her self and work" (Furr 2006, 98). The live performance was not just an arena for middlebrow, popular poets to promote themselves. Artists considered high modernists, including Amy Lowell and Ezra Pound, also marketed themselves in live readings and in print. But whether middlebrow or high modernist, the performances of public women poets were subject to nineteenth-century expectations. For example, audiences "could only suppose that [Lowell] was a frail, nerve-wracked poetess"—until they actually saw her perform (Bradshaw 2000, 146).[21] In addition, Furr describes a reading at Bowdoin College in May 1925 where the program included Millay and other authors such as Robert Frost and Willa Cather. Millay was listed on the program as "poetess," whereas Cather is "novelist, author" (qtd. in Furr 2006, 99). This description implies that the public gendered women who wrote poetry but not those women who wrote novels. Millay, I contend, explicitly played off these expectations of poetic femininity in her readings.

Indeed, reports of Millay's performance suggest that her description as "poetess" was the result of the particular persona she cultivated. Millay's performances explicitly hearkened back to nineteenth-century models of poetic femininity in their figuration of childlike innocence combined with womanly feeling. For example, one 1924 review in the *Christian Science Monitor* describes Millay's ladylike appearance. On this evening, Millay was costumed as she often was, in a long dress of rich fabric—a "gown of green and gold brocade with a train." But once Millay begins to read, she morphs into another feminized persona, "a little girl of 8 or 10, a bright New England child, with 'pig-tails' perhaps and a sailor suit" (I. F. 1924, 6).[22] These personas charm audiences because of the seemingly authentic feminine figures they present—elegant lady and precocious child. Millay's fickle femininity, in the guise of "a laughing and capricious poet," actually suggested to viewers an underlying authenticity, one that accurately "reveal[s]," in the words of this reviewer, "the heart of woman" (6). As this account suggests, Millay's mutability allowed audiences to believe they were discovering her essential nature.

While offering audiences the enticing possibility of observing Millay's womanly "heart," the public exposure inherent in such performances posed an ongoing risk to women poets. According to Parker, Millay "complain[ed] of feeling 'like a prostitute' at one heavily attended private reading." Her reaction, Parker argues, rehearses a familiar trope among "many nineteenth-century women writers, who often conceptualized literary fame as a dangerous denudation before the public gaze" (Parker 2016, 390). Because the public was all too eager to believe in a one-to-one correlation of women with their works, Millay's performances enhanced the sense that her body *was* her work. To make matters worse, neither her body nor her works belonged to Millay but were available to her audiences. This dispossession signifies a twentieth-century continuation of the Poetess's primary problem and, in turn, what Millay identified as her primary asset.

Millay confronts the expectations that her performances made her somehow more possessable in the sonnet "Bluebeard," which discusses the violation of the poet-performer's "backstage."[23] Placing her speaker inside Bluebeard's secret chamber, Millay asserts that there is nothing to be gained about her essential self because this self does not exist—it is the performance of a fantasy. The fable, in which Bluebeard kills his wives and stores their bloody bodies in a hidden chamber, was widely referenced in turn-of-the-century U.S. poetry.[24] These poems typically approach the Bluebeard story as a parable, a moral tale about hidden, private conditions within us or within society. Millay revokes the sense that there is any difference between performance and privacy, that there is any lesson to be learned. By reading the speaker in "Bluebeard" as a woman, we can understand how the poem connects the Poetess's privacy to modern women poets. The speaker maintains some private, publicly inaccessible space for herself. But this backstage is penetrable by the public.[25] In the room discussed in the poem, the sonnet calls forth the false promise of privacy for the poet performing as Poetess:

> This door you might not open, and you did;
> So enter now, and see for what slight thing

You are betrayed. . . . Here is no treasure hid,
No cauldron, no clear crystal mirroring
The sought-for Truth, no heads of women slain
For greed like yours, no writhings of distress;
But only what you see. . . . Look yet again:
An empty room, cobwebbed and comfortless.
Yet this alone out of my life I kept
Unto myself, lest any know me quite;
And you did so profane me when you crept
Unto the threshold of this room tonight
That I must never more behold your face.
This now is yours. I seek another place.
—E. Millay 1956, 566

There is, this speaker's public persona suggests, some withheld treasure or scandal, enticing a "greed like yours" to pry beyond her performance. And the public wins, as the speaker appears to lose her last vestige of privacy: "Yet this alone out of my life I kept / Unto myself, lest any know me quite." The room was a touchstone for self-preservation, and she has been so "profane[d]" that the entire operation must be abandoned. Here Millay encourages readers to think of publicity as backed by an alluring privacy, full of unauthorized insights into the public figure. However, Millay is using the association to foreground the emptiness of those supposedly inaccessible areas of the self.

"Bluebeard" trades on the Poetess's utter transparency and availability to audiences, from whom she can hold back nothing. But Millay revises this convention by instead showing the barrenness of idealized feminine privacy: it is an "empty room." The speaker explains, "Here is no treasure hid, / No cauldron, no clear crystal mirroring / The sought-for Truth, no heads of women slain." Though there is nothing shocking in this private life, what is shocking is that privacy is so "empty"—there was nothing to it anyway. The privacy audiences expect or seek out points to a false female essentialism and, with it, a modernist anxiety about the disappearance of privacy in the modern era. Such modernist anxieties are, Millay insists, ungrounded. Individual agency could not be penetrated by outside influences because there never was any difference between public and private.

By discussing not just a private but an empty room, the speaker concedes the husk of privacy to an expectant, prying public. Indeed, the empty room becomes the site of Millay's own fantasy: she invites an invasion whereby the intruder confronts only himself, and not some inner sanctum of privacy and purity. No one was ever there, not Bluebeard or the woman poet; the room was occupied only by a disappearing speaker who scolds her reader for invading a blank backstage. Where we expected to see "Truth" or "heads of women slain," the speaker instead leaves us with a symbolically empty stanza or "room." At the same time, this fantasy confirms that Millay does not bewail the absence of the public/private divide, or view this absence—contra the modernists—as an obstacle to authorial autonomy. After all, the exposure of her perceived sovereign privacy to an invading presence does not in any way attenuate the speaker. Like "The Unexplorer," this uninteresting, uninsightful privacy works to obscure the subject, therefore preserving autonomy. In fact, the speaker moves on, determined to "seek another place" for her self. On final review, the room and the poem are the sites of a vanishing act.

Even so, Millay spoke to the "sought-for truth" pursued in "another place," and she employs another medium, radio, to exploit this tension between embodied presence and symbolic absence. While live readings might seem to most clearly expose Millay to her public, it was actually the stripped-down medium of radio that suggested the greatest intimacy to the greatest number of people. Unlike a staged, public performance, radio was thought to directly transmit Millay into people's homes, and Millay was one of the first American poets to read her own works over the radio (Wheeler 2008, 41). During the winter of 1932–33, she gave eight readings on NBC's radio broadcast network. Millay was, of course, popular prior to these readings—people even bought radios for the purpose of hearing her program, and afterward, NBC received upward of fifteen hundred fan letters (Furr 2006, 100). Wheeler argues that Millay perhaps convinced others—not just poets—of radio's ability to replicate the relationship between speaker and audience; by March 1933 "Franklin Delano Roosevelt began his 'fireside chats,' capitalizing politically on this technology of intimacy and sincerity" (Wheeler 2008, 48). Indeed, Millay recognized radio as what I would describe as a lyrical technology, one that promised to deliver poetic sincerity directly to listeners. For a female poet, reading over the radio also reinforced the conventions more specific to the Poetess—namely, her utter availability. Wheeler writes that radio recalled for Millay "nineteenth-century domestic reading practices: a voice delivering words at a normal volume in the family parlor, to a small group" (56). Evoking the "metrical poetry recited in parlors, recitation clubs, [and] school auditoriums," such a voice was, no doubt, refreshingly comforting, especially in comparison to "the deliberate jolts and disharmonies of modernist *vers libre*" (57).[26] For such listeners, the radio enlivened the Poetess's inaudible voice. Millay's broadcasts conveyed natural, authentic, feminine feeling, and

"Millay's listeners assumed that the poet's voice embodied her poetry and her true self" (Furr 2006, 95).

For her part, Millay was quick to recognize potential analogies between published poetry and radio broadcasts. As Wheeler puts it, "Radio possesses an inherent likeness to the printed lyric poem—a medium similarly haunted by impossible presence" (Wheeler 2008, 39). Her poetic play with physical presence and absence—should she stay or go?—was exaggerated via radio's transmission of a bodiless voice, a voice that was both present and absent.[27] Take, for example, the sonnet "Not in a Silver Casket Cool with Pearls," a piece Millay read during her Sunday evening broadcasts in the winter of 1933.[28] Wheeler notes that the poems selected for these programs "invoke human voices and/or natural sounds" (Wheeler 2008, 52). Indeed, this poem relies on the openness of the human voice to convey its themes about the availability of love:

Not in a silver casket cool with pearls
Or rich with red corundum or with blue
Locked, and the key withheld, as other girls
Have given their loves, I give my love to you.
Not in a lovers'-knot, not in a ring
Worked in such fashion and the legend plain—
Semper fidelis, where a secret spring
Kennels a drop of mischief for the brain:
Love in the open hand, no thing but that,
Ungemmed, unhidden, wishing not to hurt,
As one should bring you cowslips in a hat
Swung from the hand, or apples in her skirt,
I bring you, calling out as children do:
"Look what I have!—And these are all for you."
—E. Millay 1956, 640

The figured speaker debunks the idea that immediate emotional availability is less precious than restrained, earned affection. While the unavailability of love is supposed to prove its worth, Millay here shows that utter availability is the most invaluable form that love can take. In fact, the poem contends that love that is withheld in order to make it more valuable becomes less sincere, not more. When "other girls" at long last gift their love, the delay is meant to signify its incredible value, as if the present were encrusted with precious materials. But this ornamentation attenuates love's purity. Indeed, this form of love contains a hint of "mischief," especially when compared to the speaker's "ungemmed, unhidden" love.

Millay's selection of this poem for radio broadcast is not, I would argue, accidental. For Millay's audience, the act of listening to—and not reading—the poem underscores the differences between the two forms of love. For instance, Millay's reading of line five over the airwaves would reiterate the inferiority of overwrought modes of expression. Reading out loud "not in a lovers'-knot, not in a ring" blurs the distinction between "not" and "knot," and suggests that worked forms of affection are associated with negation. The echoing negative reinforces the assertion that contorting love into ornate objects contradicts love's whole purpose, which is to say, its availability. In fact, the sonnet self-consciously calls attention to the medium of radio by suggesting that love's ultimate form is the perfectly transmitted lyrical voice. Whereas the octave presents the complicated and clandestine nature of insincere love, the sestet shows true love's radio-like immediacy. In opposition to the finely wrought objects in the octave, the sestet's cowslips and apples are offered in their simple, natural form—like a voice heard over the radio. To further emphasize its purity, the human voice is then associated with children. The speaker's profession—"Look what I have!—And these are all for you"—evinces the perfect transmission of emotion promised by the lyrical voice, a perfection foregrounded through the medium of radio.

Certainly radio broadcasts offered Millay the opportunity to give her readers what they wanted—intimate access to her very voice. But given the legacy of female writers and the consumption of their personas in the literary marketplace, we must also consider how Millay attempts to thwart notions of her accessible, authentic persona, especially in the mediums that seem to most directly offer it. The voice—whether the metaphorical one depicted in the poem or the one transmitted in Millay's broadcast—poses its own problematic interplay of presence and absence. The imaginary utterance that underpins lyrical poetry is not there at all, and the poem fabricates a "voiced" presence that also winks at its actual nonexistence. Millay even encourages us to apply the poem's message to the medium of radio itself, questioning the transmission of pure voice. For example, the "casket" that starts the poems is oddly reminiscent of a 1920s–1930s radio, with its boxy shape, wood paneling, and often ornate inlays. In which case, the medium of the radio would actually commemorate the death of the lyrical voice. In other words, the transmission of poetic voice will always be mediated by elements that gesture to its inauthenticity. The doubleness of voice in this poem—its availability and impossibility—is why Millay chooses it for radio reading.[29] As we have seen with her use of other media forms, radio provides the means to destabilize authenticity in a medium that would seem to ensure it.

Modernism and Liberalism

Working against the assumption that her media presence would fulfill fantasies of an authentic, stable self, Millay demonstrated that self-sovereign individuality was a fantasy. As I argue above, modernist writers were likewise concerned with the subject's sovereignty: modernism's impersonality was a means to ward off the impositions of aesthetic and formal conventions on individual consciousness. Yet the practice of modernist impersonality also pivoted away from poetic convention in order to reflect on the complexities of modernity and liberalism. Understood in this context, modernist methods attempted to preserve the foundational privacy of the liberal subject in the face of invasive changes wrought by the modern state. In this concluding section, I want to examine how Millay uses the presence of the Poetess tradition in a modernist and modernizing twentieth century in order to further question the sovereign privacy of the liberal subject. The fantasy of perfect and pure feminine privacy depicted in Millay's poetry and media presence problematizes the isolated individualism that liberalism and modernism tried to preserve. Such selfhood was also a fantasy projected in response to growing evidence of the individual's utter dependence on social, political, and economic forces.

My examination depends on understanding the complex innovations that marked modernism and liberalism in the early twentieth century. Modernism and liberalism registered the ongoing economic, industrial, and social shifts—the former in its emphasis on prominent style, and the latter as its American and European iterations underwent massive revisions in order to accommodate and consolidate those same shifts. In the United States specifically, a burgeoning corporate economy meant that liberal self-sovereignty was under threat; people felt that control was out of their hands. The liberal solution was to revise the terms of that very sovereignty; as a result, "equality of opportunity to climb the economic ladder to the position of self-rule, authority, and independence was replaced by the opportunity to fulfill one's desires through consumption" (N. Cohen 2002, 223). Modernism emerges, at least in some part, as a protest against the prevailing liberal solutions to the crises of modernity. For the modernists, as Janice Ho has observed, "the consequences of the culture of economic liberalism also proved distasteful" inasmuch as "capitalism [was] perpetuating only a crass and vulgar commercialism" (Ho 2011, 50). Understood as such, we can see how modernist anxieties grew out of a political economy that seemed to encourage mass consumption as a means of liberal self-development.

But policy- or even polemic-driven denunciations of modernity were not the modernists' modus operandi. For the modernists, Greg Barnhisel contends, "explicit, timely political statements were not worthy of 'true' poetry, and poetry written for any but a purely aesthetic purpose was by definition second rate" (Barnhisel 2015, 38). For that reason, political critique persisted only as a tone or mood, as a shared feeling of "disappointment, disapproval, or disgust with Western bourgeois life and values" (38). Millay, alternately, spoke out about political issues across her career.[30] For example, her poem "Justice Denied in Massachusetts" was published in the *New York Times* in 1927, the day before the execution of Nicola Sacco and Bartolomeo Vanzetti (T. Jackson 2008, 323). Her 1940 collection of political verse, *Make Bright the Arrows,* urged American intervention in World War II. Her outspokenness came at the cost of her legacy, which lost the "high-cultural prestige" associated with modernist literature (Barnhisel 2015, 38). While Millay's exclusion from the modernist canon has been established, it is worthwhile to look at her political poetry in order to see how she nevertheless reflected modernist misgivings about liberal ideology in the twentieth century.

In Millay's interventionist poetry, it becomes clear that her political commitments are legible as an extension of her poetic ones. Consider her poem "There Are No Islands, Any More," which warns against isolated individualism in the lead-up to World War II. This poem suggests that an isolationist position must be abandoned because its liberal premise of circumscribed individualism promises citizens a dangerous fantasy. A self, or nation, for that matter, whose actions do not affect others is an impossibility; as her poems about feminized, fickle subjects show, there is no autonomous self-sovereignty, because the private self was always formed by public input. Millay here invokes the radical publicity of the Poetess to deflate the fantasy of insularity. Indeed, when the *New York Times* printed the poem, they acknowledged that they were "indebted" to Millay, the "distinguished poetess," confirming the connection between Poetess and public, political speech.

Though the poem opens with the statement "Lines Written in Passion and in Deep Concern for England, France and My Own Country," the first stanza seems to drop any thought of gravitas for Millay's simple, "clever" verse:

> Dear Isolationist, you are
> So very, very insular!
> Surely you do not take offense?—
> The word's well used in such a sense.

'Tis you, not I, sir, who insist
You are an Isolationist.
—E. Millay 1940, 3

It is tempting to see a disjunction between a political declaration made on the eve of a world war and a poem in iambic tetrameter couplets. "Passion and Deep Concern" seem trivialized by the childlike frustration in the repetition "very, very insular!" But this trivialization is the crux of Millay's political statement. She is employing this simple tone to criticize simplistic isolationist policies. The uncomplicated language and rhyme diminish isolationist belief by suggesting that it is naïvely selfish. Millay replicates the Poetess's professed innocence in the childlike tone of this opening stanza; the speaker merely states what she observes to be true. The blunt repetition of the facts—"'Tis you, not I, sir, who insist / You are an Isolationist"—simplifies foreign policy to the point of its absurdity.

In so doing, this late poem transforms individual drama into global tragedy. The fantasy of liberalism, the poem claims, has dangerous implications for the democratic world. Millay avows the failure of the liberal self: no person is an island, and the private self is no more special or sacred than the public self:

Dear Islander, I envy you:
I'm very fond of islands, too;
And few the pleasures I have known
Which equaled being left alone.
Yet matters from without intrude
At times upon my solitude:
A forest fire, a dog run mad,
A neighbor stripped of all he had
By swindlers, or the shrieking plea
For help, of stabbed Democracy.

Startled, I rise, run from the room,
Join the brigade of spade and broom;
Help to surround the sickened beast;
Hear the account of farmers fleeced
By dapper men, condole, and give
Something to help them hope and live;
Or, if democracy's at stake,
Give more, give more than I can make;

And notice, with a rueful grin,
What was without is now within.

(The tidal wave devours the shore:
There *are* no islands any more.)
—E. Millay 1940, 3

As in the sonnet "Bluebeard," the speaker has attempted to preserve a private space but acknowledges that this backstage is never completely sealed off. Despite all the "pleasures" of privacy, "matters from without intrude," and people cannot help but react. The scenarios the speaker first imagines are answered by actions in the following stanza: fires are put out, dogs are contained, fleeced neighbors are helped. The inclusion of "Democracy" in this list of unfortunate but mundane events suggests that this political system is also part of everyday life, and, for that reason, ordinary people, not just the heads of nations, can come to its aid. The speaker can therefore "give more than I can make"—with this act of self-depletion, the poem is insisting that an isolationist stance is incompatible with democracy altogether. Crucially, democracy is not altogether incompatible with liberal self-circumscription, as the speaker wryly notices that "what was without is now within." This is followed by the poem's refrain, which reasserts that insularity will result in the destruction of all "islands" or individual nations and people. Perversely, the poem's refrain warns of a tidal wave that democratizes by destruction. This lesson exemplifies the constituting contradiction of liberalism: the self, and now the nation, cannot be sovereign over what is within unless it expands into that which is outside its borders.

In one of its best-known stanzas, the poem extends the island imagery to continue warning against an isolationist approach:

This little life from here to there—
Who lives it safely anywhere?
Not you, my insulated friend:
What calm composure will defend
Your rock, when tides you've never seen
Assault the sands of What-has-been,
And from your island's tallest tree,
You watch advance What-is-to-be?

(The tidal wave devours the shore:
There *are* no islands any more.)
—E. Millay 1940, 3

Using the example of a "little life" to symbolize national policy, Millay asks if her country can isolate itself and yet remain safe. As Millay has demonstrated in her invocation of the Poetess's radical publicity, there is no essential insularity associated with the self; each "little life" is always partially public. Because America has mistaken that fantasy of privacy for a reality, the refrain, "There *are* no islands any more," poses a grim prediction for the future of the country, "What-is-to-be." Indeed, the refrain predicts that isolationism in the face of fascism engenders a world in which no person or country retains sovereignty. In effect, Millay urges the United States to adopt the Poetess's reasoning, to recognize the fantasy of insularity and the reality of its destructive privacy in a worldwide crisis. Like the Poetess, America risks obliteration if it does not acknowledge its radical, global accessibility:

> No man, no nation, is made free
> By stating it intends to be.
> Jostled and elbowed is the clown
> Who thinks to walk alone in town.
>
> We live upon a shrinking sphere—
> Like it or not, our home is here;
> Brave heart, uncomprehending brain
> Could make it seem like home again.
>
> —E. Millay 1940, 3

Millay offers a new logic of sovereignty and safety, replacing liberalism's emphasis on the individual with a domestic rhetoric of collectivity. Indeed, treating the world like a public place for the circulation of atomized individuals renders each person a "clown." By addressing the entire "shrinking sphere" as our "home," Millay repurposes the domestic themes that had theretofore defined the Poetess tradition. The privacy-rendered-public that formerly posed a problem for the female poet now figures a solution to global crisis: the whole world is every individual's private space, meant to be shared with others. Millay makes liberalism's protection of privacy into the protection of the world, a selfless, yet self-sustaining, act.

CHAPTER FIVE

E. Pauline Johnson's Poetics Acts

From the beginning of her literary career in the 1880s, E. Pauline Johnson was praised by Canadian and American audiences as the Canadian Mohawk "Poetess." An 1897 interview in the *Chicago Daily Tribune* titled "Poetess of the Iroquois" finds Johnson rehearsing familiar tropes (*Chicago Daily Tribune* 1897, 8). For example, her description of how she composes poetry relies on notions of inadvertent inspiration: "My verses just sung themselves in my head until I had to write them" (8). Johnson's appeal to this feminized cliché is important because it puts into relief just how differently she talks about performance. As she makes clear, the poetry may be unintentional, but her performance is not: "Then, of course, I wanted to read them to people. That is all there is to tell" (8). By the end of the nineteenth century, Johnson's acknowledgment that she craved publicity was no longer a shocking departure from the antebellum Poetess's privacy. Like that of Edna St. Vincent Millay, Johnson's popularity as a Poetess persona resulted from careful self-promotion in print and performance. Just as Millay performed a feminine authenticity expressly constructed by and for the public sphere, Johnson offered a performative Indian identity for commercial consumption. Thus, in keeping with the Poetess's consumer-friendly femininity, Johnson is the appropriate mix of exotic and ladylike. The article features a drawing of Johnson in her "Indian" performance costume, complete with bear-claw necklace, but the reviewer explains that, offstage, such Indianness is hard to locate. It is obscured by Johnson's obvious propriety—that is, white middle-class femininity. The interviewer reports, "It takes a careful study of the square chin, high cheek bones, and dark hair to convince the casual observer that she really is of Indian stock" (8). Just as Millay's picture offered yet another layer of possessable, public intimacy, this reading of Johnson's visage connects her to the generic pleasantries of the antebellum Poetess.

As the interview title suggests, Johnson inherited the legacy of the antebellum American Poetess, including the expectations associated with this imagined persona as well as the devices of the genre. Indeed, her publicity materials and reviews often combined the word "Poetess" with references to her ethnic identity—she was the Mohawk Poetess, the Indian Poetess, the Iroquois Poetess, and so forth. In what follows, I argue that Johnson did not regard this model of female subjectivity as limiting. By instead embracing such expectations, Johnson manipulated the Poetess figure in order to advocate on the behalf of Native people. Granted, this political advocacy takes forms that, at first glance, appear minimalist. In that same 1897 interview, Johnson refuses to discuss "nineteenth century topics" and instead asserts that she is "only a Mohawk with an ambition to show that even an Indian can do something in the world" (*Chicago Daily Tribune* 1897, 8). This seeming quietism is the result, I argue, of the interplay between Johnson's political commitments and the conventions of the Poetess. For Johnson, the aim was to draw attention to injustices against her people, but political recognition first relied on her recognition as a Poetess. This was not a setback, however. Poetess performance allowed Johnson to exploit slippages between fantasy and reality, and she used this critical distance to assert Native rights.

Like Millay's popular appearances, Johnson's performances in print and on the stage seemed to promise audiences' possession of the Poetess's feminine feelings. At the same time, she confronted audiences with the utter unavailability of any such authentic selfhood. In this respect, both Millay and Johnson are expanding on the strategies discussed in chapter 1; Elizabeth Oakes Smith acknowledged the intimate emotions of her poetry's figured speakers but, crucially, refused to divulge such emotions to readers. Yet it is important to note that Millay and Johnson do not simply reiterate Oakes Smith's strategies. Whereas Oakes Smith sought to symbolically preserve women's agency by barring access to intimate interiors, Millay and Johnson flattened any distinction between public and private in their self-conscious performance of intimacy. By collapsing this public/private divide, Johnson is able to offer an explicitly commercial and consumable version of "Indian" womanhood. Her performance foregrounded the constructedness of a Native—and native—feminine intimacy thought to "just sing itself."

In addition to embodying commercially circulating ideas of Indianness, Johnson effected this ersatz authenticity through her complex use of lyrical devices. Indeed, such devices in Johnson's poetics allowed audiences to believe that they "eavesdropped" on the private thoughts of the Indian Poetess. In other words, the lyrical strains in Johnson's poetry enabled her profession of a seemingly authentic interiority that self-consciously displayed its availability to readers. As I argued in the introduction and in chapter 3 on Frances Ellen Watkins Harper, the fantasy of the overheard lyrical speaker was a rhetorical pose meant to draw audiences closer. Johnson's poetic performances thus exploited lyrical fantasies; she knowingly offered a profession for audiences to "overhear" at the same time that she fashioned a synthetic poetic persona that audiences would understand as authentic. By exaggerating lyric's performance of interiority, Johnson showed that the lyrical subject was as much an act as the Mohawk Poetess. The results are ironic, as the perception that lyric "turns its back" on readers actually allowed Johnson to fully confront international audiences with the injustices committed against indigenous peoples.

In Johnson's biography, these political imperatives mixed with the financial exigencies of life as a professional woman writer. Johnson got her start as a poet in the 1880s, publishing poems in "mass circulation American magazines" as well as widely circulating poetry anthologies (Strong-Boag and Gerson 2002, 78).[1] She began to perform after a fateful recitation at a "Canadian Author's Evening" in Toronto in 1892, or so the story goes.[2] Thereafter, Johnson enjoyed fame in Canada and the United States, where she gave reading tours that took her to the major cities of the Northeast and Midwest.[3] Reviews of these performances were printed in mainstream newspapers and, for better or worse, serve as the primary source of information on Johnson's recitations—details from Johnson's point of view do not exist.[4] Her performance tours provided sorely needed income plus "fresh subject matter" for her writing, another revenue stream (79). However, as Johnson came to realize, not *all* types of print publication were profitable. During her fifteen years of touring, Johnson published a number of poetry volumes; her first book, *The White Wampum,* appeared in 1895; in 1912, *Flint and Feather,* her "best-selling [and] so-called complete poems," was published before her death from breast cancer the next year (Strong-Boag and Gerson 2002, 6). That said, Johnson recognized that the poetry collection "was hardly likely to make her a fortune," and she turned to "better paying, more popular outlets for her work" (77). To that end, Johnson's "publication of poetry virtually ceased" after 1903, and she began writing prose for periodicals with "distinct markets" such as *Boys' World* and *Mother's Magazine* (137).[5] During the twenty years from roughly 1890 to 1910, "she drove herself ruthlessly," touring and writing original material for both performances and periodicals (79). In 1907, Johnson and her performance partner, Walter McRaye, again took their show on the road, hoping to make some quick money with a stint on the notoriously demanding Chautauqua circuit.[6]

Starting in 1904, and until their decline shortly after World War I, Circuit Chautauquas set up big brown tents in small midwestern towns for a few days each summer.[7] For the price of admission, rural middle-class Americans enjoyed a range of uplifting performances—lectures, music, theater—that taught self-improvement while reinforcing traditional, even nostalgic, values. These performances were not simply backward-looking but were attempts to address pressing contemporary problems; indeed, the tour endeavored to brace its midwestern audiences' fragile sense of autonomy. During the Gilded Age and the Progressive Era, transformations in the U.S. political economy shook the foundations of American selfhood. A complex mixture of industrial, technological, and political changes altered even the smallest facets of everyday life. For the largely agricultural midwesterners, innovations such as the introduction of automobiles to family farms, the advent of electricity in rural areas, and the establishment of new train lines suggested that the power of autonomous individualism had ceded primacy to unfamiliar technological and corporate forces (Jablonsky 2017, 59).[8] In fact, such changes were yoked to the growing power of corporations, which appeared an even bigger threat to liberal selfhood by the century's end (Sklansky 2002, 3). This was due in part to Supreme Court decisions granting corporations the status of people; in the 1880s corporations received "the equal protection of laws" originally associated with people, specifically freedpeople, under the Fourteenth Amendment (Kazin 2017, 451).[9]

Unsurprisingly, the same industrial and financial capitalism that put selfhood into crisis also implied the very inability of white, middle-class, and rural midwesterners to affect policy and culture. As a result, Chautauqua programming worked to reassure rural midwesterners that their rugged individualism was integral to maintaining American values and to shaping the nation's future.[10] In the early twentieth century, in other words, Circuit Chautauquas worked to articulate a patriotic rhetoric that affirmed foundational liberal practices: selfhood develops out of an authentic core, and such self-reliance confers on individuals an autonomy that allows them to determine their own fate.[11] Or, in the words of a promotional poster from 1915, Chautauquas were "INSPIRATIONAL, AND LIFE BUILDING" (Canning 2005, 176–77).

But if Circuit Chautauquas were meant to revive a spirit of heroic liberalism among their audiences, then what was E. Pauline Johnson, a Canadian Mohawk Poetess, doing there? In 1907, Johnson performed on a tour that took her to "Michigan, Iowa, Nebraska, Colorado, Kansas, Missouri, Illinois and Oklahoma"; she traveled the same route as William Jennings Bryan, who was the most famous name on any of the Chautauqua circuits (Johnston 1997, 168; Maddox 2005, 31). As a Canadian and a nonwhite, Johnson seems doubly removed from the American brand of uplift purveyed by Chautauqua, which was known for being "the most American thing in America" (Canning 2005, 227). In some respects, the reason for her presence on the circuit is obvious, since she was an internationally popular performer in Canada, the United States, and England. But, as I suggest above, this authenticity was always specious, as Johnson performed her poems in an "Indian" costume modeled on Minnehaha, Henry Wadsworth Longfellow's Native American princess. Like Johnson's surprising presence on the Chautauqua circuit, this fact might give us pause: Johnson was a Canadian Mohawk who dressed up like a fictional and generic Indian princess.

In this chapter, I focus on the complex relationship between Johnson's poetry and her performances on the Chautauqua circuit. While Johnson is primarily known and studied within a Canadian context—she is considered Canada's "most widely known woman poet of her time"—I situate Johnson specifically within the United States (Jones and Ferris 2017, 125). This intersection of artist, venue, and historical moment offers critical insights into the continuing development of liberal political philosophy and lyrical poetry in America across the "long" nineteenth century. While the United States and Canada each "maintained distinctly different ways of regulating Native identity," I am interested in what Johnson's Chautauqua tour tells us about social and political efforts to legislate American Indianness (Lawrence 2004, 6). Rather than focus on "how external definitions and controls on Indianness have impacted [Native people's] identities," I discuss the reverse—how Johnson ascertained a commercially circulating and commercially successful construction of Indianness in the United States and gave it back to her audiences (1). My approach, in other words, is more concerned with American cultural history than with Johnson herself, who viewed herself as a Canadian of British descent and was happier touring in England than in the United States (especially given the rigors and dangers of a Chautauqua tour).[12] Because she explicitly adopted stereotypes of Indianness based on the cultural circulation of Longfellow's *Hiawatha*, this chapter will focus on how American perceptions of Indianness influenced Johnson's performances—and, in turn, how Johnson manipulated these stereotypes in order to assert the agency of Native women.

For audiences that yearned for a type of American selfhood that seemed increasingly irrelevant to the fate of the nation, Johnson's poetic performances appear to have served a retrograde—if not demeaning—political purpose by bringing to life the figure that perhaps best embodied a bygone American self: the Indian. With performances that so closely conform to what I would describe as the "Minnehaha model," Johnson appears to predicate the authenticity of her Native identity on the expectations and tastes of her white audiences. Put another way, her poetic performances exploit the social function of Indianness in the popular cultural imagination of the late nineteenth and early twentieth centuries; they embody what Frederick Hoxie calls "the romantic Indian of Cooper and Longfellow" (Hoxie 2001, 94). Native Americans were perceived as living anachronisms representing "virtues the nation risked forgetting in the headlong pursuit of wealth and power" (99). Considered to be a primitive people, Indians demonstrated to modern Americans the power of a restorative past.[13] More than just powerful, that supposedly restorative past had commercial appeal as well; like Johnson, many Indians participated in America's Native nostalgia by performing as themselves in public. Like Johnson, many Indians across the nineteenth and twentieth centuries "participated in white people's Indian play" by performing as themselves in the sense that they were performing an Indianness ascribed *to them* by white tastes. In other words, Native performers enacted a version of Indianness crafted by and for white audiences, thereby "assisting, confirming, co-opting, challenging, and legitimating the performative tradition of aboriginal American identity" (Deloria 1998, 8).[14] Indian entertainment became increasingly popular at the turn of the century at sites such as Buffalo Bill Cody's Wild West shows, world's fairs, summer camps, and organizations like the Boy Scouts, where children learned to "play Indian."[15] These entertainments were gendered as well; the aforementioned examples depicted a kind of rugged masculinity, whereas performers like Johnson resonated differently, reflecting a tradition of demure, helpful Indian womanhood couched in the figure of the Indian "Princess."[16] Despite their widely divergent depictions of Native Americans—from wild warriors to innocent children—these spaces served the public imagination by reminding audiences of a supposedly simple, bygone, and authentic life

Current scholarship in Native American literary history has renewed its interest in Johnson precisely because of the complicated relationship that she strikes with both white and indigenous cultures. In general, this scholarship investigates how Johnson's work articulates a form of autonomy by employing stereotypes that call attention to the treatment of Native peoples in the United States and Canada in the late nineteenth century.[17] For example, Jace Weaver explains that "Johnson sought not so much to represent the stereotypical Indian as to (re)present the Native to Amer-European and Canadian society" (Weaver 1997, 83). Such self-conscious processes of (re)presentation, Martha Viehmann suggests, signify a form of agency and, furthermore, a warning for overly nostalgic critics: "If we read native literature looking only for specific criteria that constitute 'authentic' native writing, then we lose a sense of Indian people as actors in history and of the history of the literature they have produced" (Viehmann 2012, 261). Johnson's apparent acquiescence to white stereotypes of Indians raises questions about resistance and assimilation, that is, whether she was "subversive or not," but her "self-presentation was," Cari Carpenter argues, "more complicated than any such binary would suggest" (Carpenter 2008, 55). Likewise Mishuana Goeman writes that "Johnson often fluctuates in terms of her politics and beliefs," and as a result she provides "complicated glimpses into what is too often disciplined into neat 'historic' packages" (Goeman 2013, 44). That Johnson spoke through convention to level a critique of American and Canadian policy is a conclusion often reached by those who study her prose. For example, Beth Piatote argues that her stories assert "Mohawk autonomy in the face of external control" (Piatote 2011, 100).

Scholarship on Johnson, however, has not focused on the close relationship between her poetry and her poetic performances.[18] This chapter will explore, in the words of Tyler Hoffman, "the meanings that emerge in particular performance contexts" and the specific ways that the performance of stereotypes can confer forms of agency (Hoffman 2011, 4). To that end, I suggest using Johnson's performances as the basis for a subtle but significant shift that may, as Manina Jones and Neal Ferris argue, "spectacularize a kind of cultural 'ambidexterity' in the dynamic representation and revision of identities by individuals of the Mohawk community" (Jones and Ferris 2017, 149). However, my approach does not emphasize authentic identity but the performance of an Indianness that was *inauthentic* in the first place—or authentic according to white, middle-class cultural fictions. For that reason, I am less concerned with navigating the relationship between Johnson's Native advocacy and white acquiescence, and more interested in the ways that she developed a commercially viable Indian persona. In some respects, this approach likewise sidesteps the tendency to formulate a politics of authenticity that uses the credibility of her performances to answer the question of whether Johnson advanced or hindered the legislation of Native rights. Rather, I want to draw our attention to the techniques she used to make herself legible as "Indian," even when that legibility relied on stereotypes. The publicly circulating models of Indianness—demure princesses and wild warriors—that Johnson drew on were problematic cultural stereotypes, but her presentation did not attempt to parse a line between performativity and authenticity. Johnson's performances were always explicitly performative, suggesting that she crafted a performance persona according to a commercial public sphere in which any potential dilemma between authenticity and performativity had dissolved.[19] Johnson describes the condition of an "Indian" product whose value has now, according to the desires of the public, turned its back on any referent to the real/unreal. I look to Johnson to see how Indianness functioned by the early twentieth century, when the notion of a "tribal realit[y]" was secondary to commercial viability (Vizenor 1994, 8).[20] She offered a synthetic Indian self, and in so doing, the opportunity to interpret and understand "Indian" thought that was emblematic of a new commercial logic of Indian representations.

Indeed, Johnson created an entirely performative persona whose qualities signaled an ersatz "Indianness" to audiences precisely because there was commercial demand for explicit inauthenticity. Audiences most enjoyed those aspects of her performance that indicated their inauthentic quality, from her dress, to her movements, to her voice. Due to her success, Johnson demonstrates the commercial logic for Indianness among the white middle class in the early twentieth century: consumers were attracted to an uncomplicated, reproduceable Indian wife—that is, to an Indian to match a poeticized Minnehaha.[21] Johnson defines autonomy as the ability, it would seem, to manage, produce, and reproduce commercial stereotypes. By accessorizing herself and inspiring others to do the same, Johnson shows us that performance can exceed the expectations of the role, and thereby result in new, unexpected "parts" for Native women.

This chapter discusses the possibilities created by what I consider to be Johnson's most effective performance practice: playing dress-up.[22] While it is well known that Johnson "cross-dress[ed] as both a Native and a Victorian lady at her recitals," I focus on her performances as the Indian wife because this seems to be the primary persona adopted during her Chautauqua tour (Jones and Ferris 2017, 143–44). Perhaps she did spend part of these recitals as the "Victorian lady," but because her Chautauqua promotional pamphlet focuses solely on her Indian performance, I am doing the same. In order to illustrate the modesty and vacancy associated with the Native woman, my analysis begins with Longfellow's depiction of Minnehaha, the consummate Indian wife. With this figuration, Longfellow launches the most culturally prominent model of Indianness, and one that indelibly informs Johnson's poetry and performances. With such a modest Indian figure at her disposal, Johnson endeavors to achieve a goal that appears, on first glance, to be counterintuitive: to create a new kind of stereotype. To that end, Johnson's poems "The Legend of Qu'Appelle Valley" and "A Cry from an Indian Wife" do reproduce white fantasies of Indianness, but only as a prelude to critiquing appropriations of Native culture. Such contestations of prevailing white fantasies also extend to include her poetic performances, which self-consciously engaged with the commercial sphere in order to secure, not dissolve, Native autonomy. My discussion of Johnson's complex use of Indian stereotypes concludes with a reflection on the commercial and political legacies of her poetry and public performances. More specifically, I focus on a manual prepared by Mrs. Frederick W. Pender for staging a performance of Johnson's poem "Ojistoh." Pender's 1911 guide was designed to allow white women to inhabit Johnson's position as performer of Indian stereotypes. But Pender's reinterpretation encouraged participants to embody an Indian wife who drastically departed from the Minnehaha model. In so doing, Johnson initiated an alternate form of advocacy because her poetic performances—and the reproduction of these performances—implicitly questioned the authenticity that her Indianness was meant to undergird.

Hiawatha's "History"

Johnson's performance in a Minnehaha costume most clearly attests to the ongoing popularity of Longfellow's *The Song of Hiawatha* (1855). Angela Sorby has described *Hiawatha* as "the most popular book-length poem of the American nineteenth century" (Sorby 2005, 4). Its cultural influence outstripped even its popularity, as the poem indelibly shaped perceptions of the romantic Indian. By 1900, *Hiawatha* had become a "compulsory" pedagogical tool, a work "taught in almost every school in America" (Sorby 2005, 3). In American schoolrooms, *Hiawatha*—as well as other Longfellow favorites such as "A Psalm of Life" and "Paul Revere's Ride"—taught students the counterintuitive lesson that they shared an "archaic point of origin," a common past that served as the basis for formulating an American identity (Sorby 2005, 10). The poem successfully instilled this sense of a national lineage by encouraging readers to "feel as if what 'Indian Legends'—indeed, what Indians—vanish into were *them*" (V. Jackson 1998, 477). *Hiawatha* famously concludes with the titular protagonist canoeing into the sunset in order to make way for the white man. The poem, in other words, was instrumental in encouraging students to believe that Indians were the remnants of an ancient race on whose epoch the sun had set. By absorbing, so to speak, Indianness, readers likewise absorbed the lineaments of the American liberal self.

Of course, the peaceful eclipse of the Indians in *Hiawatha* was substituting a national narrative about the natural decline of a weaker, anachronistic race for decades of massive violence against Native people.[23] In turn, this process of effacement was not just about the past, but also the present, as it stripped contemporary Indians of political and social agency because it transformed them into artifacts of a nostalgic past. In fact, Indian rights in America diminished as the romantic Indian's popularity grew. At the same time that Johnson was achieving popularity in Canada and the United States, a so-called Indian problem presented a major Progressive Era dilemma. According to the U.S. government, the Indian was a difficult "other" who had so far resisted incorporation into American society. Government-enforced land redistribution sought to eliminate Indians' "cultural barricade" and thoroughly assimilate Indians into a white, middle-class way of life (Hoxie 2001, 42). Legislation such as the Dawes Act of 1887, the Curtis Act of 1898, the Burke Act of 1906, and other major land cessions effectively removed Native Americans from their lands by replacing reservations with private, individual, and largely white land ownership.[24] Whereas national policies undermined Indian land rights, other assimilationist programs—many undertaken by so-called humanitarian groups—targeted "the familial space of the Indian home, or the intimate domestic" (Piatote 2013, 2). The restructuring of these spaces also entailed the restructuring of young Indian minds, which was accomplished by removing children and placing them in off-reservation Indian boarding schools.[25]

Such restructuring came with no promises of uplift, as there were no plans to evenly distribute the supposed benefits of assimilation. Although reformers in the Progressive Era hoped "to shape even the most 'degraded' individuals into productive citizens," Native Americans were not being groomed for full social and political rights (Maddox 2005, 11). Rather, they were invited to develop the qualities that supported white dominance. Indeed, the "sentimental reeducation" of Native peoples in America was "designed to produce Native American subjects who adopted white middle-class values but remained subjugated within white society" (Dean 2011, 202, 207). For instance, Indian boarding schools taught Native children "the universal superiority of the middle-class white Christian 'home'" for the purposes of developing them to become "manual or domestic work[ers] in and around" these homes (Wexler 2000, 103; Dean 2011, 207–8).

Hiawatha served this American "political vision" by effectively assimilating Native Americans through processes of cultural and historical erasure (Trachtenberg 2004, 54). To that end, the popularity of the poem enacts a cruel irony. It fabricated an origin story that attributed nascent liberal values—self-reliance, self-development, self-governance—to Native Americans and then used this fiction to declare Native people pre-political, or incapable of possessing liberal selfhood.[26] Here we can see *Hiawatha* perpetuating Charles W. Mills's concept of racial liberalism: *Hiawatha* modeled a preliberal self that anticipated the idea that only white men were deserving of the full rights of liberty. The text lent itself to such lessons because it depicts Native Americans as sacrificial figures from the past whose demise served as a precondition of white dominance. For example, chapter 14, "Picture-Writing," opens with Hiawatha's lament, "Lo! how all things fade and perish!" (Longfellow 1891, 142). This line is self-reflexive inasmuch as it includes Native peoples among the "things" that have faded. Hiawatha's musings on mortality in effect defuse the political agency of Native people. Despite this result, I'd like to briefly concentrate on "Picture-Writing" as one model for the strategies that Johnson employed to "picture" her own Indianness.

Native people have no claim on a past from which to build a presence for the future, as Hiawatha realizes that "who are in those graves we know not," and that wise men's "words of wisdom / . . . Do not reach the generations" (Longfellow 1891, 142–43). Hiawatha's concerns meditate on the purpose of the text: the poem itself serves as the kind of record that Hiawatha desired and that readers now possess. In order to preserve his people's "great traditions," "achievements," and "wisdom," Hiawatha thus creates a picture language in which "each figure had a meaning, / Each some word or thought suggested" (142). But at the same time, his picture language effectively relegates Native people to the realm of the pre-political. Just as Hiawatha "show[s] unto his wondering people" the symbols he had drawn "and interpreted their meaning," Longfellow teaches readers that Indians are likewise symbols, "old, ancestral Totem[s]" from whom Americans, no matter their background, descended (145, 143). Hence readers learn that Native people are not equals, but artifacts of a lost race whose prehistory serves dominant, white culture. As artifacts, Native Americans are not accorded the autonomy granted to the future-forging American citizens that schoolroom poetry cheers on. In fact, Longfellow suggests that the very preservation of Native peoples' history and culture comes at the cost of their existence.

This picture language plays a crucial role in the racial liberal legacy of *Hiawatha* and, more specifically, the text's persistent ability to overwrite Native American cultures. *Hiawatha* did not just describe for readers its titular protagonist's production of a picture language, but made it manifest "in drawings, paintings, sculptures, illustrations, photographs, and cinema" and in "profusely illustrated editions of *Hiawatha* like Frederic Remington's" (Trachtenberg 2004, 88). This 1891 deluxe edition of *The Song of Hiawatha* featured illustrations by Remington, the famous illustrator, painter, and sculptor of Native Americans and the American West (Trachtenberg 2004, 88). While I am not arguing that this edition influenced Johnson—although we do know that some version of *Hiawatha* directly affected her performance costume—I do think it effectively illustrates how Indianness was constructed in the public sphere. Johnson crafted her ersatz authenticity by using strategies similar to those modeled in this text's "picture-writing."

Reprinted in 1906, just one year before Johnson joined the Chautauqua circuit, this edition contains "full-page photogravures"—one per chapter—and pen-and-ink drawings in the margins of every page (Longfellow 1891, x, xi).[27] Remington drew inspiration for his illustrations from his frequent trips to the American West, where he acquired Native artifacts and filled sketchbooks with images from the frontier. But rather than reveal the gulf between Remington's ethnographic data and Longfellow's Indian fantasy, Remington's rendition underscores the myth of the vanished and homogenous Indian by implying that Native identity resided in scattered bits and pieces of Indian culture, and not in its people.[28] More importantly, Remington's drawings teach readers about the kind of authenticating details that signify Indianness. The implication of this lesson is subtle but significant—provided they had the right accessories, anyone could possess Indianness. Remington's implicit pedagogy, I argue, begins to model the strategies that Johnson employs to validate her Native identity to audiences.

For Longfellow and Remington, the first step in rewriting Native history was to produce a coherent image, past and present, of a collective "Indian" people, despite "some five hundred distinct tribal entities" in America at that time (Trachtenberg 2004, xiv).[29] The commercial and cultural success of this project depended, as I have suggested, on not completely stripping Indian culture of its authenticating details. Instead, Longfellow and Remington elaborated a generalized Indianness through their attention to particularities. Remington's illustrated text uses precise ethnographic information to craft a generic Native people. For example, each Native object that decorates the margins of *Hiawatha* receives a specific tribal affiliation. According to the "Contents and List of Illustrations," one illustrated "Headdress" is listed as "Pawnee"; elsewhere, the illustrated edition features a drawing of "Blackfoot moccasin, green" (Longfellow 1891, 3, 5). While Native objects were painstakingly detailed, illustrations of Native people include no such designations. The masculine face that shares the same page with the Pawnee headdress is simply listed as a "Warrior" (3). It seems strange that we should know the color and tribal association of a moccasin, but not to whom a head belongs. This pattern persists throughout the text: most human faces are listed as "Warrior" or "Squaw," and everyday items continue to be specified—for example, a "Blackfoot legging," the "Fire-bag of Crowfoot, head chief of Blackfeet," or a "Sioux squaw's mantle, white bead work" (19, 164, 205).[30] In *Hiawatha,* this odd combination of specificity and ambiguity is trying to lard a nationalist myth with historical credibility. Indian people become vague and generic, effectively denying them the autonomy to dispute their place in this "historical" narrative.

This strategic combination of specificity and generalization should also recall the marketing of the Poetess, in which distinctive visual markers such as portraits and signatures worked to dissolve the figure into inherently womanly—but not individual—qualities. Indeed, Longfellow's text and Remington's pictorial representations mythologize the Indian wife by figuring Minnehaha through the devices of the Poetess. With Minnehaha, Longfellow models for readers a generic Native woman whose clichéd femininity replicates the Poetess's abstraction. Until she meets Hiawatha, Minnehaha's own capriciousness echoes the Poetess persona created by Frances Sargent Osgood. Recall that Osgood's poetic speakers abstracted themselves by landing on no stable subjectivity and disabled their agency by making private thoughts public. Likewise, Longfellow's descriptions of Minnehaha evoke notions of flighty femininity and inadvertent transparency. Named after the "laughing water" of the nearby "Falls of Minnehaha," Minnehaha too is variable, what with "her moods of shade and sunshine, / Eyes that smiled and frowned alternate" (Longfellow 1891, 45). Later depictions of Minnehaha confirm the Poetess's abstraction by demonstrating her lack of agency. In chapter 10, "Hiawatha's Wooing," Minnehaha's sincerity places her in a Poetess tradition—a tradition, of course, superintended by men. Minnehaha silently serves the men after Hiawatha arrives at her father's wigwam, and "not once her lips she opened" (101). But when her father asks her to consider Hiawatha's marriage proposal, he commands her to "let your heart speak." Her father's command is not a simple passing detail, but evidence that the unprocessed profession of her heart requires the supervision of more powerful men. When she does break her silence, Minnehaha accordingly expresses herself with utmost sincerity:

> Neither willing nor reluctant,
> As she went to Hiawatha,
> Softly took the seat beside him,
> While she said, and blushed to say it,
> "I will follow you, my husband!"
> —Longfellow 1891, 102

Any assertiveness in Minnehaha's declaration is undone by her gentleness and modesty. As her girlish blush suggests, the attention and autonomy that accompany decision making embarrass Minnehaha. Neither willing nor reluctant, her admission appears beyond her will. Besides her accidental utterances, Minnehaha also has no autonomy of her own (except for when it comes to following her husband)—that is, she possesses the self-abnegating femininity of the amateur Poetess. In fact, Longfellow's Minnehaha would seem to fit Jackson and Prins's assertion that the Poetess is "not a speaker, not an 'I,' not a consciousness, not a subjectivity, not a voice, not a persona, not a self" (V. Jackson and Prins 1999, 523). While I critique this definition of the Poetess in chapter 1 of this book, I agree here that Minnehaha seems more a reflection of the objects and people surrounding her than a person herself. However, the attributes that symbolize Minnehaha's demure Indian Princess combine, I argue, to create the template from which Johnson crafts her commercial version of the so-called Mohawk Poetess.

Here we can start to recognize that Minnehaha's abstraction made her an ideal "Indian" product in the same way that the Poetess's abstraction made the persona eminently consumable. Reproductions of *Hiawatha* such as Remington's illustrate—literally—how Minnehaha's emptiness had commercial appeal. This version redoubles the equivalency between the Indian Princess and the abstract Poetess by singling out Minnehaha for her genericness. Chapter 10 contains a large photogravure that shows Minnehaha's blushing declaration, "I will follow you, my husband!" In Remington's illustration, Minnehaha sits facing Hiawatha as they hold hands (Longfellow 1891, 102). In addition to her bland expression, which appears to underscore her "neither willing nor reluctant" demeanor, Minnehaha wears her hair in two plaits that fall over hoop earrings, and she wears a large, square pendant over a loose shirtdress.[31] These details remind us of Remington's authenticating hand and help illustrate Longfellow's characterization of Minnehaha as a kind of Poetess: indistinct, idealized, and vacant unless marked by the accessories of Indianness. The pages surrounding the Minnehaha photogravure continue to deepen readers' understanding of her blankness. Images of tribe-specific feminine objects (an "Apache headdress" covered in leaves), tame creatures (a "Deer"), and calm landscapes ("Falls of Minnehaha, after an old photograph") provide parallels to the non-agential Indian wife (105, 104, 95). In other words, these images offer a picture-language translation of Longfellow's text that accessorize the virtuous Poetess with the markers of demure Indian womanhood.

As the cultural history of *Hiawatha* demonstrates, the appearance of authenticity was crucial to the popularity of the text. In turn, that very concept of authenticity presented Native Americans with a seemingly unsolvable challenge. Every marker of genuineness—from the well-researched illustrations in Remington's 1891 edition to the "accurate" costume in Johnson's 1907 Chautauqua performances as Minnehaha—was instrumental in constructing an entirely synthetic Indian identity.

"I will follow you, my husband!" Frederic Remington's full-page photogravure from chapter 10 of Henry Wadsworth Longfellow, *The Song of Hiawatha*, illus. Frederic Remington (New York: Houghton Mifflin, 1891), 102.

An Accurate Performance

Johnson perhaps most visibly confronts this same dilemma: given the expectations associated with authenticity, how could she protest on behalf of her people when that protest had to be couched in the performance of Indianness? For readers and audiences, *Hiawatha* was American history and, for that reason, Indians who desired a public presence were compelled to conform to the expectations the text promoted. Johnson's adoption of the ideal Indian wife would appear to revoke her ability to speak out—especially given Minnehaha's mild manners. The seemingly contradictory pairing of Johnson's performance of a stereotype with her pressing political critique is the central concern of this section. I argue that Johnson does not define herself against prevailing institutions and mores; rather, she speaks critically to white audiences *through* those constraints. Though "invisible" as an Indian herself, her invocation of *Hiawatha* gave her a generic, albeit specious, visibility, as well as a political strategy. By self-consciously displaying the constructedness of "Indian" identity, her poems suggest that American selfhood—Native or white—is as synthetic as the Indianness it absorbs and builds upon.

As she incarnated the very text of *Hiawatha* itself, Johnson's performances worked to supersede authentic/artificial and subversive/assimilationist binaries. Much in the same way that Remington adorned the pages of *Hiawatha* to authenticate Longfellow's history lesson, Johnson "adorn[ed] herself with an eclectic combination of tokens" (Strong-Boag and Gerson 2002, 111). Long before she joined the Chautauqua circuit in 1907, her audiences enjoyed her appearance because it served to confirm white fantasies about indigenous peoples. For example, in 1893, reviewer Mary A. Taft attributed the charm of Johnson's performance to her bloodline, commenting that "her poems breathe with the wild fire of departed braves and with the pathos of later days" (qtd. in Strong-Boag and Gerson 2002, 110). Yet Taft defined Johnson's Indianness by appealing to the commercially circulating fictions that the performer replicated. Or, as Taft puts it: "In reciting these she wears an Indian costume, an exact reproduction of that worn by Minnehaha, decorated with silver brooches, heirlooms in her father's family, the ermine of the chief's daughter, Indian beadwork and old wampum belts not now made" (110). Indeed, according to Johnson's sister, parts of Johnson's "Indian costume and silver brooches were copied from a picture we had of Minnehaha" (Strong-Boag and Gerson 2002, 110).[32] What Taft takes as proof of Johnson's identity derives not from her actual heritage, but from her costume, itself an approximation of a white fantasy.[33]

For Chautauqua audiences, Johnson thus confirms the authenticity of her heritage by performing at a sort of double remove from this heritage: she replicates an illustration, and one based on a fictional text. For those watching her performances, Johnson did not need to possess a bloodline to be an Indian princess (although it certainly helped); she just needed the proper accessories. Of course Johnson was Mohawk, one of the six nations of the Iroquois Confederacy located in Canada. But for her U.S. audiences, the trappings of authenticity had become glaringly inauthentic. For instance, one reviewer even claimed that Longfellow depicted "the life of the Indian" more accurately than Johnson.[34] It is therefore not surprising that when Johnson used Longfellow's fictional account to perform according to public expectations for Indianness, viewers regarded her presentations as most authentic.

We should not necessarily measure Johnson's ability to raise awareness about Native injustice by her white audiences' reactions. While some reviews in contemporary magazines and journals sketched the crucial link between her presence and her promotion of Native rights, reviewers seemed most stunned by the power of her performance rather than her advocacy.[35] Indeed, Johnson or her Chautauqua promoters capitalized on her appearance and used it to advertise her tour. The resulting promotional pamphlet uniformly praises Johnson for her skillful construction of an Indian suited for public consumption. Nearly all of the text selected for this pamphlet associated impressions of her poetry with her vivid readings. For example, the *Graphic* (London) reports that "Miss Johnson recited with great spirit her poems of 'Ojistoh' and 'Qu-Appelle' and other pieces" while "clad in a handsome dress of buckskin and red, with silver ornaments, and blanket" ("'Tekahionwake'" 1907, 2). The *Globe* duplicates this attention to dress and address, noting that Johnson appeared "in her native costume" and "gave a vivid rendering" of these same poems (2). Likewise, a *Morning Post* reviewer finds that performance makes the poems more compelling, commenting that "these little pieces are powerfully descriptive, and they gain considerably by the admirable manner in which they are interpreted" (2). And the *Morning Leader* observes that Johnson read her poems "with much dramatic vigor," but focuses on her costume, explaining that "she appeared in the dress befitting the rank of her tribe, a curious buckskin garment, beautifully ornamented, over which was the traditional Indian 'blanket'" (2). The accompanying photos likewise hint at the kind of "Indian" performance audiences would enjoy. The pamphlet's cover features a full-length picture of Johnson in her performance dress, standing in profile with her chin lifted. The following page includes Johnson's profile in medium close-up and showcases her famous bear-claw necklace.[36]

In assembling her Chautauqua publicity pamphlet, Johnson or promoters could have manipulated or even fabricated such reviews and images. I nevertheless rely on excerpts from her Chautauqua program because, fabricated or not, these materials advertise a commercially circulating image of Indianness that Johnson or promoters thought would draw audiences.[37] A review by "Kit" perhaps best articulates the public's desire for the convincing spectacle of Indianness over meaningful content. Kathleen "Kit" Blake Coleman (1856–1915), the pioneering female journalist from the Toronto *Mail-Empire*, recognizes that Johnson deliberately moved through gestures and pulled faces; she writes, "The Indian Poetess is a very clever woman—her voice is exquisitely tender, her facial power wonderful and her gestures graceful and telling" ("'Tekahionwake'" 1907, 4). Johnson's outfit is "accurate in every detail," which is to say that it was an oxymoron: an authentic costume, an accurate reproduction of Indian dress (4). And yet all of these elements of performance thrill Kit to the extent that she "love[s]" Johnson because "she shows how passionately devoted she is to her people" (4). In other words, Kit finds Johnson to be a woman committed to Indian people because she so entertainingly simulated one.

Cover and interior of E. Pauline Johnson's Chautauqua tour promotional bill. Joseph Keppler Jr. Iroquois Papers, Collection Number 9184, box 3, "Tekahionwake," *Promotional Bill for the American Chautauqua Tour, June, 1907*, Division of Rare and Manuscript Collections, Cornell University Library, Ithaca, New York.

E. Pauline Johnson—Walter McRaye

MISS E. PAULINE JOHNSON, known as "Tekahionwake," the Iroquois Indian Poet-Entertainer, will begin an American Chautauqua tour in June, 1907, assisted by Walter McRaye, the celebrated Canadian Humorist. These great artists come fresh from their London ovation, and will be the best novelty entertainment ever offered to the Chautauqua Assemblies.

Miss Johnson will appear in native Indian buckskin costume, presenting her own poems and legends of Red Indian life. Theodore Watts said of her in the London Athenæum, "The most interesting English-speaking Poetess now living."

Assisted by Mr. McRaye she made her first London appearance on Monday, July 16th, at Steinway Hall, before a large and distinguished audience, including Lord and Lady Strathcona, Sir Charles Tupper, Sir Gilbert Parker, M. P., Sir Charles and Lady Rivers-Wilson, Sir Daniel and Lady MacMillan, Mr. Theodore Watts-Dunton the great literary critic, the High Commissioners and their Staffs of South Australia, Tasmania and Natal, Captain and Mrs. Baker, and Mr. Courtney Thorpe, and were instantly endorsed by the entire London Press, as the most *Unique, Original* and *Unhackneyed* performance of the season.

While in London, Miss Johnson—Tekahionwake—gave Recitals in many illustrious drawing rooms, among which may be named that of the Marquis and Marchioness of Ripon, Lady Edith Blake, wife of His Excellency, the Governor of Ceylon, Lady Helen Munro-Ferguson, Mr. Hamilton Aide, etc. Tekahionwake's letters of introduction while in England were given her by His Excellency, the Earl of Aberdeen, Governor General of Canada.

Given the attention these reviews pay to her appearance, it may seem that what Johnson succeeded in doing, for better or for worse, was focusing attention not on *content* (her advocacy for her race) but on *form* (the cleverness of her dress-up). Indeed, such a distinction can lead us to conclude that her spectacular performance undermined the apparent seriousness of her poetry. However, I argue that these acts were complex strategic tools. Her poems deliver a political critique by confirming the injustices experienced by Native people and explicitly disputing assimilationist practices. But these texts initiate a mode of resistance that the performances necessarily complete: performance itself was a means of asserting Native autonomy. Johnson's poetic acts may appear to acquiesce to white versions of Native "history," but this was the point of the Indianness Johnson described. It was always only synthetic, predicated on white fantasies. Johnson *does* believe in the authenticity of an Indian identity, but, importantly, she does not "practice" it in the commercial sphere. Taking advantage of prevailing liberal distinctions, one might say that Johnson reserves this authentic Indian identity for private. In public, Johnson performs a fantasy constructed for commercial circulation. Such an act, I argue, has political payoff, as her performances withdraw Native selfhood from the public sphere where it can no longer be usurped. By offering a surrogate to the public, Johnson presumes to place Indianness out of reach. Ultimately, performance confers an agency that may be invisible in the text alone.

Take, for example, "The Legend of Qu'Appelle Valley" (1898), part of Johnson's performance repertoire.[38] On first glance, there is little that recommends the poem as a critique of white fantasies. The poem replays the wooing scene in *Hiawatha,* when the speaker, an Indian suitor seeking his wife, recalls his beloved's words:

> I will be first to lay in thine my hand,
> To whisper words of greeting on the shore;
> And when thou would'st return to thine own land,
> I'll go with thee, thy wife for evermore.
> —E. Johnson 2002, 126

Fifty years after *Hiawatha*'s publication, Johnson's poetry reproduces the same self-abnegating qualities that characterized Longfellow's Indian princess. Granted, Johnson's Indian maiden is more audacious than Minnehaha inasmuch as she utters more than one sentence. But still she demonstrates the qualities of the romantic Indian. She is quiet and shy, whispering her words. At the same time that she declares her intentions, she also pledges her subservience to her future husband. In other words, Johnson's depiction of

Indian women who are willing followers seems to borrow heavily from Longfellow's iconic maiden and, in so doing, to reinforce representations of the Indian race in the white imagination.

But Johnson is using these familiar cultural stereotypes, I argue, to enable a broader critique of how white nationalist mythologies depend on Indian culture and history. Johnson goes one step further than Longfellow: *Hiawatha* claims to base its version of history on Native culture, but Johnson's poem shows how settler nations derive public history from a white culture that has been mistaken for and comes to replace Native culture. To demonstrate this appropriation, Johnson is self-consciously recalling *Hiawatha*; like the journey in "Hiawatha's Wooing," her poem is told from the perspective of the Indian suitor who travels from a great distance to claim his bride. Unfortunately, the bride-to-be in Johnson's poem—the speaker in the lines above—dies the night before the suitor reaches her home. During this night, he mysteriously hears her calling his name from miles away on her deathbed, to which he responds, "Qu'Appelle?" (E. Johnson 2002, 127).[39] The majority of the poem describes his journey, but Johnson bookends this tale with stanzas that highlight the usurpation of Native culture. These stanzas explain how "paleface settlers" have adopted the speaker's experience of lost love and turned it into tourism (128).

With opening lines that describe both the speaker's indignation and anguish, the poem initiates a broadside against the exploitation of Native interiority for the ends of white public history. Indeed, Johnson contrasts the speaker's anguish with the detached interest of the white people—not the speaker or the indigenous people—who are responsible for naming the valley "Qu'Appelle":

I am the one who loved her as my life,
Had watched her grow to sweet young womanhood;
Won the dear privilege to call her wife,
And found the world, because of her, was good.
I am the one who heard the spirit voice,
Of which the paleface settlers love to tell;
From whose strange story they have made their choice
Of naming this fair valley the "Qu'Appelle."
—E. Johnson 2002, 126

The initial use of the phrase "I am" invites audiences—no doubt, predominantly white and middle class—to share the speaker's expression of universal feeling, as the first four lines read like the heartfelt memories of a speaker of any race. But the repetition of "I am" in line five differentiates between white readers and the aboriginal speaker—only the latter has access to a "spirit voice." Even with this shift, the poem is continuing to follow the conventions of *Hiawatha*. Like Longfellow's poem, "The Legend of Qu'Appelle Valley" offers readers a would-be mixture of the familiar and the exotic; while the speaker's anguish is relatable, the mention of the spirit voice confirms racial authenticity.

What distinguishes "The Legend of Qu'Appelle Valley" from *Hiawatha*, however, are the poem's subtle insistences that its so-called authentic details are, in fact, constructed out of white expectations for Native culture. For instance, the opening stanza, as well as the very title of the poem, draws attention to the valley's specious "Indian" name. The speaker seems confused that his tragedy has become a beloved story for whites, who not merely repeat his strange tale but "love to tell" it. He continues to emphasize his distance from the valley's name by calling it "their choice." It is doubtful that the speaker would even consider the events of the poem to be a "legend"—those events are, after all, his lived experience. Finally, the title "Qu'Appelle" has colonialist origins: it is French patois, confirmed when, later in the poem, the speaker calls out "in the quaint French tongue" (E. Johnson 2002, 127). "Qu'Appelle" is not a word indigenous to the Native population but one that has been reattributed to them by white people. White "settlers" reclaim a language *that was originally theirs* when they name this valley. In other words, Johnson illustrates that "authentic" aboriginal culture is in fact the creation of white culture.

And now, Johnson insists, that same white culture seeks to consume its own history of colonialism under the guise of authentic Indianness. After the speaker recounts his journey to the valley, the last stanza interrupts his earnest expression of woe to depict how whites arrogate Native experience:

Among the lonely Lakes I go no more,
For she who made their beauty is not there;
The paleface rears his tepee on the shore
And says the vale is fairest of the fair.
Full many years have vanished since, but still
The voyageurs beside the campfire tell
How, when the moonrise tips the distant hill,
They hear strange voices through the silence swell.
The paleface loves the haunted lakes they say,
And journeys far to watch their beauty spread
Before his vision; but to me the day,

> The night, the hour, the seasons are all dead.
> I listen heartsick, while the hunters tell
> Why white men named the valley The Qu'Appelle.
> —E. Johnson 2002, 128

In these lines, Johnson cannily uses tourism to undercut issues of Indian authenticity. Every time the speaker starts to divulge his anguish over the death of his beloved, the presence of white men intrudes on his consciousness. For instance, a disturbance caused by white campers in the third line cuts short the speaker's sad musings—"Among the lonely Lakes I go no more, / For she who made their beauty is not there." The "paleface" who has "journeyed far" to see "the haunted lakes" and their "beauty" sets up a campsite, placing "his tepee on the shore" and telling this story around the "campfire." Due to this intrusion, the speaker refrains from recalling his emotions for the rest of the stanza. Only in the last three lines do we learn the extent of the speaker's devastation, which the "white men" compound by ignoring his "heartsick" life and naming the valley "Qu'Appelle." Indeed, the speaker relinquishes his experience to the white version of history—just note how the quotation marks, present in the first stanza, disappear from around "The Qu'Appelle" in the final line. While "The Legend of Qu'Appelle Valley" makes explicit how white settlers adopt a fake history as their own, the poem nevertheless yields to that white version of history: the warrior concedes the name "Qu'Appelle" for the valley.

In "The Legend of Qu'Appelle Valley," the self-conscious transformation of the speaker's heartbreak into white folklore demonstrates how Johnson's poetry exposes the fantasy of authentic selfhood that underlies much lyric theory. If personal woe becomes socially recognized as a compelling tourist attraction, then interiority, Johnson suggests, has lost its sovereign sanctity, and private feeling has become fodder for a commercial public sphere. By gainsaying the commonplace notion that lyrical expression of emotion constitutes poetic selfhood, Johnson works to fully cleave the private from the public and, by extension, to subordinate the authentic—whatever that may be—to the commercial. The result is to produce conventionalized notions of "Indianness," of Indian identity, that press readers to recognize "Indians" as synthetic, public possessions. Importantly, Johnson's conscious engagement with the commercial sphere does not come at the cost of her political advocacy. By flaunting the constructedness of this commercial Indianness, Johnson is endeavoring to preserve an autonomous, authentic form of Indian identity at one remove from the consumption and exploitation of the commercial public sphere.

As we can see, Johnson's poetry maintains a complex relationship to settler nations. To critique white culture, her poetry relies on figures that appear to acquiesce to such culture. These same practices—and their potential political complications—can be seen in her other works. In one of her best-known poems, "A Cry from an Indian Wife," the profession of "Indian" identity allows Johnson to showcase the injustices that assimilation attempts to erase. Like "The Legend of Qu'Appelle Valley," this poem engages lyrical conventions to dissolve supposed sincere interiority into popular, public Indianness. As a result, Johnson can speak through this seemingly sincere stereotype to draw attention to the injustices inflicted on Native people. While the poem was first published during the Canadian North-West Rebellion of 1885, in which the Métis allied with indigenous populations to stage an uprising over the protection of land rights, Johnson's claims were also relevant to Native American populations in the years surrounding her Chautauqua appearances (E. Johnson 2002, 292). Railroad expansion through the Midwest toward the Pacific relied on the "reallottment" of Indian lands; no doubt the very railroad tracks that brought circuit performers to midwestern audiences were built on former Indian lands (Hoxie 2001, 41–53).[40] However, "A Cry from an Indian Wife" seems to once again affirm the cultural premises of *Hiawatha*. With its noble Indian warrior, submissive wife, and hints of the imminent extinction of a Native community, the poem appears to acquiesce to the appropriation of Indian land for white uses. The poem may not be terribly subversive, but, I argue, it manipulates what was already fabricated.

As its title indicates, "A Cry from an Indian Wife" is a wife's sad "farewell" to her "Forest Brave" who has left her to fight in the North-West Rebellion (E. Johnson 2002, 14). Despite the Canadian context, which may have been lost on Chautauqua audiences, the poem is still rearticulating themes from *Hiawatha*. Since Chautauqua acts were thought to be "'pure' or 'truly' American," audiences would have assumed that Johnson's performance complemented the patriotic programming that defined the circuit (Lush 2008, 1). To that end, the poem might bolster for audiences an antiquated sense of patriotic selfhood by recognizing, alongside the Indian brave, a common British enemy.[41] But in order to align a Canadian aboriginal figure with white, middle-class American audiences, Johnson employs the conventions of Minnehaha, and by extension, the antebellum Poetess. The poem allows audiences to "overhear" the Indian wife's intimate introspection, more specifically, her uncontrolled internal struggle. For example, she exclaims, "Go; rise and strike, no matter what the cost. / Yet stay. Revolt not at the Union Jack" (E. Johnson 2002, 14). These unruly, contradictory confessions are not hypocritical but convey the Indian wife's conflicting loyalties, which in turn denote her transparency. Like Minnehaha, she is letting her "heart speak." The lines' choppy syntax indicates spontaneity and sincerity, whereas more organized, deliberate feelings would suggest rhetorical manipulation. Johnson further amplifies this sense of sincerity by exaggerating the lyrical performance of isolation: the Indian wife does not realize anyone is privy to these unorganized thoughts—thoughts that conveniently evince the exemplary interiority of true womanhood. The seeming sincerity that links lyrical and Poetess poetry is performed here to its contradictory but effective end, as Johnson self-consciously performs privacy to explicitly engage audiences. Just as Watkins Harper's enslaved mothers asserted the humanity of the enslaved in their devotion to their children, the Indian wife's fears for her husband attest to the adversity facing Native peoples, and for audiences who might not otherwise appreciate such suffering.

By exposing these supposedly sincere emotions, the Indian wife shows her similarity to her white, female audiences. Indeed, the Indian wife possesses the same moral goodness as white women because she sympathizes with those women who face a similar dilemma:

> . . . my heart is not the only one
> That grieves the loss of husband and of son;
> Think of the mothers o'er the inland seas;
> Think of the pale-faced maiden on her knees . . .
> —E. Johnson 2002, 15

But when, a few lines later, the wife exposes white hypocrisy, audiences are pushed to acknowledge this critique just as they acknowledged the wife's sentimental sincerity. As she imagines a white woman who fears her own Indian husband, the Indian wife moves to indict that same white woman for lacking a broader sympathy:

> Ah, how her white face quivers thus to think,
> *Your* tomahawk his life's best blood will drink.
> She never thinks of my wild aching breast,
> Nor prays for your dark face and eagle crest
> Endangered by a thousand rifle balls,
> My heart the target if my warrior falls.
> —E. Johnson 2002, 15

The wife draws attention to the abuse that Indians have experienced by encouraging audiences to realize that "dark face[s]" bleed, die, and pray the same as "white face[s]." By adopting Minnehaha's familiar femininity, Johnson uses her poem to convey sentimental lessons by advocating on behalf of Native people.

The poem ends with a criticism that directly implicates the appropriation of rightful lands suffered by indigenous people in both Canada and the United States.[42] Because audiences have been, so far, sympathetically aligned with the Indian wife's plight, they are positioned to fully comprehend their complicity in these transgressions. The Indian wife shakes off her hesitancy and embraces her husband's mission to preserve Indian lands and rights:

> O! coward self I hesitate no more;
> Go forth, and win the glories of the war.
> Go forth, nor bend to greed of white men's hands,
> By right, by birth we Indians own these lands,
> Though starved, crushed, plundered, lies our nation low . . .
> Perhaps the white man's God has willed it so.
> —E. Johnson 2002, 15

By invoking commercially circulating models of the Indian wife, namely, Minnehaha, Johnson can confront readers and audiences, who have begun to recognize the humanity of Native people, with the idea that they might be responsible for these atrocities. The unspecified and implied "you" in the wife's exhortation to "go forth" addresses not just her husband, but all Native people. In this linguistic "act," the Indian wife becomes as brave as her Indian warrior husband. By apostrophizing to herself, "O! coward self I hesitate no more," the wife replaces the sentimental, feminized Indian woman, modeled by Minnehaha, with the romantic, heroic, and disappearing Indian, modeled by Hiawatha. Because all she can offer as a wife is her interiority (rather than a fighting body like her warrior husband), she offers it to her people by this profession. And what she professes is her people's right to possess their tribal property—they must not "bend to the greed of white men's hands." Nevertheless, this new voice acknowledges what sounds like imminent failure in battle, and the "starved, crushed, plundered" state of Indians in the poem speaks to the contemporary status of indigenous people in North America.

Of course, *Hiawatha* was still setting the boundaries within which Johnson's poetry could be properly recognized as "Indian." For that reason, there were likewise limits on the efficacy of Johnson's advocacy, as those same boundaries prodded her to represent Indians as a generic, conquered race. And, whatever its sardonic implications, her lip service to the "white man's God" in the poem's last line still complies with patterns of erasure in *Hiawatha*, which presents Indian people, past and present, as historical fodder for the creation of American citizenry. But unlike Minnehaha, who dies crying for Hiawatha, and the Indian wife whose sacrificial apostrophe to her husband erases her individuality, Johnson's performance of the poem does not actually efface Johnson but offers her performance as proxy. Johnson's performance of this poem would assert, well, performance, suggesting that her identity was all surfaces. Her "acts" therefore attempted to prevent the commercial consumption of Native identity by seeming to offer up that very identity. By presenting an emblematic Indian wife, Johnson highlighted the impossibility of ever possessing an essentialized Native self at the same time that she spoke through stereotype to insist upon Indian presence—not absence.

Ojistoh: Illustrated Indian Woman Monologue

Johnson's poetic performances on the Chautauqua circuit can be seen, I argue, as a response to Longfellow, Remington, and the American culture that usurped Native life for white purposes. Johnson may do the same, but in her poetry and performances she foregrounds how Indian narratives were used to fabricate a public history and supposedly Native identity for her audiences. Johnson recognized the purpose that Indianness served in the public sphere, and because she understood this social function, Johnson was able to shift stereotypes. In conclusion, I want to discuss Johnson's well-known performance poem "Ojistoh" (1895). Not only does the poem itself demonstrate Johnson's control of stereotypes, but it encouraged a new performance of Indianness in which audiences, not Johnson, are responsible for enacting the agency for Native people. If Longfellow and Remington adapted Native culture to create a synthetic Indianness that served white purposes, in "Ojistoh" and its strange reproductions, Johnson takes control of that very fabricated Indianness and delivers it back to audiences with important differences.

As her reviewers confirm, Johnson developed her own commercial reputation by successfully drawing upon the most prominent commercial versions of the Indian. In turn, owing to her success, Johnson's product—which is to say, her poetry and her performance of her poetry—itself prevailed to become the commercial version of the Indian. Following her Chautauqua appearances, Johnson's poem "Ojistoh" was reproduced in much the same way as the Remington version of *Hiawatha*, with an emphasis on image and authenticating accessories. According to Johnson's promotional pamphlet, "Ojistoh" was a poem she had performed to great acclaim in London, and Chautauqua crowds likely experienced a repeat performance ("'Tekahionwake'" 1907, 2).

A few years later, those Chautauqua audiences and audiences across America could continue enjoying Johnson's performance by staging it themselves. In the 1911 booklet *Ojistoh: Illustrated Indian Woman Monologue*, Mrs. Frederick W. Pender couples the reprinted poem with her instructions about staging a performance: how to dress up like Ojistoh, how to set the stage, what gestures and tones to use when reciting the poem, and what music and dances to include after the recitation.

Pender shows us that anyone could play Indian, and, I argue, this confirms the basis of Johnson's politics: to explicitly affirm that public, commercially circulating Indian selves are a performance, a fantasy. Now that Johnson's work had succeeded in confirming the established conceptions of Indianness as entirely performative, she could move to push stereotypes toward a new figuration of the Indian wife, not one whose self-effacement offers a critique of white culture, but one whose agency draws attention to the autonomy of Native peoples. For Johnson, what was ultimately more important, then, was not just the ability to speak through stereotype. Rather, what Johnson's performances valued was her very ability to shift conventions. Johnson thereby submits to the world of conventions but defines her autonomy in her ability to make white women, such as Pender, perform commercial Indianness in a manner that she chooses. We can see this in the poem itself, which, I argue, models the process whereby the conventions of the Indian wife are exaggerated to the extent that loyalty now includes murderousness. The public participating in this "Indian woman monologue" in turn possess and perform a white version of Indianness, but now Johnson dictates the commercially circulating conventions of the Indian woman.[43]

The poem is told from the point of view of Ojistoh, another Indian wife. But Johnson engages sentimental conventions, I contend, in order to create an assertive Native woman. Ojistoh explains how she was abducted by an enemy Huron, feigned attraction to her captor, and then murdered him by "bury[ing]" a "scalping knife" in his back. With the Huron's blood on her hands and her integrity intact, Ojistoh returns to her warrior husband, proclaiming, "My Mohawk's pure white star, Ojistoh, still am I" (E. Johnson 2002, 116). While executed in the name of fidelity, the murder clearly signals a shift, to put it mildly, from the demure acquiescence of Minnehaha. That shift becomes even more startling when we consider that the poem was subsequently packaged as a performance manual and sold to American audiences. Take, for instance, the poem's opening lines, which initially replicate for readers an acceptable and appealing Minnehaha-like wife only to strike startling departures from such conventions:

I am Ojistoh, I am she, the wife
Of him whose name breathes bravery and life
And courage to the tribe that calls him chief.
I am Ojistoh, his white star, and he
Is land, and lake, and sky—and soul to me.
—E. Johnson 2002, 114

The assertion in the first line—"I am Ojistoh"—does what Minnehaha could not: claim, as a wife, an identity for herself. Johnson gives Ojistoh an autonomous presence that is nevertheless forged through her warrior husband, but now his power is internal to her—he is her "soul."

Even with this move from "dominated drudges" to "feisty natural princesses," Johnson is still trafficking in stereotypes of Native women (Deloria 2004, 4).[44] But because the expectations for the Indian wife are so widely circulated, Johnson imbues the Minnehaha model with a previously unthinkable quality: the capacity for explicit violence. This capacity is on display even before Ojistoh stabs her Huron captor, as Johnson begins to attribute to Ojistoh the violence usually associated with Indian masculinity:

Ah! but they hated him, those Huron braves,
Him who had flung their warriors into graves,
Him who had crushed them underneath his heel,
. . . .
Their hearts grew weak as women at his name:
They dared no war-path since my Mohawk came
With ashen bow, and flinten arrow-head
To pierce their craven bodies. . . .
—E. Johnson 2002, 115

Ojistoh's description of her husband's bravery contains graphic images ("pierce their craven bodies") couched in familiar sentiments ("Their hearts grew weak as women"). The Minnehaha model sanctions Ojistoh's violence: since faithfulness is the hallmark of the Indian wife, then bloodshed is acceptable. And due to this faithfulness, Ojistoh can safely demonstrate a cunning duplicity typically absent from the Minnehaha figure—a duplicity that now attributes a private/public divide to the formerly flat Indian wife.

While "Ojistoh" the poem depicts a newfound agency for the Indian wife, *Ojistoh: Illustrated Indian Woman Monologue* not only exaggerates this autonomy but advertises it to performers and audiences across the nation. The play version may still appropriate a fabricated Native identity, but it makes explicit how Johnson's commercially viable Indianness could also revise the Indian figure that American markets consumed. "Ojistoh" may seem a curious choice for reproduction, as it was derided as a sensational tale of "adventure and cheap arousal" (or perhaps this makes it a natural choice for commercial circulation) (Lyon 1990, n.p.). But given that the poem effectively "stages performance itself," it lends itself to reproductions that explicitly emphasize performance (Jones and Ferris 2017, 144).

Widely disseminating Johnson's strategies beyond the Chautauqua circuit, *Ojistoh: Illustrated Indian Woman Monologue* encouraged audiences to not simply witness but embody an Indian wife with a difference. Anyone with fifty cents and access to the publisher's catalogue could herself become Ojistoh. According to Kevin Byrne, *Ojistoh* was the product of "a mail-order, amateur-play publishing industry [that] existed in the United States for over a hundred years, from the mid-nineteenth to the mid-twentieth century" (Byrne 2014, 217). The industry's success suggests that Johnson's revised Indian wife was widely available to and accepted by performers across the United States. Indeed, according to Byrne, due to the "vast" market for these plays, "it can be said that this industry had a significant influence on the nation, shaping and reflecting its cultural tastes" (217). Pender's New York publisher, Edgar S. Werner, produced these amateur plays at the turn of the century, and *Ojistoh*'s price and form emphasized that it was designed for nationwide circulation.[45] Written explicitly for amateurs, these plays were destined for unprofessional settings such as fundraisers. Given such amateurism, "the scripts and accompanying supplementary materials had to provide all such information"—indeed, Pender's instructions included an incredible level of detail (Byrne 2014, 218). Sometimes the authors of these plays tacitly acknowledged the amateurs putting them on and tried to allay the performers' anxieties. For example, Byrne cites the 1929 play *The Lady Minstrels from Dixie*, in which one character explains to another, "You don't have to be an actress to be in a minstrel show. All you do is sing songs and say funny things" (218–19). Indeed, in the commercial public sphere's circulation of racial identity, you don't have to be a member of a specific race or even a professional actor in order to play someone of a different racial or ethnic identity. Amateur actors merely needed to "sing songs" or "say funny things"—or put on the right costume, or make the appropriate gestures, or speak in an assumed tone. If Johnson took her cues from the commercial public sphere in designing an entirely performative Indian, then Pender gave the same figure back to the public.

Pender's appropriation of Johnson's poem presents its own challenges to scholarship on Johnson. As far as I can tell, Johnson had no knowledge of this dramatized version of her poem and received no royalties or recognition beyond her mere listing as the poem's author. Indeed, it is possible that Pender was taking advantage of both Johnson's fame and absence from the stage. By 1911, when *Ojistoh* was published, Johnson was no longer performing in public because she was dying from breast cancer in Vancouver.[46] Furthermore, it is not precisely clear how Mrs. Pender became familiar with Johnson's work, even though it is not surprising that she did. Johnson had spent time in New York, and reviews of her performances were printed in mainstream newspapers. Her poems were also included in "mass circulation American magazines" and poetry anthologies (Strong-Boag and Gerson 2002, 78).[47] And while Johnson's "publication of poetry virtually ceased" after 1903, her prose output surged, as she began writing "for distinct markets" such as the readers of *Boys' World* and *Mother's Magazine* (Strong-Boag and Gerson 2002, 137).[48]

Nevertheless, it's clear that Pender encountered Johnson's poetry, so the more relevant inquiry might focus on why she considered the Mohawk artist's work amenable to adaptation. Here a turn to Pender's own biography might prove helpful, but, once again, the historical record is scant. It does appear that Mrs. Frederick W. Pender was an elocution teacher living in Manhattan, and, no doubt, she would have been attracted by their shared professional expertise: the dramatic reading.[49] Johnson was herself never considered an actress—her self-characterizations and publicity materials described her as "The Indian Poet-Reciter," "The Iroquois Author-Entertainer," and "The Mohawk Author-Entertainer" (Strong-Boag and Gerson 2002, 105). Such terms—reciter, entertainer—place Johnson in the tradition of elocution. Those same terms also place her in the growing field of musical melodramas, a popular form from 1880 to 1935 whose chief performers were women (Kimber 2016, 61). With the publication of stand-alone plays through the Edgar S. Werner Company, Pender entered this same competitive marketplace in the first few years of the new century. Her plays often included "lesson talk" and musical accompaniment—indeed, Pender's *Ojistoh* supplies music for a "Great Feather Dance-Song" and a "Squaw's Dance-Song" (Pender 1911, 2).[50]

A look at the title page of *Ojistoh: Illustrated Indian Woman Monologue* will find no copyright information about the original Johnson text that Pender has repurposed.[51] On first glance, the implication seems clear. Pender's dramatic appropriation of Johnson's poetry is just another example of the white appropriation of Native culture for white entertainment and edification. By adding music or lesson-talk, the dramatic text has established its originality, at least in the eyes of copyright law.[52] It's only a small consolation that Johnson was certainly not the only author whose work was commercially repurposed without credit for dramatic recitation. With such low legal barriers to appropriation, these mail-order dramatic publishers made quick commercial use of existing works in dialect or works about the experience of ethnic minorities.[53] In short, these melodramatic products often turned to commercially constructed images of Indianness—*Hiawatha* and other white-authored accounts of Native life were popular choices for dramatic repurposing.[54] Because Johnson's "Ojistoh" already possessed the markers of commercially circulating Indianness, it is no wonder then that Pender would find the piece ideal for adapted performance in an industry built on repackaging circulating stereotypes.

Pender's appropriation would seem to suggest that any efforts to preserve Native autonomy or culture would ultimately succumb to stereotypical representations of white Indianness. However, I would like to suggest that Pender's adaptation actually clarifies how commercialism abets Johnson's political project. Indeed, Pender's work not only asserts Johnson's power over stereotypes but also suggests how Johnson presumes to shield authentic identity from the commercial public sphere. In "Ojistoh," Johnson created a template from which white audiences could embrace revised Indian stereotypes. We can see the adoption of that template in Pender's version of the poem. Pender provides detailed "Points" for the costumes and makeup of the "Indian Woman" who will recite Johnson's poem. Among (many) other instructions, one should wear "Buckskin, embroidered with beads. Leggins [*sic*] and moccasins beaded to harmonize with dress. Necklace of wild animals' teeth. Strands of colored beads. Leggins and moccasins beaded to harmonize with dull silver bands of metal" (Pender 1911, 6). Performers should darken their skin with two coats of "brown grease-paint" in order to perform in a sort of red-face. In addition, participants could even emulate Johnson's noted physicality—the booklet contains detailed "Directions for Presentation" that include instructions for how to enunciate the poem and how to punctuate certain lines with precise gestures (6, 8).[55] Indeed, Pender moves meticulously through each stanza to explain the movements, poses, and pronouncements the performer should employ. And were this not specific enough, the directions include photographs of Pender dressed as Ojistoh in the very poses she has just described. In other words, the instructions for this commodity describe for amateur performers the same details that both the 1891 *Hiawatha* and Johnson used to authenticate themselves.

Pender's detailed instructions may seem to foreclose interpretation, but her reading attests to Johnson's successful creation of a template that stretched the cultural boundaries defining the Indian wife. The *Hiawatha* tradition that

Cover to [Mrs.] Frederick W. Pender, *Ojistoh: Illustrated Indian Woman Monologue* (New York: Edgar Werner, 1911).

influenced Johnson necessarily persists in Pender's reinterpretation. At several points in the poem, when the action veers toward sexual explicitness or violence, Pender tells us how to interpret the poem in a way that excuses actions uncharacteristic of the Minnehaha model. In her attempt to perpetuate the demure Indian wife stereotype, Pender makes herself, audiences, and performers complicit with Johnson's revisions. For the lines where Ojistoh attempts to manipulate her way to freedom by flattering her captor, Pender offers this explanation:

> Recoiling from fate awaiting her, and despairing of ever again seeing her beloved Mohawk, rouses all her faculties, the cunning of her race comes to her aid, and with lightning rapidity she plots to escape. As if by magic

> her whole manner changes. Instead of defiance and arrogance, her voice shows sweetness, as she leans forward to rest her "cheek against his back." In winsome manner she entreats him to "loose" her "hands" and slacken their rapid "pace." During the last four lines she does her utmost to convince her captor that she admires his "courage," and that she has transferred her affection from her Mohawk chief to him.
>
> —Pender 1911, 24

Pender often interprets Ojistoh's motivation by extrapolating from Johnson's poem. It's not explicit in Johnson's poem that Ojistoh is "recoiling" or "despairing"; "sweetness" and "winsome manner" are Pender's words. Pender also reinforces racist stereotypes that we know Johnson publicly opposed. In this interpretation, Pender does what so many other white authors have done to Native culture; she takes it and overwrites it with her own, and at times racist, interpretation. Nevertheless, this interpretation does proliferate the possibility of a new take on Minnehaha. Pender condones the character's duplicity and violence and shows us that Johnson's Indian wife is justified in her actions because she is underpinned by the proper, harmless Minnehaha figure. Even at the most violent moment of the poem, Pender accepts this new element of the Minnehaha myth. For the lines "His knife-hilt in my burning palm I felt; / One hand caressed his check, the other drew / The weapon slowly—'I love you, love you,'" Pender explains: "Skillful, subdued yet intense dramatic action is required in drawing knife higher to R. oblique; voice thrills with intoxicating passion . . . the words forming a strangely weird contrast to her movements" (Pender 1911, 27). Ojistoh's actions are "strangely weird" because this artifice and assault are not what white audiences have come to expect from Minnehaha, the consummate Indian wife. Even though she has been quick to explain away Ojistoh's problematic actions, this time Pender offers no explanation beyond the "strangely weird contrast." The contrast holds—it simply exists in this tale, a new element absorbed into the Indian wife. Johnson has taught us how to play the figure, and in her lesson she has made room for a lot of "weird" new actions.

Even though this poem perpetuates white stereotypes of Native simplicity and savagery, it confronts audiences with a new Indian maiden whose bravery they may embody by following Mrs. Pender's instructions. Indeed, these movements were not meant to simply entertain audiences but to enhance the vicarious experience of the performer. Pender's poses are applications of the Delsarte method, in which "posing was to be personally transforming as well as performative." Through the combination of poses, physical movements,

PICTURE XIV.

"One hand caressed his cheek, the other drew
The weapon softly—"

Mrs. Frederick Pender as Ojistoh. [Mrs.] Frederick W. Pender, *Ojistoh: Illustrated Indian Woman Monologue* (New York: Edgar Werner, 1911), 28, picture 14.

and recitation, "a Delsarte student would come to feel the emotion expressed" (Kimber 2016, 71).[56] Through her instructions, then, Pender helps the performer internalize the revised stereotype of an agential Indian wife. For instance, the delivery of the last lines of the poem, Pender insists, should "thrill with pride" and give a "glimpse of [Ojistoh's] noble womanhood, as she throws her heart into the last line" (Pender 1911, 30). In her adoption and embellishment of Johnson's performance practices, Pender's pantomime highlights how Johnson combined stereotypes in ways that contradicted the Minnehaha model. Pender's attention to detail in these instructions must draw from Johnson's own performances, and how she accessorized her way to recognition as an Indian wife. As in Remington's illustrations and Johnson's Chautauqua costume, the Indian can be accumulated, put on, and performed with the right accessories. But Johnson's works offered an alternate form of advocacy by teaching others the radical performativity of the Indian wife. By fulfilling the public's desire for a performative Indian, Pender, perhaps unintentionally, became complicit in Johnson's advocacy. Pender pushes audiences—audiences well beyond the Chautauqua circuit—to recognize an explicitly synthetic Indianness that, nevertheless, was not the submissive model that supported white fantasies.

By teaching others the radical performativity of the Indian wife, Johnson works to trouble the authentic core residing, so the story goes, at the center of the liberal self. Johnson's works offered an alternate form of advocacy because her poetic performances—and the reproduction of these performances—implicitly questioned the "authenticity" of the American self that her Indianness was meant to undergird. These poetic acts imply that selfhood exists on the same level as performance; American character is in fact a character that can be performed with the right accessories. The American liberal self is not fixed by any historical weight when history can be rewritten through artifacts, images, and accessories.

Scholarship on Johnson's performances has not focused on Pender's reinterpretation, and I do not dwell on it here to privilege the settler nations that have arrogated indigenous culture. By attending to this adaptation of Johnson's work, I have emphasized the extent to which the poet successfully repurposed stereotypes' function. Indeed, Johnson created a model in which embodying stereotypes does not remove the Native artist's agency, but grants her the power to present and preserve what she chooses. Furthermore, this analysis indicates that Johnson's work has important consequences for other women writers who performed or read publicly in the early twentieth century. While poetic performances could enact female self-dispossession, Johnson demonstrated that women could simultaneously call attention to a manipulated persona whose supposedly pure, private form was ultimately unavailable. In their performances, poets such as Johnson, Alice Dunbar-Nelson, Amy Lowell, and Edna St. Vincent Millay self-consciously dissolved poetic personas into the very public sphere that created them. In so doing, these authors complicate gendered conventions by assuming the critical distance that performance enabled.

Ultimately, such poetic performances serve as literary responses to American settler colonialism, responses that call for greater consciousness about how America constructs its own history. Calling "the conquest and decimation of American Indians" one of the "constitutive" "fact[s]" of America, Mahmood Mamdani argues that "what is exceptional about America, the USA, is that it has yet to pose the question of decolonization in the public sphere" (Mamdani 2015, 608). As Mamdani prods his readers to acknowledge the nation's earlier colonialism, Elvira Pulitano points to the persistence of colonialism today: "America never became postcolonial, and what is usually considered Native American literature still operates in an ongoing process of colonialism" (Pulitano 2003, 10). In this context we can begin to understand the political legacy of Johnson's performances in a distinctly non-Native public sphere. These performances testify to that "ongoing process" by self-reflexively meditating on American settler culture—which is to say, on the indigenous cultures it fabricates to obscure its own colonialism. Johnson urges us to consider that the performance of acquiescence is not acquiescence at all—it is a dynamic response to settler power.

Afterword

This book has mounted a defense of lyric reading on several fronts. First, it has presumed to demonstrate the social value the practice offered to nineteenth-century readers and writers. This demonstration defines lyric in terms of imaginary subjects and expressive utterances because such an approach allows us to discuss, compare, and make meaning out of lyric as a nineteenth-century genre. Jonathan Culler illustrates the more extreme version of this logic with his comment that "a compelling argument for lyric as a genre is that we have no better alternatives" (Culler 2015, 87). Culler's quip is polemical, and I hope to have shown that lyric is, in fact, better than nothing because it simply makes more ideas possible. When he's not expressing exasperation, Culler illustrates such an approach when he writes that genres resist "the logic of historical determination." While "political, social, and economic systems have moved on in ways we think of as irreversible," the possibilities of a genre nevertheless remain "potentially available" (89). This openness to generic ahistoricism means openness to more ideas; or, in the words of Joshua Adams, Joel Calahan, and Michael Hansen, "The concept of genre itself does not require univocal and hierarchical exclusions (Adams, Calahan, and Hansen 2016, 7). Indeed, they write "it should be possible to describe and interpret features common to poems over time" (7).

Lyric promotes a poetic accessibility and generic un-exclusivity that will not dissolve all genres back into lyric, or attribute lyrical devices to all genres. I hope that my metaphor for lyric bears out these conclusions and offers a useful tool for the future of poetry studies: genres have strains. We can locate notes of one genre in other verse forms by closely attending to trace devices or tropes. We can think about generic strains infecting other poems and manifesting in symptoms that do not entirely deplete the original verse form. "Strain" offers further analogies for thinking about genre—a stretch, a filter, an exertion, even a pain.

My argument comes down to the idea that anachronicity can be a provocative, not unattractive, approach to poetry. Far from encouraging irresponsible analysis, I hope this book shows that the border between historically accurate and imaginative interpretation is productive; applying twenty-first-century ideas to nineteenth-century texts appears anachronistic but is actually generative. Talking about ahistorical genres may seem outmoded; likewise, defining lyric as an imaginary speaking subject may seem obsolete. But the connection between lyric and subjectivity provides an innovative way to address the discourse of selfhood in a variety of poetic texts and contexts.

Lyrical subjectivity is, yes, idealized, but it also has historical connections to political definitions of the self—specifically, as I argue, liberal subjectivity. That said, I want to suggest the possibility that there can be other types of subjectivity associated with poems and poetic genres in the nineteenth-century United States. In my argument, lyrical poems figure a subjectivity that corresponds to the subject imagined by liberalism, but what other kinds of subjects are possible, not just in lyric, but in other types of poetry? I have not had the time to explore early American poetry and the creation of a republican citizen, or the blurriness between republicanism and liberalism at the turn of the eighteenth to the nineteenth century and how poems might address that ambiguity. I hope to encourage other scholarly considerations of the different types of subjectivity enabled by lyrical reading. And the reverse: How might liberalism influence the constitution of different poetic genres? What about forms like the ballad, which function in the postbellum United States as "carriers of group identity, collective history, and social meaning"—did liberal thought react against these collective impulses or did the ballad develop in response to liberal individualism (M. Cohen 2015, 200)?

To illustrate how historicized forms of lyric reading could influence future studies in nineteenth-century American poetry, let's consider the georgic, an example with no relationship to the lyrical or the liberal. Margaret Ronda's discussion of American georgic shows how genres have historical and transcendental applications. Our shared methodology demonstrates that a new approach to nineteenth-century American poetics is starting to cohere. This poetic form focuses on labor and the environment; its self-referential poetics of cultivation suggests that the georgic imagines the state of American work and artwork across the nineteenth century (Goodman 2012, 556). Ronda illustrates georgic's historical resistance and evolution when she argues that "a version of georgic" exists in nineteenth-century American poetry that "derives" from Virgilian roots but "is substantially reformulated under the historical conditions of capitalist modernization" (Ronda 2013, 61). Georgic "derives" from an older and idealized literary tradition, but in the context of nineteenth-century and twentieth-century America, these transcendental aspirations take on significance as a response to "capitalist modernization." Or, as Ronda argues, "new forms of agrarian and industrial capitalism" result in "the emergence of a georgic strain specifically responsive to these social and economic upheavals" (61). Like lyric, georgic is implicitly idealized, but its poetic practices respond to the forces shaping American lives. Expanding Ronda's use of "georgic strain," we can take the devices and ideologies that signal georgic and apply them to poems that may not seem to be in a Virgilian tradition. There could be georgic strains in poems such as Lydia Sigourney's "To a Shred of Linen," or we can even return to Frances Sargent Osgood's "Laborare Est Orare" and read for georgic instead of lyric. In which case, the model of lyric reading I have proposed in this project has utility across genres. Readers can bring different generic reading strategies to specific verse forms. When we read a poem for lyric, georgic, or other forms, our identification of specific generic instances does not deny the poem's fundamental generic hybridity.

Such arguments apply to subjectivity in addition to genre. For instance, in his discussion of the georgic, Timothy Sweet makes this connection between genre and self-creation, writing that "we must labor to produce our lives. We can do so in a variety of ways, and this is what the American georgic attempts to work out" (Sweet 2002, 5). The georgic work ethic could have emerged from liberal individualism, or perhaps a transatlantic and transhistorical tradition of georgic helped shape liberal thought. We could even understand Watkins Harper's depictions of slavery as critiques of the georgic "disenchantment" that Ronda associates with Walt Whitman's and Robert Frost's poetics of labor (Ronda 2013, 61). In other words, the work ethic implicit in the georgic suggests the influence of a racial liberalism whose fiction of self-reliance is symbolized in the dignity and difficulty of labor—a dignity only afforded to white men.

My discussion of lyric concerns not only the history of American liberalism but also its future. As I have argued, Poetess poems were uniquely positioned to respond to the freedoms denied to nineteenth-century women and people of color. These works continue to demonstrate their relevance today due to their ability to diagnose liberal injustices. The tropes and practices of the Poetess remain pertinent—only consider current discussions of wellness and self-care, which are almost always directed at women. This emphasis on "well-roundedness and well-being" implies that wellness is the solution, supposedly, to unfulfilling commitments in the public sphere (Rottenberg 2014, 147). The implication here is that happiness is only possible when public circulation is matched with domestic recuperation. Women, therefore, always already have some foot in the domestic realm and all its encumbrances. These imperatives have thus come to replace liberalism's liberty with affective conditions that restrict women's agency (147). Catherine Rottenberg calls this "the transmutation of liberal feminism into a discourse of positive affect" (148). The "task of pursuing happiness" inevitably yokes women to the domestic realm and, in so doing, perpetuates the public/private divide (167).

But Poetess poetry has long eyed the claim that the affective well-being of women relies on domesticity. Here Poetess poems presage women's twenty-first-century problems—for instance, Osgood ironically asserts, in a poem of the same name, that women are "happy at home." In the first stanza of "'Happy at Home,'" a female speaker proclaims the virtues of the home in response to a publicly circulating "maiden":

> Let the gay and the idle go forth where they will,
> In search of soft Pleasure, that siren of ill;
> Let them seek her in Fashion's illumined saloon,
> Where Melody mocks at the heart out of tune;
> Where the laugh gushes light from the lips of the maiden,
> While her spirit, perchance, is with sorrow o'erladen;
> And where, 'mid the garlands Joy only should braid,
> Is Slander, the snake, by its rattle betray'd,
> Ah! no! let the idle for happiness roam,
> For me—I but ask to be "happy at home!"
> —Osgood 1850b, 359

Happiness is found at home and, for that reason, the speaker seems to imply that domestic duties serve as a corrective to the inauthenticity and vulnerability of public life. Indeed, the maiden puts on a happy face to cover up her sorrowful interior, an action meant to imply that the sadness and insincerity attending public life are absent from the home. The public sphere poses further liabilities. In salons and saloons alike, women are subject to "Slander, the snake," endangering their reputations in the name of fashion. At first glance, Osgood seems to endorse women's association with domesticity. In other words, she confirms liberalism's narrative about women's inability to withstand the pressures of the public sphere. Such public life will produce sorrow in women, and authentic happiness is generated only at home. Current imperatives that professional life requires some kind of private corrective seem to echo this logic.

But, as we know by now, Osgood does not merely reflect cultural expectations; in this case she helps diagnose the problems with privacy that persist in the twenty-first century. Osgood ends all four stanzas with the rhyming of "roam" and "home"; the rhyme is meant to highlight the opposition of these concepts. But their constant pairing suggests doubts that puncture the hermetic ideology of the domestic. By insisting that there is nowhere to roam at home, the association creates a kind of claustrophobic atmosphere for the woman whose life is limited to the duties of a wife and mother. In other words, life at home may be no happier than life in the saloons. Furthermore, the phrase "happy at home" always appears in quotation marks, even in the poem's title. While this marker could indicate that Osgood is quoting a popular catchphrase, it also suggests the irony of an empty platitude. Ultimately, Osgood criticizes the idea that there needs to be some kind of balance to public life, and that the domestic offers such benefits. Osgood's exaggeration of the opposition between sorrow and happiness, roaming and home-ing, is meant to criticize the very existence of a divide designed to limit women's autonomy. Osgood therefore anticipates Rottenberg's argument that the spatial split between public and private is a liberal fiction working to hinder women's freedom; such a "gendered split," she argues, "is constitutive of the very way space is established and organized in the liberal imaginary" (Rottenberg 2014, 167). The happiness supposedly found at home "orients us away from attempting to imagine spatiality and social relations in new ways" (167). Poetess poetics have worked to reimagine liberalism's "spatiality and social relations"—from Aunt Chloe's house to Eva's forest; from Ojistoh's duplicity to Bluebeard's disappearing act. Such works not only extend liberal spaces and subjectivities to those excluded on the basis of gender and race but also help identify the fantastic premises of twenty-first-century liberalism.

Notes

Introduction

1. Michael Cohen writes that "poems long occupied a complex position in the history of social life and sociality," and this idea of a poem's social life is a key concept for my work (M. Cohen 2015, 9). Not included in this nineteenth-century social life, he argues, is the notion of "poetry" as a generic category: "in the nineteenth century, poetry is not a genre" because the concept of "poetry" had no historical purpose or function (13). "Poetry" did not "do" anything the way that specific poems and genres did; people could not use "poetry" to accomplish anything (10). Rather, Cohen notes, "there were many poetic genres that operated hierarchically but also in dynamic tension with one another. Poems were not all equal, but their relative values and functions could change over time" (14). I build on Cohen's historicization in order to argue that the lyrical strains in nineteenth-century poems are part of their social life. As a familiar term in the gift books, poetry collections, newspapers, and other print media of the nineteenth century, lyric had a social purpose.

2. As film scholar Rick Altman writes, "It should be possible to outline the major principles of genre theory established by two millennia of genre theorists. Yet this is precisely what we cannot do" (Altman 2011, 11). In this work, I will approach genre as a set of ideological boundaries against which poetic practices take shape; or, as Lauren Kimball writes, I see genre as "a structure of meta-poetic idealization" (McGill et al. 2015, 166). I am also aware of the problems that seemingly stable concepts of genre pose, and I find these problems productive. As Isaac Cowell comments, "Nineteenth-century poetic genres already contain within themselves the potential for their own unmasking, exposing the artifice of the critical limits we set for them. After all, genre takes its conceptual unity from the fundamental premise of the transgression of boundaries" (McGill et al. 2015, 166).

3. Cristanne Miller writes that "to read a genre historically in relation to a particular poet's work, therefore, requires knowing when we retroproject contemporary genre, or other, expectations for reading upon earlier norms and how our norms differ from those of, say, the mid-nineteenth century in the United States" (C. Miller 2012, 19). M. Cohen, discussing the ballad form, likewise contends that scholars create an "illusion of a false stabilization of terms, which locks it within the projections of the reader's own historically dependent position, typically that of a professionally trained expert working in some system of higher education" (M. Cohen 2015, 154).

4. Like Wolosky, Jackson agrees that "the nineteenth century was the period in which the shift from many verse cultures articulated through various social relations gave way to an idea of poetry devoted to the transcendence of those relations (via beauty, say, or truth, or Literature, or Culture, or Poetry)" (V. Jackson 2011, 57).

5. Of course, there is no literal voice in the lyrical poem. As Eliza Richards explains in her entry "Voice" in *The Princeton Encyclopedia of Poetry and Poetics*: "Voice is an oral metaphor employed in the description and analysis of the written word. . . . Regardless of how much

one insists that writing is not speaking and that voice is not literally present in the poem, literary critics have persistently relied on metaphors of voice to analyze writing. It is difficult to imagine how one would go about discussing poetry in particular if we were forbidden to use the terms *voice, speaker,* and other vocal terms" (Richards 2012, 1525).

6. Recent scholarship by Paula Bernat Bennett, M. Cohen, Virginia Jackson, Mary Louise Kete, Mary Loeffelholz, Meredith McGill, Cristanne Miller, Yopie Prins, Elizabeth Renker, Richards, and Claudia Stokes, to name a few, historicizes the communicative function of nineteenth-century poetic genres. These scholars examine specific verse forms and contexts in order to recover the history of poetic communication as it changes over time.

7. Essays on lyric were abundant in the nineteenth-century periodical press. Many articles discuss lyric in the context of church music, while other works examine what the classical lyric, especially works by Horace, could teach contemporary readers. Efforts to explore lyric's attributes was also a popular topic. For instance, in 1888, the Raleigh, North Carolina, *News and Observer* reports on the establishment of a Seminary of Literature and Philology at the nearby University of North Carolina, Chapel Hill. The very first subject for this meeting was "Lyric Poetry," with papers discussing Greek lyrists such as Sappho, Horace, the French lyric, and William Wordsworth (*News and Observer* 1888, x).

8. *The Golden Treasury* was reprinted four times in 1861 alone. First published in Great Britain, it was then made available around the world in more than twenty subsequent reprintings from 1861 through 1896. Sales of the collection continued in the tens of thousands through World War II (Palgrave 1992, 444).

9. Rather than exploring other political subgenres, this book focuses on the ways nineteenth-century Americans engaged with liberalism's own inchoate "strains" as they consolidated across the nineteenth century. Since it is beyond the scope of this book to account for the different ways that different liberalisms have been understood in the United States, I will focus on one type of liberalism—namely, what Ryan calls "modern" liberalism (Ryan 1998, 294). "With its romantic appeal to an individuality which should be allowed to develop itself," modern liberalism is most concerned with these social, cultural, and humanistic ideas of the self (294). I employ Ryan's definition of "modern" as opposed to "classical" liberalism; modern liberalism "focuses on the idea of limited government, the maintenance of the rule of law, the avoidance of arbitrary and discretionary power, the sanctity of private property and freely made contracts, and the responsibility of individuals for their own fates" (293). Furthermore, my discussion takes "liberalism" in its most literal sense: a political philosophy concerned with liberty or freedom from life-limiting fears. Judith Shklar's concept of the "liberalism of fear" in her essay of the same name argues that "every adult should be able to make as many effective decisions without fear or favor about as many aspects of her or his life as is compatible with the like freedom of every other adult" (Shklar 1989, 21). Ryan likewise writes that liberalism's "aim is to emancipate individuals from the fear of hunger, unemployment, ill-health and a miserable old-age, and positively, to attempt to help members of modern industrial societies to flourish" (Ryan 1998, 295).

10. For example, Nancy Cohen writes, "Liberalism defined man as an autonomous being, human because of his ownership of his own person and his own capacities and free in his lack of dependence on the will of others. The individual possesses himself and hence possesses rights upon which neither society nor the state can trespass" (N. Cohen 2002, 6). Brian Connolly agrees, explaining that "the liberal subject, that autonomous, rational indi-

vidual who acted on his own desires, was endowed with the capacity for consent, was not dependent on others, and had his choices and desires ratified in contracts" (Connolly 2014, 2). Elizabeth Maddock Dillon likewise argues that "liberalism also, by implication, constructs and relies upon a strong definition of the modern subject as one who is free, autonomous, and capable of self-government" (Dillon 2004, 2).

11. In chapter 5 of his *Autobiography*, Mill describes his "dry, heavy dejection of the melancholy winter of 1826–7." To try to alleviate his depression, he turns to poetry, reading "the whole of Byron." He "got no good from this reading, but the reverse." However, Wordsworth "proved to be the precise thing for [his] mental wants at that particular juncture." In fact, the lyrical qualities of Wordsworth's poems made them "a medicine" for Mill: "They expressed, not mere outward beauty, but states of feeling, and of thought coloured by feeling, under the excitement of beauty. They seemed to be the very culture of the feelings, which I was in quest of. In them I seemed to draw from a source of inward joy, of sympathetic and imaginative pleasure, which could be shared in by all human beings" (Mill 2003, n.p.).

12. Scholars such as Jonathan Culler, Northrop Frye, Timothy Jackson, Kerry Larson, and David Russell, to name a few, have grappled with Mill's essay on poetry, and each have their own interpretation.

13. Mill and other nineteenth-century scholars in the liberal tradition were concerned with how individual desire could overrun the restrained, rational liberal subject and, potentially, the nation. Connolly writes, "If the liberal subject was the foundation of political sovereignty, then the desire of the liberal subject often figured as a threat to the nation, given the unpredictability of desire" (Connolly 2014, 8). This desire, however, was "tempered by reason and rationality" (7). Each subject was capable of self-regulating these private passions into acceptable forms for public interaction. According to Connolly, "It was the family, more so than any other institution, that was called on to discipline the excesses of the liberal subject. The family became a potentially effective site of encumbrance and constraint as it formed the liberal" (10).

14. Indeed, Russell writes that "poetry . . . is the kind of liberal individual expression that rescued Mill from his crisis and which he wants in *On Liberty*—through the means of a principle of liberty—to ensure for everyone" (Russell 2013, 21).

15. Culler explains that there are "two quite different historical operations" when it comes to understanding the figured lyrical speaker. He argues that "first, there is the process in the nineteenth century where the expressive lyric—lyric as the intense expression of the poet—becomes the norm. . . . Quite different is the critical operation by which Anglo-American New Criticism, after the 1940s, takes the poem away from the historical author and treats it as the speech of a persona" (Culler 2015, 84). This study connects these two historical approaches by showing that the nineteenth century's figured "poet" was the historical construction of an imaginary persona. As I will explain in the discussion of the Poetess in chapter 1, nineteenth-century readers conflated the author with her poems, imagining a public persona attributed to the historical author. As a result, the nineteenth-century poem was understood as the "speech" of this publicly created and circulated figure.

16. I focus on Emerson's views in his *Essays: First Series* and *Essays: Second Series*—that is, works from what scholars consider his "early" period in the 1840s (Levine and Malachuk 2011, 4, 9). However, the years after the Civil War were actually the peak of Emerson's popularity, and it is important to note that his views on self-reliance shifted significantly after the

Civil War. Robert Yusef Rabiee writes that "medievalism influenced his later life and thought," and "of the many possible developments latent within the young Emerson's Transcendentalism, an authoritarian tendency emerged" (Rabiee 2016, 83). By the time of his popular essay "The Progress of Culture" (1867), Emerson's "self-reliant, self-authorizing American Scholar" had become "the corporate lord, whose wealth imbued him with sovereign powers that Emerson once reserved for the poet and religious seer" (Rabiee 2016, 86).

17. For example, Emerson's essays were originally delivered as public lectures, directed to an audience. Rather than apostrophizing to an imagined other, Emerson addressed people. As a result, his prose communicated a strong selfhood in order to assist "you," his listeners. It was Emerson's civic duty to inspire the public's belief in the ideal, autonomous self.

18. This rise came at the expense of republican philosophy, so the story goes. Grounded in the virtues of civic participation, the republican good life gave way to an individual pursuit of happiness primarily defined by individual labor and wealth accumulation. However, the transition was messy, and the distinction between liberalism and republicanism blurred across the century. For example, Meredith McGill, in *American Literature and the Culture of Reprinting, 1834–1853*, explains how publishing practices in the antebellum period disrupted the narrative of a straightforward switch. Copyright law favored a "theory of authorship" that was "grounded in a republican belief in the inherent publicity of print and the political necessity of its wide dissemination" and "stressed the interests of the polity over the property rights of individuals" (McGill 2003, 47). Her discussion of literary property illustrates "the resistance a republican theory of authorship can offer to the forward march of possessive individualism" (48).

19. Such changes, N. Cohen notes, included "the first real confrontation with the implications of universal suffrage and mass democracy, the transformation of the majority of the citizenry into wage earners, the rise of the corporation as a new type of property, the devastating fluctuations of the international market economy, and the growth of the administrative capacity of government," all of which gave rise to "problems and questions about society, economy, and state" (N. Cohen 2002, 4).

20. T. J. Jackson Lears writes that "as more and more people became enmeshed in the market's web of interdependence, liberal ideals of autonomous selfhood became ever more difficult to sustain" (Lears 1983, 7).

21. The Progressive Era and the Gilded Age saw government and corporate involvement in liberalism's typically laissez-faire ideology. Sidney Fine argues that "what was needed was a new philosophy of the state, a new liberalism embodying something of the spirit of Jeffersonianism but ready to use government as an agency to promote the general welfare. Industrial America made necessary the evolution of the general-welfare state" (qtd. in N. Cohen 2002, 10). This was not a return to republicanism; rather, as N. Cohen writes, "the progressives' new liberalism . . . sought to use state power to regulate the capitalist economy and to improve the living conditions and 'security' of the citizenry, without abolishing private property or revolutionizing liberal-democratic political institutions" (5). The Gilded Age concretized the Progressive Era's social welfare programs and economic regulation in an effort to uphold an idealized liberal self that was free from the encroachments of society (255). R. Jeffrey Lustig agrees, noting that "between 1890 and the First World War a decisive shift took place in the point of view of American liberalism" (Lustig 1986, 4). The

result was "a third alternative" that was corporate in nature: "It was pro-business *and* pro-state, dedicated to private profit *and* regulatory reform. It was both corporate and liberal, and not only because it arose in defense of the corporation; it also tried to apply individualist modes of reasoning to the problems of an organized society" (6, 7).

22. The idea of "encumbrance" comes from Wendy Brown: "The putative autonomy of the liberal subject partakes of a myth of masculinity requiring the disavowal of dependency, the disavowal of the relations that nourish and sustain this subject" (qtd. in Dillon 2004, 15).

23. As late as 1884, newspapers excitedly anticipate her forthcoming autobiography (which was never actually published) (*Literary World* 1884, 308).

Chapter One

1. A Google Scholar search reports that the article has been cited thirty-nine times from 2008 to 2018.

2. More recently Tricia Lootens writes, "I speak of 'the Poetess'; but, in fact, I have come to believe there is no such thing" (Lootens 2016, 3).

3. Lootens names such indistinguishableness the "Poetess parallax" (Lootens 2016, 8). She argues that her "shifting, flickering alternations mobilize a dynamic that does not, and indeed cannot, settle," and it is therefore impossible to see the figure "in perspective" because her "instabilities" "always remain subject to historical alteration" (218–19).

4. This idea of vacillation comes from Socarides, who writes, "Twentieth- and twenty-first-century criticism has vacillated between recovering the identities of individual women poets and arguing that the poetess was never really a person at all, but was, instead, a type, a trope, an idea, a figure, a category, or an occasion" (Socarides 2018, 131).

5. This was also due to an increase in printed material. Melissa Homestead writes that "the United States of the 1850s represented the largest potential literary market ever up to that time, with more literate adults than in any other country. The large number of potential consumers, combined with advances in book manufacturing technologies (steam printing presses, stereotype plates, case-binding) and the advent of steam railroads to transport books quickly and inexpensively throughout the country, made the true national 'bestseller' possible for the first time" (Homestead 2005, 108).

6. For more on the antebellum reprinting practices, see McGill 2003.

7. As Homestead explains, the practice of editors lifting—or literally snipping out—poems from other papers to print in their own was the norm, aided by postal regulations that allowed editors to exchange their newspapers with each other without having to pay for postage (Homestead 2005, 155).

8. Due to the fame of many Poetesses, periodicals did make an effort to provide the author's name in order to entice fans to buy their publications.

9. Both male and female antebellum writers were often placed in the position of married women, in that they "could simultaneously claim their literary property and find themselves dispossessed of it" (Homestead 2005, 191). For instance, Seba Smith, Elizabeth Oakes Smith's husband, was well known for his pieces written as the fictional character Major Jack Downing. However, Jack Downing became so popular that he was frequently imitated. Because Seba Smith could not or did not obtain a copyright for his writing, other writers were able to publish as and profit from his creation (Neal 1843, xviii–xxii).

10. According to Eliza Richards, "Women were imagined to be receptacles of emotion untainted by worldly concerns"; antebellum women who wrote poetry therefore "were portrayed as fonts of unmediated emotion. . . . Their poems were cast as identical offspring, incarnations of the Poetess' intimate feelings" (Richards 2004, 16).

11. The notion of property in the self or a "property in being" can be traced in part to Ralph Waldo Emerson (Dolan 2011, 354). Neal Dolan writes that "Emerson looked within, to a nonmaterial intensification and enhancement of a central liberal value—individual ownership" (354). For instance, Emerson comments in his essay "Nature" that "there is a property in the horizon which no man has but he whose eye can integrate all the parts, that is, the poet" (qtd. in Dolan 2011, 356).

12. In the article, "Frances Sargent Osgood," published shortly after her death 1850, Griswold explains that "all that was in her life was womanly, 'pure womanly,' and so is all in the undying words she left us" (Griswold 1850, 131). In fact, Osgood's consummate womanliness causes Griswold to make his famous statement on women's nature; women who give up "feminine refinement" for "masculine energy" are "hermaphroditish disturbers of the peace" (131).

13. For instance, "To My Pen" appeared in the *Columbian Magazine* as well as the *Ladies' Repository* in 1847; it was also included in Griswold's *Female Poets of America* in 1849. "To a Slandered Poetess" was published in *Sartain's Union Magazine of Literature and Art* in March 1849. "To an Idea That Wouldn't 'Come'" was also published in 1849 in *Graham's Illustrated Magazine of Literature, Romance, Art, and Fashion.*

14. These echoes are not accidental, as Bradstreet was a well-known and popular poet. She was considered to be America's first female poet, and her works were also included in Griswold's *Female Poets of America*. Furthermore, "Prologue" was published in Bradstreet's 1650 collection *The Tenth Muse,* which would have been available to readers in Osgood's time.

15. For an alternate reading of this poem, see Richards, who argues that "the speaker juxtaposes discursive modes while suspending resolution, mimicking and transmitting cultural perspectives that are not her own" (Richards 2004, 88).

16. "Caprice" appeared in *Graham's American Monthly Magazine* in February 1846 and in the *Harbinger* in February 1848.

17. Some notable exceptions include Felicia Hemans and Letitia Elizabeth Landon (Coppée 1860, 87, 117).

18. By the turn of the century, Martha Patterson writes, "increasing numbers of women demanded a public voice and private fulfillment through work, education, and political engagement" (Patterson 2008, 1). Women were involved in the fight for suffrage through membership in the National Woman Suffrage Association, the National Woman's Party, or a number of other political organizations (M. Patterson 2008, 6–7). Women who may not have wanted to involve themselves in politics founded other means of public, social engagement in the form of women's clubs, whose membership rapidly expanded at the turn of the century, with upward of two million participants (10). The social restrictions confining women to the domestic realm through marriage were also changing. Patterson describes "a greater willingness to take advantage of liberalized divorce laws, [and] more options for women to support themselves through paid labor if they left a marriage" by the early twentieth century (17).

19. A cursory search of the Making of America databases through the University of Michigan and Cornell University turns up, respectively, 751 and 362 mentions of the "poetess," with forty-eight hits between 1890 to 1924 (Michigan) and sixty-one hits between 1890 to 1901 (Cornell).

20. For example, in *American Song: A Collection of Representative American Poems, with Analytical and Critical Studies of the Writers* (1894), editor Arthur Beaman Simonds prefaces Osgood's section by stating that she "was the first woman to write good poetry in this country" (Simonds 1894, 166).

21. Anne E. Boyd explains that "in the 1880s and 1890s, as [the *Atlantic*] responded to increasing competition in the literary market by reinforcing the reputations of its elite male writers. Rather than encourage women writers to ascend to the ranks of Hawthorne and Emerson, it rewarded those who conformed to its assumptions about women inhabiting a separate sphere in literature and in life. Thus, women writers gained the highest praise from editors and reviewers for their local color literature, which was deemed of 'minor' importance in comparison to the great works that would be enshrined as America's high literature" (Boyd 1998, 10).

22. For instance, it was published in *The Cambridge Book of Poetry and Song* in 1882 and listed in Edith Granger's *An Index to Poetry and Recitations* in 1918 (Bates 1882, 402; Granger 1918, 161). It can be found in newspapers from the *Raleigh Register* to the *Ohio Farmer* (Osgood 1850a, n.p.; Osgood 1859, 328).

23. The article begins by describing how Lincoln liked to read *Macbeth, Hamlet,* and *Richard II* out loud, and then reports that Lincoln enjoyed British poets Robert Burns and Thomas Hood. On the American side, "he read Bryant and Whittier with appreciation; there were many poems of Holmes that he read with intense relish." The article admits that Lincoln "made no attempt to keep pace with the ordinary literature of the day"—he famously could recite William Knox's "Mortality" by heart (*Christian Science Monitor* 1914, 17).

24. According to Barry Schwartz, Lincoln's image in the early twentieth century "was pulled in contrary directions: toward stateliness, authority, and dignity on the one hand, and toward plainness, familiarity, and homeliness on the other" (Schwartz 1991, 301–2).

Chapter Two

1. The version of "A Human Life" that I quote from is that transcribed by Leigh Kirkland from Oakes Smith's own manuscript, held by the New York Public Library, Rare Books and Manuscript Division (Oakes Smith 1994). Kirkland includes plain-text transcriptions of the cancellations and additions made in Oakes Smith's own hand, such as strike-throughs and carets.

2. The broader strokes of Oakes Smith's life and works would have been well known to fans and critics. She married the poet and humorist Seba Smith in 1823 when she was sixteen. After he lost his fortune in the Panic of 1837, she began to write poetry to support the family—and she was a hit. In 1842, her poem *The Sinless Child* made her famous, and she wrote in all sorts of forms—poems, novels, short stories, essays, lectures—spanning nearly the entire nineteenth century. Her marriage at such an early age had a profound impact on her life, and in *Woman and Her Needs,* parts 5 and 7, Oakes Smith pleads that women not be married when they are adolescents (Oakes Smith 1851, 49–57, 70–79).

3. It appears that "A Human Life" was meant to be published, but it never came out. Oakes Smith alludes to it in her own writing and in interviews. For example, the column Table Talk from 1884 reports that Oakes Smith "is making reasonable progress with her autobiography, which will teem with recollections of the most eminent men and women in all vocations in the last generation" (*Literary World* 1884, 308). Oakes Smith even pre-publicizes the work when she states, "As I look back . . . it would seem that half the thought of fine thinkers and actors has in some way circled within the radius of my experience" (308).

4. To speak "soundly of myself" refers back to the manuscript's epigraphs from Michel de Montaigne, Blaise Pascal, and Johann Wolfgang von Goethe (Oakes Smith 1994, 71). Montaigne's quote, the first listed, reads in part, "Not to speak soundly of a man's self implies some want of courage; a firm and lofty judgement . . . makes use of his own example upon all occasions" (71). Pascal's and Goethe's quotes follow, and all of these excerpts describe the importance of self-circulation in public (71). They suggest that private self-reflection made publicly available benefits both the individual and society. In essence, Oakes Smith is justifying her autobiographical work.

5. As Richards notes, "Women poets' ability to recast reception on their own terms is limited by forces beyond their control" (Richards 2004, 153).

6. See Richards for more about Oakes Smith's "arboreal" names (Richards 2004, 152).

7. This scrapbook is available in the Elizabeth Oakes Prince Smith Papers, found on microform in the Manuscripts and Archives Division of the New York Public Library. On the clipping of the article, Oakes Smith wrote, "Evening Leader, Wilkes-Barre, Pa, July 13 1855" (Dickinson [1855]).

8. In her day, Oakes Smith was well known as a poet and as an activist, but history has not recognized her contributions in either role. By the twentieth century, her name was primarily found in reprints of Edgar Allan Poe's collected literary criticism. That said, Mary A. Wyman published *Two American Pioneers: Seba Smith and Elizabeth Oakes Smith* in 1927 (Wyman 1927).

9. Other women's rights activists shared the same philosophy as Oakes Smith. Paulina Davis, for example, shared concerns about the possibility of "individual development and universal cultural reform" (Wayne 2005, 52).

10. In the first volume, published in 1881, Oakes Smith is named as a speaker at various meetings, in lists of convention officers, for her contributions to the suffragist periodical the *Una*, for her remarks at the 1852 convention, and in numerous other capacities in the history of the movement. *History of Woman Suffrage* was later expanded to include six volumes, going up to 1920 (Stanton, Anthony, and Gage 1881).

11. For example, in *Females and Their Diseases: A Series of Letters to His Class*, published in 1848, renowned Philadelphia physician Dr. Charles Meigs taught his male medical students that "a woman's 'sexual destiny' was to mature into a 'reproductive agent,'" that woman's "'intellectual and moral perceptivity and powers' were as 'feminine as her organs are,'" and that "home is her place," since "a woman lacked 'great administrative faculties'" (qtd. in C. Patterson 2016, 517).

12. Men are not the single guilty party; women also promote an incorrect image. For example, Mrs. S. C. Hall criticizes literary women, concluding that "*still the woman would have been happier had she continued enshrined in the privacy of domestic love and domestic duty, so perfectly is she constituted for the cares, the affections, the duties, the blessed duties of unpublic*

life." Oakes Smith counters, "If Mrs. S.C. Hall really thought this—really believed that a human being is happier for holding the greater part of its nature in abeyance, she ought herself never to have written—she should have buried her fine talents, and shut out from her eyes all the freshness and freedom of vision which help to make our life a well spring of happiness" (Oakes Smith 1851, 87).

13. Angela Ray explains that "between 1829 and 1878 women constituted 3 percent of the total number of presenters at the Concord Lyceum, and only five women gave lectures: Elizabeth Oakes Prince Smith in 1851, Caroline H. Dall in 1859, Mrs. Van Benthuysen in 1865, Lucy Stone in 1876, and Mary Ashton Rice Livermore six times between 1872 and 1878" (Ray 2006, 191). In fact, Ray found that "the *New York Tribune*'s list of available lecturers for 1853–54 included only one woman, the author-lecturer Elizabeth Oakes Smith" (192).

14. For a different reading of this quote, see Dorri Beam's discussion of Margaret Fuller's and Oakes Smith's investment in Mesmerism. Oakes Smith's applications of the philosophy are important to keep in mind. Beam argues that in this passage, "we see the importance of Mesmerism to Oakes Smith's feminism: women must release themselves from their assigned sphere, itself a kind of Mesmerized slavery in which they 'see and hear through [man's] senses.' Once women achieved the higher visionary encounter with their own souls, however, they would slough off the 'effigies' of the socially defined women's sphere" (Beam 2013, 52).

15. In "Bill of Rights" from 1853, which she includes in "A Human Life," Oakes Smith confronts the hidden labor that supports the existence of white, male subjectivity; she says, "Strike out this mass of labor performed by women, and we apprehend our Brothers would be driven to their wits" (Oakes Smith 1994, 308). Because women perform the labor that sustains a liberal citizenry, they should thus "be accepted as a citizen [*sic*]": "I contend that public opinion and human laws should recognize women in this necessity for labor, and, as she must, through this labor, depart from the seclusion and protection of our Brothers. . . . She must redeem her civil responsibilities as rigorously as her Brother; consequently she should share his privileges and immunities" (308).

16. For example, in the sketch "Evenings with Some Female Poets" by "J. S.," a character named Johannes comments, "No one homages genius, whether in man or in woman, more than I do; but really, after reading volume after volume of female writing . . . I think that it is once in an age that a woman with even respectable talent appears" ("J. S." 1852, 212).

17. I quote from the version published in *Godey's Magazine and Lady's Book* (Helfenstein 1844). This essay was published and republished across various outlets in 1844, with one clipping preserved in Oakes Smith's scrapbook under the handwritten title "Genius and Talent" (Oakes Smith, n.d.). Of the many items Oakes Smith had published in her lifetime, the presence of this item in her scrapbook suggests that it held a special meaning for her.

18. According to Richards, Oakes Smith makes this point in her diary (Richards 2004, 218). Indeed, writing under a different name allowed women writers to place more works than they otherwise could have under their single name, which was often under exclusive agreement with certain publications or associated with certain types of writing.

19. Poe criticizes *The Sinless Child* for being too rough in its current form; it needed further refinement in order to be a great poem: "With a good deal more deliberate thought before putting pen to paper . . . with more rigorous discipline in the minor merits of style, and of what is termed the school-prospectuses composition, Mrs. Smith would have made of 'The Sinless Child' one of the best, if not the very best of American poems" (Poe 1895, 308).

20. "*His own name*" could be understood as a wink from Keese for presuming to publish Oakes Smith's works with his name attached (Keese 1843, xii). Indeed, prior to these concluding remarks, Keese demonstrates a self-depreciating humor by stating, for example, that he does not possess "one particle of that literary discernment" (ix).

21. This sketch and others included in this edition and elsewhere are quite frank about Seba Smith's financial ruin. As Neal explains, "He was ruined—lock, stock and barrel" (Neal 1843, xxi).

22. My contention that *The Sinless Child* was participating in this liberal public sphere is an underlying but unstated assumption of recent scholarship. For example, Kete suggests a connection between the self-fashioned Poet figure and the self-fashioned liberal subject by arguing that Eva is "Oakes-Smith's version of the Emersonian poet imagined as a woman; she is the namer, the one who re-connects things to themselves and makes even the ugly beautiful" (Kete 2000, 249). Richards links Oakes Smith's efforts to male "genius" poets by noting that she "graft[ed] a masculine capacity for philosophical contemplation on to the figure of a female child" (Richards 2004, 157). We learned in Oakes Smith's essay on the topic that genius is free from the pressures and encroachments of society, and such independence is a key component in the idealized liberal subject. Kete emphasizes such liberty by arguing that "[Eva's] heroism is signaled by successful resistance to integration with the conventional social world" (Kete 2000, 249).

23. In which case, is it impractical to discuss lyric when it comes to a long narrative poem? I am not advocating that we collapse the entire poem into the category of lyric, rather that we look for the lyrical strains in the poem. By taking a closer look at the spots where the poem lends itself to lyric reading, spots that correspond with expectations of the Poetess's sincere profession, we can discern where and how Oakes Smith made the case for her status as Poet.

24. Eva was the inspiration for numerous other literary figures, most notably Eva in Harriet Beecher Stowe's *Uncle Tom's Cabin* and the title character of Henry Wadsworth Longfellow's poem *Evangeline*.

25. Among her many other essays on the nature of marriage and the legality of divorce, see "Woman and Her Needs," part 7 (Oakes Smith 1851, 70–79).

26. Indeed, Kete writes that "Oakes-Smith depicts the figure of the mother as trying to corrupt the daughter by insisting that the daughter fulfill the conventional expectations of feminine behavior which have so crippled her" (Kete 2000, 251).

27. In his essay, Tuchinsky discusses how Oakes Smith's Transcendentalist philosophy influenced her views on divorce. Oakes Smith believed that "indissoluble marriage" was necessary to combat the selfish individualism that could tear families apart (Tuchinsky 2016, 56). Tuchinsky explains, "Within a context of rapid economic and cultural change, the reconsideration of marriage reflected the larger tension within market society between individual choice, emancipation, and personal fulfillment, and more communitarian and familial ideals that prized organic, dependent, and reciprocal relationships" (56).

28. Duquette discusses Emerson's essay "Napoleon." In this work, Emerson "offers a crucial, widely disseminated corrective to the emphasis on triumphant individualism seemingly celebrated in 'Self-Reliance'" (Duquette 2015, 650). Emerson illustrates not the self-reliant, liberal hero, but "the liberal nightmare (or neoliberal ideal *avant la lettre*) in which access to possessions and their consumption displaces other understandings of equality" (652).

29. For more on disembodied sprites or figures of "fancy" in women's poetry, see Richards (2004, chap. 2, 60–106).

30. Another version of this poem, in which Oakes Smith incorporates Indian names and legends, was being published at the same time as the version I consider here. This alternate version removes the "I" speaker and replaces it with "him of the shell" (Oakes Smith 1845, 123). This name is accompanied by a footnote stating, "'You shall be called Wa-dais-dis-imid, or he of the little shell.'—Schoolcraft" (123). Oakes Smith refers to Henry Rowe Schoolcraft, whose antebellum studies of Native American cultures influenced literary works, most notably Longfellow's *The Song of Hiawatha*. This second version of the poem can be found in Oakes Smith's *Poetical Works* (1845).

31. For more on the gendered, transcendent forms in this poem, see Richards 2004, 182–83.

Chapter Three

1. Scholars have pointed out the importance of names when writing about Frances Ellen Watkins Harper. As Andreá N. Williams argues, simply using "Harper" does not distinguish "the single, married, and widowed phases of the author's long life" (Williams 2014, 120). For instance, Watkins Harper was unwed during her first six years of activism and went by the surname Watkins (120). Meredith McGill notes that failing to differentiate between "Watkins" and "Harper" "insists on a single identity across the radical personal and political changes of midcentury," resulting in the assumption that "her writing is all of a piece" (McGill 2012, 56). Keeping these distinctions in mind, I will refer to Frances Ellen Watkins Harper as Watkins Harper in this chapter in order to, in the words of Koritha Mitchell, "remind readers that she was a public figure even before she was married and even without benefiting from the social acceptance that later came with being a widow" (K. Mitchell 2018, 13).

2. In addition to the discursive elements of enslavement, the material effects of legislative changes regarding slavery and freedom were a problem for Watkins Harper. After 1853, she was prohibited from returning to Maryland, her home state, because of a law change forbidding the entry of free blacks. Frances Smith Foster writes that this legislation signaled a "major turning point" in Watkins Harper's antislavery activism (Foster 1990, 10).

3. Loeffelholz and Carolyn Sorisio represent one strand in the recent and lively study of Watkins Harper, which discusses Watkins Harper and the black female body in public (Loeffelholz 2004; Sorisio 2010). Related criticism by Stephanie Farrar focuses on black women's maternity and republican motherhood (Farrar 2015). Meredith McGill and Eric Gardner have recovered the various contexts in which Watkins Harper's work appeared, including antislavery lecture performances, ephemeral pamphlets handed out at such lectures, and publication in newspapers like the *Christian Register* (McGill 2012; Gardner 2018). In addition, Gardner, Rebecka Rutledge Fisher, and others discuss how Watkins Harper strove to rewrite racist histories against the backdrop of Reconstruction (Fisher 2008). Perhaps the most prominent approach in Watkins Harper criticism examines her efforts to question or reform American democracy, as seen in scholarship by Michael Bennett, Lauren Berlant, Derrick Spires, and Ivy Wilson (M. Bennett 2005; Berlant 1993; Spires 2019; Wilson 2001). This list is far from comprehensive, but I hope

to have suggested how Watkins Harper's oeuvre offers diverse and exciting opportunities for future study.

4. While Mills's discussion of racial liberalism underpins my argument about Watkins Harper's poetics, I want to identify potential blind spots in the application of such theory. According to Shatema Threadcraft, contemporary Afro-Modern theorists such as Mills "have developed conceptions of black liberation from constraint and conceptions of racial equality that are most focused on black action in civic space" (Threadcraft 2016, 27). But this focus, Threadcraft suggests, too often privileges the black male body. As a result, the "realm of intimate relations and its associated capacities" is overlooked, and black women's bodies and experiences are diminished (27). In order to challenge "the laser focus on masculine agency and civic space within the tradition," thinkers like Threadcraft focus on "women's writing and resistance" (29, 28).

5. Lauren Berlant also describes "the slave's two bodies," but in terms of a public/private divide—"sensual and public on the one hand; vulnerable, invisible, forgettable on the other" (Berlant 1993, 556). I argue that this twoness is contained and further complicated by enslaved mothers.

6. I borrow this notion of "capacities" from Threadcraft, and her discussion of how racial liberalism constrains the black body's ability to act within and control its environment (Threadcraft 2016, 27). However, the restriction of capacities was different for enslaved men and women. In her discussion of the intimate restrictions that impacted enslaved women, Threadcraft explains that "whites exercised considerable power over enslaved women's capacities for reproduction, nurture, and care in a manner not typically experienced by black men" (38).

7. Dawson writes that political discourse within the black community "differed from discourse in the American polity at large," at the same time that "it influenced and was influenced by discourses in American society" (Dawson 2001, 5).

8. I refer to Isaiah Berlin's famous distinction between positive and negative liberty, found in *Four Essays on Liberty* (Berlin 1969). However, I want to qualify the positive/negative liberty distinction with a point from Threadcraft and Nancy Hirschmann, whom Threadcraft discusses. Threadcraft writes that theorists like Berlin have overlooked "cultural and contextual barriers that shape women's desires and function just as effectively to limit women's freedom of action" (Threadcraft 2016, 61).

9. In her explanation of republican motherhood, Sarah Robbins writes that a "successful republic" was aided by mothers who worked as "reproducers and nurturers of civic virtue" in young men (Sarah Robbins 2002, 565) Literature was a key part to this process, and women readers and writers could therefore shape the nation through the citizens they were helping to raise (564).

10. Watkins Harper's essay "Enlightened Motherhood" explicitly engages a rhetoric of republican motherhood. For instance, Watkins Harper states that "the moment the crown of motherhood falls on the brow of a young wife, God gives her a new interest in the welfare of the home and the good of society" (qtd. in Foster 1990, 287). But, I argue, the republicanism in her address works to affirm a black liberalism. Watkins Harper ends her remarks by insisting that "we need mothers . . . whose homes will be an uplifting power in the race. This is one of the greatest needs of the hour" (qtd. in Foster 1990, 292).

11. Indeed, this hybrid lyrical/ballad format has been recognized since early Watkins Harper scholarship. For instance, Elizabeth Ammons describes Watkins Harper's ballads in

terms of the lyric: "Usually choosing the ballad as her form, [Watkins Harper] wrote, as was the convention, to stir her readers' hearts. The poems are frankly emotional, most frequently evoking anger, pity, horror, exaltation or compassion" (Ammons 1985, 63).

12. McGill proposes "format" as an alternative to "medium" because the former term "directs our attention to the set of choices printers and publishers make in publishing a work, with the potential field of a book's reception very much in mind. Format is where economic and technological limitations meet cultural expectations" (McGill 2003, 55).

13. Catherine Casey's "Woman's Column" in the 1888 *Christian Recorder* illustrates how the abstract Poetess persona proved an asset for Watkins Harper. It is through the generic Poetess persona that readers recognized Watkins Harper's exceptionalism. For instance, Casey laments that Watkins Harper's poems have not been more widely and prestigiously recognized. But this complaint demonstrates how the generic Poetess provided a template from which Watkins Harper proved her genius:

> Why are not Mrs. Harper's poems bound in blue and gold and lying upon our library shelves? Her exquisite poem, describing the life and times of Moses, bears testimony that she has true poetic genius, and she has written so many lyrics which eminently deserve to be preserved as a contribution to our literature. Like Whittier, Mrs. Harper always writes upon choice subjects, and her rhythm is always simple and musical. Why is it always necessary when we want to quote a poetess to go all the way back to Phillis Wheatl[e]y, when we have such poems as those of Mrs. Harper's shining in our faces from the newspapers and magazines of the present day?
>
> —Casey 1888, 5

Casey's use of "poetess" may seem casual, a name applied to poets who are female. But her word choice illustrates the link between the Poetess persona and lyrical practices. Lyrical expression and simplicity signal the work of the Poetess, and Watkins Harper's "shining" works, Casey argues, will be sought by "aspiring school girls" "a hundred years from now" (5).

14. All of Watkins Harper's work quoted in this chapter comes from Foster, *A Brighter Coming Day* (1990).

15. In fact, other scholarly accounts participate in the lyric reading of Watkins Harper's poems, perhaps unintentionally. Take for instance Wilson's discussion of the "narrative form" in Watkins Harper's poetry, which, he writes, frequently evokes "a solitary subject, as if to approximate a recitative" (Wilson 2001, 63). Wilson has noticed what I would identify as a lyrical device, or feint—a speaker turning her back on the audience in order to draw them closer. While this operatic practice might be used to offset a character's solitary musings or a dialogue, or to move the plot, it mimics a speech act and is only ever "sung" by one person at a time. In other words, the recitative-like quality of Watkins Harper's poems, in which a solitary speaking subject performs with no knowledge of a listening audience, is an indication of its lyrical qualities.

16. This shading of Eliza's face from dark to light is, Geoffrey Sanborn points out, one of the few physical characteristics that Watkins Harper describes in her writing (Sanborn 2005, 691). He argues that Watkins Harper gives us "a body that becomes visible only when it flushes or goes pale" (693). While Sanborn extends this observation to argue that Watkins Harper's flushing or blanching characters resist "white standards of beauty," I argue

that darkening or paling faces are connected to the ownership, or lack thereof, that Watkins Harper's figured mothers have over their own bodies (698).

17. I borrow "remix" from Wilson, who explains that "the decisive mark of a 'remix' is that repetition is always transformative and always solicits retransformation. The remix is, thus, not derivative but a form of active engagement" (Wilson 2001, 9).

18. For another reading of Watkins Harper's use of voice in this poem, see Barrett. She argues that Watkins Harper "layer[s] her own public voice onto the private voice of Margaret Garner in order to build a rhetorically forceful direct address to the American nation" (Barrett 2012, 120–21).

19. The sentimental family was idealized as the force that exerted a rational restraint upon the whims of the liberal subject. "Protected by a newfound privacy," the family, Brian Connolly writes, "was called on to discipline the excesses of the liberal subject. The family became a potentially effective site of encumbrance and constraint as it formed the liberal subject" (Connolly 2014, 10). However, the sanctity of the private sphere held no protection for enslaved families, and, as a result, the family's rationalizing function was removed.

20. While Watkins Harper seems to suggest that the slave mother has lost all reason, Threadcraft argues that the infanticide was Garner's last possible form of meaning-making. Recall that Garner "lives in the body forced to reproduce—forced to use the reproductive capacities of her body to carry, sustain, and produce a being—but powerless to determine what it is that she produces" (Threadcraft 2016, 57). Threadcraft acknowledges that the infanticide is "problematic" but argues that it ultimately "remains so powerful because of Garner's decision as a dramatic and desperate move to have final say over the meaning of her sexual, reproductive, and caretaking actions" (60).

21. According to Wilson, Watkins Harper responded to *Uncle Tom's Cabin* on at least two other occasions: "To Mrs. Harriet Beecher Stowe" appeared in the January 27, 1854, number of *Frederick Douglass's Paper*; the poem "Eva's Farewell" closes the original edition of *Poems on Miscellaneous Subjects* (Wilson 2001, 67).

22. I am not suggesting that Watkins Harper sequenced her writing of these poems in order to show the development of a black liberal subject. "The Slave Mother," "The Slave Auction," and "Eliza Harris" all appeared in the first edition of *Poems on Miscellaneous Subjects*, published in 1854; these three poems plus "The Slave Mother (A Tale of the Ohio)" were then published in the 1857 edition. In addition, these poems likely circulated in pamphlets and spoken lectures well before either edition of *Poems on Miscellaneous Subjects*.

23. Hartman writes, "The ascribed responsibility of the liberal individual served to displace the nation's responsibility for providing and ensuring the rights and privileges conferred by the Reconstruction Amendments and shifted the burden of duty onto the freed. It was their duty to prove their worthiness for freedom rather than the nation's duty to guarantee, at minimum, the exercise of liberty and equality, if not opportunities for livelihood other than debt-peonage" (Hartman 1997, 118).

24. For example, in one of her lectures in 1865, Watkins Harper tells her audience that "there was a great deal more to be done, so that the oppressed might have not only bare freedom, but be clothed with all the rights that are necessary to complete citizenship" ("Mrs. L" 1865, 35).

25. Other scholars see Watkins Harper's works as more explicitly autobiographical. For instance, Barrett writes that "a personal 'I' permeate[s] Frances Harper's poetry," and that

"traces" of this "I" suggest "her conflicting allegiances as a free black educated woman dedicated to the struggle for African American rights" (Barrett 2012, 112, 128–29).

26. Indeed, Fisher writes that Chloe is "an individual encircled by an empathetic community" that "opens the way for Chloe to communicate to the world beyond her own" (Fisher 2008, 62).

27. Watkins Harper herself was single for the majority of her public career. She was married for only four years before her husband died, so it is worth noting, according to Williams, that Watkins Harper "spent most of her adult life uncoupled" (Williams 2014, 100).

28. Williams explains that "marital status may impact everything from an individual's social esteem to labor practices"; single individuals are a "civil[l]y disadvantaged class in relation to the state, so far as they are excluded from the benefits accompanying marriage" (Williams 2014, 101–2). Nevertheless, "the concept still maintained that a woman's life was most meaningful when expended in the service of others . . . even as unmarried women claimed a measure of independence and respectability, they remained tethered to certain feminine expectations" (Williams 2014, 104).

29. Hartman calls emancipation a "nonevent" due to the "the perpetuation of the plantation system and the refiguration of subjection" in the United States (Hartman 1997, 116).

Chapter Four

1. Lesley Wheeler's discussion of modernism is instructive inasmuch as it demonstrates the reasons why Millay has been overlooked: "Modernism claims the new for itself. Because a fractured, spare, allusive free verse is modernist poetry's signature style, formal verse has often been regarded by poets and critics as modernism's antithesis. Received forms, according to this logic, are feminine, retrograde, and populist, while the disjunctive modernist aesthetic occupies a violently masculine world, manifests innovative genius, and subverts the cheap sentimentality of mass culture" (Wheeler 2015, 628). Suzanne Clark explains that "when Edna St. Vincent Millay wrote, modernism was getting desperate to make those barriers work—excluding 'feelings' and 'the private' (or autobiographical) and 'intentionality' from a poetry that could only be 'original,' could only 'make it new,' by strictly delimiting the constituting *difference* of the poetic text" (Clark 1996, 160).

2. Robert Johnson suggests that Millay's sonnets "reflect the artistic problems of her age. . . . They often balance the urgency of human emotional responses and the concomitant need to name what one feels against the limitations of attempting to describe the felt moment" (R. Johnson 1995, 117). Jane Stanbrough argues that Millay's public image hides internal anguish, "an overwhelming sense of personal vulnerability . . . to victimization by uncontrollable conditions in her environment" (Stanbrough 1993, 214). Thus Millay avoids modernist "freedoms of form" and favors the sonnet, "a fit vehicle to convey her deepest feelings of woman's victimization" (227).

3. Modernism's concern with the private and public, the subjective interior and objective exterior, echoes the Poetess's problem of public privacy and a poetic self created for public consumption. Popular access or availability was a key modernist issue. For example, in *A Survey of Modernist Poetry* from 1927, Laura Riding and Robert Graves comment that modernist poetry "seems to say: 'Keep out. This is a private performance'" (Riding and Graves 1927, 9). They explain that "what we have to do, then, is to discover whether or not the poet

means to keep the public out" (Riding and Graves 1927, 10). T. S. Eliot contemplates the place of private feeling in public poetry, famously arguing in "Tradition and the Individual Talent" that "poetry is not a turning loose of emotion, but an escape from emotion; it is not the expression of personality, but an escape from personality" (Eliot 1920, 53). In the words of J. Hillis Miller, Eliot determines that "an act of self-surrender has expanded the private mind of the poet into the universal sphere" (J. Miller 1965, 172).

4. "Renascence" was published in *The Lyric Year* in 1912.

5. While all periods of American history can be characterized by massive changes, this one seems particularly turbulent due to changes in technology, political economy, and society; indeed "a nation that just forty years before had been primarily rural and inward-looking, still recovering from a devastating civil war, emerged as an urban, industrial giant" (Nichols and Unger 2017, 1). Such developments in industrialization made the nation a global power. At the same time, "the shift from the cotton economy to domestic industrialization, the expansion of railroads and manufacturing, the intensive exploitation of natural resources, and the commercialization of agriculture" attest to the drastic changes occurring domestically (Maggor 2017, 210). One could argue that drastic swings in the political economy were met with cultural attempts to create stability, reflected in attitudes about masculinity and femininity.

6. According to Hamlin, "The number of women working for wages had almost tripled since 1870," with "women comprising 20% of the paid labor force by 1910" (Hamlin 2017, 92). Women's access to higher education constitutes one of "the most significant and controversial developments of the post–Civil War era"; Hamlin writes that "in 1870, women made up 21% of college students" but "by 1910 this had risen to 40%" (94).

7. Take, for instance, the Miss America pageant, which began in 1921, the year after passage of the women's suffrage amendment. Instead of affirming women's advances in political equality, the pageant "promote[d] 'traditional' womanhood—'unpainted' and 'unbobbed'—together with women's domestic role" (Hamlin 2017, 95).

8. Nancy Milford's biography is the primary source documenting Millay's early influences, and it provides few details on what the poet may have read at school or at home (Milford 2002). The Edna St. Vincent Millay Society (www.millay.org) has largely restored and preserved Steepletop, Millay's upstate New York home. The site contains her library, but the archive is not yet open to the public.

9. In her 1910 diary, Millay mentions reading Elizabeth Barrett Browning's *Sonnets from the Portuguese* and Palgrave's *Golden Treasury*, whose 1907 edition contained work by various Poetesses. This diary is located in the Edna St. Vincent Millay Papers at the Library of Congress (E. Millay 1910).

10. Also see C. Millay's published poetry clippings, along with her daughter's scrapbooks, in the Edna St. Vincent Millay Papers, Library of Congress (E. Millay 1910).

11. C. Millay wrote stories for children and dispatches as a sort of traveling correspondent around New England. A number of children wrote to the Young Folks' Column of the *Maine Farmer* to say how much they enjoyed "Mrs. Millay's" stories, asking her to write more—and to invite them to the parties she hosted at her home.

12. Millay was so well known that she became a kind of genre unto herself, the prototype for poetry by young, modern women. Hervey Allen claims in a 1926 issue of the *North American Review* that a new book of poems by a young woman "owes a great deal for its now stock attitudes to Edna St. Vincent Millay" (H. Allen 1926, 364); Marie Luhrs in *Poetry*

explains that Millay's poetry "has been so studied, so quoted, so admired that unfortunately it has robbed many young poets of their voices" (Luhrs 1926, 281).

13. In 1924, Monroe's continued praise for Millay's youthful independence promotes the Poetess's unadulterated—and therefore unprofessional—insight. In "Comment: Edna St. Vincent Millay," also from *Poetry*, Monroe conserves the sincerity associated with women poets: "Always one feels," Monroe writes, "the poet's complete and unabashed sincerity. [Millay] says neither the expected thing nor the 'daring' thing, but she says the incisive true thing as she has discovered it and feels it" (Monroe 1924, 265). Monroe's mention of a "discovered" or surprise "thing" echoes the reception of the Poetess: she is not a skilled artist but an inadvertent mouthpiece for what she feels.

14. Indeed, the modernist poetics that resulted in knitted brows were "at odds with Millay's poetic practices"; Suzanne Clark writes that "modernism assumes an estrangement between the poem and the reader—difference, not familiarity. Exile, not community" (Clark 1996, 145).

15. For other works that expand the scope of modernist interpretation, see, to name a few, Edward S. Cutler, *Recovering the New: Transatlantic Roots of Modernism* (2003), and Douglas Mao and Rebecca L. Walkowitz's collection *Bad Modernisms* (2010).

16. This poem "traveled" into the homes of middlebrow readers across the country, first appearing in *Vanity Fair* in September 1920 and later published in the second edition of *A Few Figs from Thistles* in 1921 (T. Jackson 2008, 297).

17. Timothy Jackson's dissertation, "Selected Lyrics and Dramatic Verse of Edna St. Vincent Millay: A Critical Edition," contains comprehensive information on the publication of Millay's poems (T. Jackson 2008).

18. She "was photographed by the celebrated photographers of her day such as Arnold Genthe, Man Ray, Herman Mishkin, Carl Van Vechten, and Berenice Abbot" (Parker 2016, 380).

19. In *American Poetry since 1900* (1923), Louis Untermeyer comments on the artistic shift between Millay's first volume, *Renascence*, and her second, *A Few Figs from Thistles*. In that second volume, "Miss Millay seems to have exchanged her birthright for a mess of cleverness; it is nothing more than a pretty talent that gives most of these light verses the quality of a facile cynicism, an ignoble adroitness" (Untermeyer 1993, 117–18).

20. Keyser notes that "the captions and articles describing Millay in *Vanity Fair* suggest a connection between the ethereal beauty of the poet and the success of her lyrical verse" (Keyser 2007, 81). This connection extended to other women writers in the early twentieth century. Parker comments that "physical appearances, enshrined in photography, may indeed be proven to have had a largely unacknowledged influence on the reception of women poets"; for instance, Amy Lowell's weight might have affected her "waning critical fortunes" (Parker 2016, 397).

21. Lowell's "props, theatrics, and a flamboyant personality" decidedly undercut expectations for female poetic performance (Bradshaw 2000, 145).

22. Other *Christian Science Monitor* reviewers were likewise intrigued by Millay's range of feminized personas. For instance, a 1927 reviewer describes Millay as "looking like a little girl dressed up in a trailing gown of Renaissance brocade. She stares out of wide eyes at her audience" (*Christian Science Monitor* 1927, 2).

23. Millay's work with the sonnet form further links her to traditions of women's writing. The sonnet became the culturally appropriate form for women's public expression in the

eighteenth and nineteenth centuries in both England and the United States. It "signified a generic role for sincere feeling, a gendered cultural script" (Rosenbaum 2007, 100). For further discussion on this point, see Curran 2002 and Robinson 1995.

24. Poets such as Rose Terry Cooke, Emily Dickinson, Edgar Fawcett, Bret Harte, James Russell Lowell, and Edwin Arlington Robinson alluded to the tale to describe something wondrous, hidden, or deadly. In brief, the story follows these lines: No women want to marry the nobleman Bluebeard because he has an ugly blue beard. Despite the disappearance of his seven former wives, he convinces an eighth wife to marry him. The young woman joins him in his castle, but shortly thereafter he leaves for the country. Bluebeard gives his wife the keys to the castle, including a key to a small room she is forbidden to enter. Curiosity overcomes her, and she enters the room, discovering the bloody bodies of the seven former wives. Bluebeard returns, discovers the entry, and tries to kill her, but her brothers save her at the last moment. The website SurLaLune Fairy Tales provides an excellent annotated version of Charles Perrault's tale.

25. My use of "backstage" draws from Millette Shamir's discussion of middle-class womanhood in the nineteenth century. She writes, "What the records of domesticity often reveal, however, are the psychological pressures brewing within middle-class women, who did not have at their disposal such backstage areas, ironically, at the very moment when they were figured as icons of privacy" (Shamir 2006, 41).

26. Furr listened to recordings of these broadcasts and explains how "inauthentic" Millay's speaking style sounds today: "a parody of seriousness at best, maudlin and histrionic at worst" (Furr 2006, 102). But for the time, Furr argues that "the vocal techniques we might consider artificial drew Millay's audience in" (102).

27. Wheeler comments that "even her print work displays a persistent concern with authorial presence, the way a poet is 'there' and 'not there' at once, and how deeply the lyric depends on this tension" (Wheeler 2008, 40).

28. This broadcast from the winter of 1933 included eight poems drawn from *Renascence* (1917), *Second April* (1921), *The Harp Weaver* (1923), and *Fatal Interview* (1931) (Wheeler 2008, 49–52). "Not in a Silver Casket Cool with Pearls" appears in *Fatal Interview*.

29. Furr explains that "listening to Millay, therefore, involves holding in tension two opposing aesthetics, one that appreciates Millay's theatricality as theatricality and Millay as artful poseur, and another that understands Millay as sentimental poet, guardian and promoter of the beautiful" (Furr 2006, 103).

30. For example, in a 1942 *New York Times* article, John K. Hutchens acknowledges Millay's political outspokenness, observing that "through most of her distinguished career she has been a perfectionist, but never a tenant of an ivory tower. As long ago as 1927, the Sacco-Vanzetti case moved her to bitter wrath. In the late Nineteen Thirties, with more prescience than most people, including poets, displayed, she was writing the verses collected in 1941 as 'Make Bright the Arrows,' among them her 'There Are No Islands Any More" (Hutchens 1942, X12).

Chapter Five

1. Her initial fame in Canada and the United States came from her verse, but, as Veronica Strong-Boag and Carole Gerson point out, the opportunities for publishing in each country had different barriers. They write, "The fact that Johnson's first verses appeared in *Gems*

of Poetry, an American periodical issued in New York, illustrates the embryonic state of Canadian culture in the early 1880s" (Strong-Boag and Gerson 2002, 100). As Johnson made a name for herself in American periodicals, she was simultaneously establishing a Canadian literary tradition, becoming one of the writers "who were constructing a distinct national identity for former colonies struggling towards collective consciousness" (101).

2. For more on this event, see Strong-Boag and Gerson 2002, 102–3.

3. Johnson was and still is a beloved Canadian poet; according to George W. Lyon, "her collected poems, *Flint and Feather*, remains the largest selling Canadian book of poetry, one which remains in print in a popular edition" (Lyon 1990, n.p.).

4. Strong-Boag and Gerson, whose research is foundational for current studies on Johnson, explain the paucity of information on Johnson's performed poems: "Skits and dramatic presentations composed for performance experienced a particularly high mortality rate, surviving only in accounts by newspaper reviewers" (Strong-Boag and Gerson 2002, 6).

5. Both magazines were owned by the David C. Cook Publishing Company in Elgin, Illinois.

6. Betty Keller, describing the tour from the performer's point of view, notes that "entertainers on the circuit needed hardy constitutions since they were fed on campground meals, the ability to cat nap in odd corner[s] since their schedules were often rearranged on short notice, and great reserves of sincerity since 'uplift' is hard to fake . . . even when, at the end of August, they had already given the same speech forty-seven times in as many towns and did not believe a word of it anymore" (Keller 2015, 232).

7. Circuit Chautauquas were spinoffs of the original Chautauqua Institution, held on Lake Chautauqua in western New York in 1874. Organizers and promoters from the Lyceum lecture circuit of the nineteenth century saw the appeal of a Chautauqua experience adapted into a traveling, lecture form. Keith Vawter of the Redpath Lyceum Bureau offered the first Circuit Chautauqua in 1904. While his original endeavor was largely a failure, from there the circuit system developed, offering a set of routes that visited rural midwestern towns over the summer. The company offering the tour would set up tents and book the talent, and each city on the route would be visited in turn by the tour's performers (Canning 2005, 6–11).

8. For instance, the "corporatization" of the railroad industry left many midwestern farmers feeling like "pawns in the unfettered accumulation of wealth by East Coast and European interests" (Jablonsky 2017, 62).

9. Thanks to rulings in cases such as *Santa Clara County v. Southern Pacific Railroad* in 1886, "the 'person' whose 'life, liberty, or property' the Fourteenth Amendment secured was not the freedman but the corporation" (Beatty 2008, 110).

10. For those "whose lives were bound by agriculture," Chautauqua programming "reflected a desire to address farming's waning dominance as the quintessentially American way of life" (Canning 2005, 37).

11. For more on Jacksonian liberal individualism, see McClay 1994.

12. Keller writes that Johnson's midwestern audiences perceived "good" Indians as those who were "either dead or captive. They rather enjoyed seeing one now and then in a side show or circus, because it gave them an opportunity to show their children what the enemy looked like" (Keller 2015, 234).

13. Discussing "modernist constructions" of the Indian at the turn of the century, Philip Deloria writes that "the Indian that Americans desired no longer resided completely within

national identity. Now, that desire rested in some distant time and place in the form of a pure authentic Indian who meant hope for modern society" (Deloria 1998, 120).

14. Concepts from Deloria's *Playing Indian* provide the foundation for many of this chapter's claims: the impulse of white Americans to create an essential, homogenous Indianness; the idea that Indianness changes over time and reflects the desires and anxieties of American culture; the irony that a fabricated Indianness comes to represent authentic, natural identity; the idea of Indians as not just "other," but living anachronisms (Deloria 1998, 5, 98, 103, 105–6).

15. See chapter 4 of Deloria's *Playing Indian* for more on the establishment of the Boy Scouts and its roots in the performance of Indianness (Deloria 1998, 108–27).

16. The figured American Indian princess can be traced back to colonial times (Deloria 1998, 51–53). While I focus on Minnehaha, the Indian princess figure is also, and perhaps originally, associated with Pocahontas. For instance, Betty Bell writes that "the first Native women writers, in the nineteenth century, did borrow Pocahontas' nobility, authority, and visibility to make their self-representations coherent and acceptable to white audiences" (Bell 2002, 313). Native artists contemporaneous with Johnson, such as Narcissa Owen, Sarah Winnemucca, and Zitkala-ša, also performed the Indian princess figure for white readers and audiences.

17. For a current discussion of the politics of the Haudenosaunee or Iroquois Confederacy and political sovereignty across the Canadian and American borders, see Simpson 2014.

18. A notable exception is the 2017 article by Manina Jones and Neal Ferris.

19. I borrow a definition of the "commercial public sphere" from film scholar W. J. T. Mitchell, who describes it as a sphere "with advertising, publicity, mass media, and other technologies for influencing a consumer public" (W. Mitchell and Kruger 1991, 434).

20. Such ersatz Indianness is acknowledged by Indian performers' own awareness of their "mimicry of the white man's Indian," as Ruth B. Phillips explains (Phillips 2001, 28). Precisely by playing "fictive or negative roles pre-scripted for them," Native performers could draw attention to the "shallowness and arbitrary nature of the signs of Indianness" (Phillips 2001, 28). I am arguing that Johnson's performances were always explicitly performative, suggesting that she crafted a performance persona according to a commercial public sphere in which any potential dilemma between authenticity and performativity had dissolved. My argument takes for granted what scholars such as Miles Orvell have worked out at length. While an early twentieth-century culture of authenticity was developing in response to an "implacabl[e]" and "vast consumer culture," Orvell points out that imitation "remained (and remains even now) a significant component of twentieth-century culture" (Orvell 1989, 141). In other words, the "real thing" can exist only as an idealization of the unreal. The authentic, Deloria writes, "is a culturally constructed category created in opposition to a perceived state of inauthenticity. The authentic serves as a way to imagine and idealize the real, the traditional, and the organic in opposition to the less satisfying qualities of everyday life" (Deloria 1998, 101). I apply these conclusions to Johnson's performance. Audiences valued "authentic" Indianness, but what they took as the "real" was created according to popular, fictional representations of the Indian in commercial culture.

21. In this respect, my approach to Johnson echoes current scholarly approaches to Sarah Winnemucca, the Northern Paiute author and activist of the late nineteenth century. As

Carolyn Sorisio points out, Winnemucca performed for her white audiences dressed as an Indian princess, despite the fact that this performance persona reflected "neither the Winnemucca family's status among the Northern Paiutes nor Northern Paiute structures of leadership" (Sorisio 2011, 10). In giving back to audiences the simulation of Indianness they desired, Sorisio, borrowing a term from George Vizenor, calls Winnemucca a "postindian warrior," that is, one who "exposes, through performance and irony, the simulation itself" (Sorisio 2011, 12). Sorisio's discussion of Winnemucca can be applied to my discussion of Johnson, who has not yet been discussed as a kind of "postindian warrior" whose explicitly synthetic performance self-consciously showcased its constructedness.

22. Goeman writes that "dress becomes a way to engage with the artificial production of race through reconstituting gender" (Goeman 2013, 64).

23. My focus on the late nineteenth and early twentieth centuries is not meant to understate the atrocities committed against Native peoples that began with European contact. For the purposes of this chapter, I will focus on a small part of Native history: the legislation of the Progressive Era that replaced physical violence with a kind of psychological and domestic violence. For more on the domestic assimilation policies of the late nineteenth century, see Piatote 2011. I must also point out that the violence against Native people continues today. See, for example, the 2007 Amnesty International report *Maze of Injustice*, which discusses sexual violence against Native American women and the government's failure to provide protection or justice. An update reports that while some advances have been made, significant concerns remain (Amnesty International, n.d.).

24. For more on U.S. assimilation policies, see Hoxie 2001, 41–81. The Canadian Indian Acts of the late nineteenth century sought assimilation through similar methods. This legislation granted political rights resembling those of settler citizens so long as aboriginal people ceded land and gave up tribal affiliations. For instance, if aboriginal women married white men, they effectively severed kinship and legal ties to their tribal bands (Piatote 2011, 98–99, 114–15; Goeman 2013, 59–60). As Rick Monture points out, Canada's Indian Acts were being created and implemented "at around the same time that Pauline Johnson began to develop her literary voice" (Monture 2014, 68–69). While distinct "ways of controlling Indianness have developed in two otherwise very similar settler states" (Lawrence 2004, 7), I argue that Johnson's works can be understood to critique reprehensible legislation in both Canada and the United States.

25. For more on Native people's critique of and resistance to Indian boarding schools in the United States and Canada, see Sarah Ruffing Robbins 2017, 135–79.

26. The "pre-political" is a term I borrow from Elizabeth Dillon, who writes that "in the fiction of liberalism," this realm is "populated primarily by women" and "people of color" (Dillon 2004, 15).

27. The 2004 David R. Godine paperback reprint of the Remington edition evinces not only *Hiawatha*'s continuing popularity but also the ongoing appeal of Remington's own picture-language.

28. The edition's "Introductory Note" makes a point to acknowledge the discrepancies between the poem and images of Indian life. Longfellow "used his imagination to emphasize the central truths of his poetic inspiration of Indian life," and Remington's pictures "have a basis of reality from his long and close study of the Indian in many other situations, but sometimes are fanciful in their treatment" (Longfellow 1891, x–ix).

29. As Alan Trachtenberg notes, "Longfellow dipped into many pots in fashioning a faux indigenous hero who performs his feats not as Ojibway . . . but as 'Indian'" (Trachtenberg 2004, 60).

30. In quoting this edition's use of the word "squaw," I would like to acknowledge, in the words of Piatote, the "obscenity of the term" (Piatote 2013, ix). Piatote uses "sq—w" in order to "denaturalize its use" and call attention to the dash as "a marker of violence": "the term is not free of the physical and sexual violence it directs at indigenous and aboriginal women" (ix).

31. Remington's illustration of Minnehaha is one in a long line of popular and fine-arts representations of the figure across the nineteenth century.

32. One image that likely crossed Johnson's path was *Minnehaha Feeding Birds*," completed in 1874 by the Canadian artist Frances Anne Hopkins. In it, a woman wearing a beige tunic covered in beads and shells and a turquoise necklace sits in a canoe. She extends her hand to the birds perching on the gunwales of her craft (Hopkins 1874). Given her passion for canoeing, Johnson might have found this picture quite appealing.

33. In an 1892 letter to W. D. Lighthall, Johnson reveals how she came by these kinds of items. She writes, "I want a pair of moccasins, worked either in colored moose hair, porcupine quills, or very heavily with *fine colored beads*, have you ever seen any such there? I have written to Chief [Jacks?] about getting some bead work done of my dress, and to several N.W. Reserves, for bears teeth necklaces, etc., but if you see anything in Montreal that would assist me in getting up a costume, be it, beads, quills, sashes, shoes, brooches or indeed anything at all, I will be more than obliged to know" (qtd. in Strong-Boag and Gerson 2002, 110). The Hudson's Bay Company in Winnipeg also assisted her in this request. They supplied her with "moccasins and a buckskin top and skirt, plus cuffs, collar and belt decorated with beads, moose hair and porcupine quillwork" (Grey 2002, 157). Thanks to additional styling advice from her sister, Eva, Johnson's performance costume was complete (157).

34. In a review of "The White Wampum" in the *Bookman* from 1895, the unnamed reviewer comments that "[Johnson's] art, strange to say, bewrays her, and, after all, we get nearer to the life of the Indian through Longfellow and Whittier. Especially is this so where she deals with human nature; there is none of the strange fascination that creeps over us as we read *Hiawatha*" (*Bookman* 1895, 236).

35. Take this 1897 *Emerson Journal* review: "[The Indian poems] picture in tender words their savage state and how they might be bettered but that the greed of gain grasps all in exchange for the poor Indian's body and soul. . . . Dull indeed is the man that cannot be aroused by Miss Johnson's recitations" (Strong-Boag and Gerson 2002, 107). In addition, one reviewer claims that "the Indian poems themselves tell of the hardships of the Indian at the hands of the white man," and another argues that "Miss Johnson is a stalwart enthusiast over her Indian ancestry" ("'Tekahionwake'" 1907, 6). Even the beloved Schoolroom Poet John Greenleaf Whittier echoes such comments: "Thy poems have strength as well as beauty; it is fitting that one of their own race should sing the songs of the Mohawk and Iroquois in the English tongue" (6).

36. Strong-Boag and Gerson note how these poses strayed from the "full-frontal documentary photographs of historical First Nations male leaders" whose "direct stares challenge the observer" (Strong-Boag and Gerson 2002, 113). Johnson's photos instead "heighten her artfulness as a performer" by "display[ing] the details of her outfit as well as her feminine figure" (113). "Her uplifted gaze towards an invisible horizon" served symbolic

and practical purposes, "signall[ing] her engagement with a story extending beyond the frame of the picture" and "eventually concealing a sagging chin as she tried to remain forever youthful" (113).

37. Furthermore, I rely on this information because accounts of Johnson's performances are not widely available. Researchers such as Strong-Boag and Gerson and Linda Morra have noted the "paucity" of reviews that specifically describe her performance (Jones and Ferris 2017, 143).

38. While the title of the poem suggests folklore, the name "Qu'Appelle" denotes geographical locations in Saskatchewan: a town, a fort, a river, and the valley that contains the aforementioned sites.

39. Johnson again echoes *Hiawatha*'s plot: in chapter 20, "The Famine," Hiawatha hears Minnehaha calling his name from her deathbed although he is "far away amid the forest, / Miles away among the mountains" (Longfellow 1891, 204).

40. Also see Hoxie 2001, 216–19. Indian property was actually seized or lost under the expansion of "federal guardianship" that would supposedly ensure the "protection" of land.

41. For more on how Britain figured in the formation of America's national identity across the nineteenth century, see Onuf 2012.

42. Johnson's poem "The Corn Husker" likewise critiques settler colonialism through the central figure of a Haudenosaunee woman (E. Johnson 2002, 121). Like "A Cry from an Indian Wife," the poem "presents Indians as a people of the past," but also "calls attention to the present," citing "might's injustice"—that is, settler nations—for the decline of indigenous culture (Strong-Boag and Gerson 2002, 151).

43. Some critics, such as Lorraine York, have concluded that Johnson "ultimately lost control over her self representations and, instead, slavishly fed her public whatever image they desired" (York 2002). Given the poem's seemingly stereotypical representation of Native savagery, the creation and subsequent reproduction of "Ojistoh" might indeed suggest Johnson's "need to satisfy a non-Native audience's preconceptions about Native people" (York 2002). However, I argue that this poem demonstrates Johnson's ability to work through those desires in order to assert her agency and the agency of Native peoples.

44. As Monture points out, while the poem "depicts a courageous and strong Indigenous female figure at a time when few such images circulated, it can also be interpreted as perpetuating the sensationalized image of a highly sexual and violent Native woman" (Monture 2014, 88). I maintain that Johnson is asserting Native autonomy in her ability to manipulate the stereotype of the Indian wife, and even if the result is a "sensationalized image," she nevertheless revises prevailing models.

45. Byrne explains that these scripts were "flimsy," "lightweight," and cheap, with the more expensive scripts selling "at the comparatively high price of sixty cents" (Byrne 2014, 217–19). The cover to *Ojistoh* shows a price of fifty cents—if this edition was slightly pricier, it was most likely due to the photographs.

46. During this time, the proceeds from her book, *Legends of Vancouver*, were put into the Pauline Johnson Trust Fund to provide an income for Pauline's last months and to pay for her hospitalization (Grey 2002, 371–88).

47. For instance, "Ojistoh" appears in volume 41 of Charles Dudley Warner's *Library of the World's Best Literature*, which was reprinted multiple times and in multiple volumes at the turn of the century (Warner 1897, lxii).

48. The juvenile readers of *Boys' World* may have very well overlapped with Pender's own elocution students, while *Mother's Magazine* seems likely to have crossed Pender's path.

49. An advertisement in the *Brooklyn Daily Eagle* from October 22, 1908, reads "MRS. FREDERICK W. PENDER, teacher elocution, oratory. Voice brought out and strengthened" (*Brooklyn Daily Eagle* 1908, 14). The advertisement told interested students that they should send an application letter to her address on West 128th Street (14).

50. Sometimes Pender just contributes the lesson talk, as she does for *Ain't It Awful, Mabel* (Library of Congress 1911a, 3142). In other instances, she individually authored the drama and included elocutionary advice in her detailed stage directions—*His Exceptional Mother-in-Law* is one such example (Pender 1905).

51. Indeed, the copyright entered for Pender's *Ojistoh* in 1911 suggests that the addition of "lesson-talk" renders it a new text; the copyright is attributed to the Edgar Werner company, but the entry is found in the "J" section under "Johnson (E. Pauline)" (Library of Congress 1911b, 5556). Crucially, though, the copyright entry reads "poses and lesson-talk by Mrs. Frederick W. Pender" (5556).

52. The Copyright Act of 1909 overhauled the previous statute, in place since 1790. But this did not ensure protection for Johnson's original work. "Ojistoh" first appeared in Johnson's collection *The White Wampum*, published in London in 1895 (Strong-Boag and Gerson 2002, 16, 225). American appropriations after 1909, such as Pender's, seem to treat such works as public domain.

53. Take for instance *Werner's Readings and Recitations No. 48*, a magazine of collected dramatic works. The table of contents for this issue lists works by category; in the lengthy section labeled "Dialect," the ethnicity of the assumed speaker is listed alongside the text's title. For example, "Honey-Bug Baby (negro)" is followed by "Jes' Whistle Up a Song (Yankee)" ("Honey-Bug Baby" is by Emma C. Dulaney, and "Jes' Whistle Up a Song" has no author listed). While there is no listing for "Indian" in this volume, these descriptors indicate that assuming the ethnic identity of another was an appealing prospect for would-be reciters (Schell 1911, 6).

54. For instance, the pamphlet for *His Exceptional Mother-in-Law*, the stand-alone amateur play that Pender wrote and published with Werner in 1905, contains a page-long advertisement for "Hiawatha Entertainments" by Stanley Schell (Pender 1905, i). In addition, the same *Catalogue of Copyright Entries* for 1911 that contains *Ojistoh: Illustrated Indian Woman Monologue* lists entries for "Indian" works. Marion Thomas from Newark copyrights texts that include "Little Indian Child and You" and "Real Little, True Little Indian Girl" (Library of Congress 1911b, 6643). "An Indian Wooing," a "dramatic sketch in one act," is entered into copyright by Minna Aydelotte of Santa Cruz (Library of Congress 1911b, 6749).

55. Pender also includes instructions for a second performer, the "Indian Chief," who is there for "scenic effect but who does no talking" (Pender 1911, 6). The booklet devotes most of its "Points" to instructions for costuming the Indian Woman—nearly a full page compared to the Indian Chief's single paragraph (6).

56. The pamphlet for Pender's *His Exceptional Mother-in-Law* also contains an advertisement for a "Delsarte Recitation Book" (Pender 1905, 8).

Bibliography

Adams, Oscar Fay. 1915. "Frances Sargent Osgood." *Christian Register* 94: 9–10.

Adams, V. Joshua, Joel Calahan, and Michael Hansen. 2016. "Reading Historical Poetics." *Modern Language Quarterly* 77, no. 1: 1–12.

Allen, Hervey. 1926. "Review." *North American Review* 223, no. 831: 360–66.

Altman, Rick. 2011. *Film/Genre*. London: British Film Institute.

Ammons, Elizabeth. 1985. "Legacy Profile: Frances Ellen Watkins Harper." *Legacy: A Journal of American Women Writers* 2, no. 2 (Fall): 61–66.

Amnesty International. n.d. "Ending Sexual Violence against Indigenous Women in the U.S." Accessed October 18, 2019. https://www.amnestyusa.org/the-fight-to-end-sexual-violence-against-indigenous-women-and-girls-in-the-u-s/.

Appleby, Joyce. 1992. *Liberalism and Republicanism in the Historical Imagination*. Cambridge, MA: Harvard University Press.

Barnhisel, Greg. 2015. *Cold War Modernists: Art, Literature, and American Cultural Diplomacy*. New York: Columbia University Press.

Barrett, Faith. 2012. *To Fight Aloud Is Very Brave: American Poetry and the Civil War*. Amherst: University of Massachusetts Press.

Bates, Charlotte Fiske, ed. 1882. *The Cambridge Book of Poetry and Song*. New York: Thomas Y. Crowell.

Beam, Dorri. 2013. "Fuller, Feminism, Pantheism." In *Margaret Fuller and Her Circles*, edited by Brigitte Bailey, Katheryn P. Viens, and Conrad Edick Wright, 46–64. Durham: University of New Hampshire Press.

Beatty, Jack. 2008. *Age of Betrayal: The Triumph of Money in America, 1865–1900*. New York: Vintage Books.

Bell, Betty. 2002. "Gender in Native America." In *A Companion to American Indian History*, edited by Philip Deloria and Neal Salisbury, 307–20. Malden, MA: Blackwell.

Bennett, Michael. 2005. *Democratic Discourses: The Radical Abolition Movement and Antebellum American Literature*. New Brunswick, NJ: Rutgers University Press.

Bennett, Paula Bernat. 2003. *Poets in the Public Sphere: The Emancipatory Project of American Women's Poetry, 1800–1900*. Princeton, NJ: Princeton University Press, 2003.

———. 2007. "Was Sigourney a Poetess? The Aesthetics of Victorian Plenitude in Lydia Sigourney's Poetry." *Comparative American Studies* 5, no. 3: 265–89.

Berlant, Lauren. 1993. "The Queen of America Goes to Washington City: Harriet Jacobs, Frances Harper, Anita Hill." *American Literature* 65, no. 3 (September): 549–74.

Berlin, Isaiah. 1969. *Four Essays on Liberty*. New York: Oxford University Press.

Blasing, Mutlu. 2007. *Lyric Poetry: The Pain and the Pleasure of Words*. Princeton, NJ: Princeton University Press.

Bookman: A Review of Books and Life. 1895. "The White Wampum." November, 236. American Periodicals, search.proquest.com/docview/124752771?accountid=7098.

Boston Daily Advertiser. 1877. "Three Forms of Poetry." February 24.
Boston Notion. 1843. Review of *The Sinless Child*. In *The Sinless Child*, by Elizabeth Oakes Smith, edited by John Keese, xxxiii–xxxiv. New York: Wiley and Putnam.
Boyd, Anne E. 1998. "What! Has She Got into the 'Atlantic'?" *American Studies* 39, no. 3 (Fall): 5–36.
Bradshaw, Melissa. 2000. "Outselling the Modernisms of Men: Amy Lowell and the Art of Self-Commodification." *Victorian Poetry* 38, no. 1: 141–69.
Bradstreet, Anne. 1967. *The Works of Anne Bradstreet*. Edited by Jeannine Hensley. Cambridge, MA: Harvard University Press.
Brooklyn Daily Eagle. 1908. "Mrs. Frederick W. Pender." October 22, 14.
Brown, Margaret Wise. 2003. *Mister Dog: The Dog Who Belonged to Himself*. New York: Random House Children's Books.
Byrne, Kevin. 2014. "'Simple Devices Are Always Best': An Examination of the Amateur Play Publishing Industry in the United States." *Papers of the Biographical Society of America (PBSA)* 108, no. 2: 217–37.
Canning, Charlotte. 2005. *The Most American Thing in America: Circuit Chautauqua as Performance*. Iowa City: University of Iowa Press.
Carpenter, Cari. 2008. *Seeing Red: Anger, Sentimentality, and American Indians*. Columbus: Ohio State University Press.
Casey, Catherine. 1888. "Woman's Column." *Christian Recorder*, February 9, 5.
Castiglia, Christopher. 2008. *Interior States: Institutional Consciousness and the Inner Life of Democracy in the Antebellum United States*. Durham, NC: Duke University Press.
Chicago Daily Tribune. 1897. "Poetess of the Iroquois." January 28, 8.
Christian Science Monitor. 1914. "Lincoln a Reader of Poetry." January 5, 17.
———. 1927. "Memories of Maine Days Flavor Readings of 'Little Millay Girl.'" *Christian Science Monitor*, November 14, 2.
Clark, Suzanne. 1996. "Jouissance and the Sentimental Daughter: Edna St. Vincent Millay." In *Gendered Modernisms: American Women Poets and Their Readers*, edited by Margaret Dickie and Thomas Travisano, 143–88. Philadelphia: University of Pennsylvania Press.
Clarke, Helen. 1890. "Notes and News." *Poet-Lore* 2, no. 12: 666–72.
Cleveland, Charles D., ed. 1862. *A Compendium of American Literature*. Philadelphia: E. C. & J. Biddle.
Cohen, Michael C. 2008. "Whittier, Ballad Reading, and the Culture of Nineteenth-Century Poetry." *Arizona Quarterly* 64, no. 3 (Autumn): 1–29.
———. 2015. *The Social Lives of Poems in Nineteenth-Century America*. Philadelphia: University of Pennsylvania Press.
Cohen, Nancy. 2002. *The Reconstruction of American Liberalism, 1865–1914*. Chapel Hill: University of North Carolina Press.
Cone, Helen Gray. 1890. "Woman in American Literature." *Century Illustrated Magazine* 40, no. 6: 921–30. ProQuest. https://search-proquest-com.lib-e2.lib.ttu.edu/docview/125511079?accountid=7098.
Connolly, Brian. 2014. *Domestic Intimacies: Incest and the Liberal Subject in Nineteenth-Century America*. Philadelphia: University of Pennsylvania Press.
Coppée, Henry. 1860. *A Gallery of Distinguished English and American Female Poets*. Philadelphia: E. H. Butler.

Culler, Jonathan. 2001. *The Pursuit of Signs: Semiotics, Literature, Deconstruction.* Ithaca, NY: Cornell University Press.

———. 2015. *Theory of the Lyric.* Cambridge, MA: Harvard University Press.

Curran, Stuart. 2002. "Mary Robinson and the New Lyric." *Women's Writing* 9, no. 1: 9–22.

Cutler, Edward S. 2003. *Recovering the New: Transatlantic Roots of Modernism.* Lebanon, NH: University Press of New England, 2003.

Dawson, Michael C. 2001. *Black Visions: The Roots of Contemporary African-American Political Ideologies.* Chicago: University of Chicago Press.

Dean, Janet. 2011. "Reading Lessons: Sentimental Literacy and Assimilation in *Stiya: A Carlisle Indian Girl at Home* and *Wynema: A Child of the Forest.*" *ESQ: A Journal of the American Renaissance* 57, no. 3: 200–240.

Deloria, Philip Joseph. 1998. *Playing Indian.* New Haven, CT: Yale University Press.

———. 2004. *Indians in Unexpected Places.* Lawrence: University Press of Kansas.

Dickinson, Susan E. [1855]. "Women Writers: A Chapter on Their Ephemeral Reputations." In Elizabeth Oakes Prince Smith Papers, MssCol 2780. Manuscripts and Archives Division, New York Public Library.

Dillon, Elizabeth Maddock. 2004. *The Gender of Freedom: Fictions of Liberalism and the Literary Public Sphere.* Stanford, CA: Stanford University Press.

Dolan, Neal. 2009. *Emerson's Liberalism.* Madison: University of Wisconsin Press.

———. 2011. "Property in Being: Liberalism and the Language of Ownership in Emerson's Writing." In *A Political Companion to Ralph Waldo Emerson,* edited by Alan Levine and Daniel Malachuk, 343–82. Lexington: University Press of Kentucky.

Dupre, Daniel S. 2006. "The Panic of 1819 and the Political Economy of Sectionalism." In *The Economy of Early America: Historical Perspectives and New Directions,* edited by Cathy D. Matson, 263–93. University Park: Pennsylvania State University Press.

Duquette, Elizabeth. 2015. "The Man of the World." *American Literary History* 27, no. 4 (Winter): 635–64.

Duyckinck Evert A., and George L. Duyckinck. 1881. *The Cyclopedia of American Literature.* Vol. 2. Philadelphia: Baxter Publishing.

Eliot, T. S. 1920. "Tradition and the Individual Talent." In *The Sacred Wood: Essays on Poetry and Criticism,* 42–53. London: Methuen.

Emerson, Ralph Waldo. 1910. *Journals of Ralph Waldo Emerson: With Annotations.* Vol. 3. New York: Houghton Mifflin.

———. 2001. *Emerson's Prose and Poetry.* Edited by Joel Porte and Saundra Morris. New York: W. W. Norton.

Farrar, Stephanie. 2015. "Maternity and Black Women's Citizenship in Frances Watkins Harper's Early Poetry and Late Prose." *MELUS* 40, no. 1 (Spring): 52–75.

Fisher, Rebecka Rutledge. 2008. "Remnants of Memory: Testimony and Being in Frances E. W. Harper's Sketches of Southern Life." *ESQ: A Journal of the American Renaissance* 54, nos. 1–4: 55–74.

Foster, Frances Smith. 1990. *A Brighter Coming Day: A Frances Ellen Watkins Harper Reader.* New York: Feminist Press.

Fraser, Nancy. 1992. "Rethinking the Public Sphere: A Contribution to the Critique of Actually Existing Democracy." In *Habermas and the Public Sphere,* edited by Craig Calhoun, 109–42. Cambridge, MA: MIT Press.

Furr, Derek. 2006. "Listening to Millay." *Journal of Modern Literature* 29, no. 2: 94–110.

Gardner, Eric. 2018. "African American Literary Reconstructions and the 'Propaganda of History.'" *American Literary History* 30, no. 3 (Fall): 429–49.

Garrison, Theodosia. 1904. "The Literati." *Smart Set* 13, no. 1 (May): 149–50.

Goeman, Mishuana. 2013. *Mark My Words: Native Women Mapping Our Nations*. Minneapolis: University of Minnesota Press.

Goodman, Kevis. 2012. "Georgic." In *The Princeton Encyclopedia of Poetry and Poetics*, 4th ed., edited by Stephen Cushman et al., 556–57. Princeton, NJ: Princeton University Press.

Graham's Magazine. 1844. "Our Contributors.—No. XV. Mrs. Anne S. Stephens." 26, no. 4 (October): 234–36.

Granger, Edith, ed. 1918. *An Index to Poetry and Recitations*. Chicago: A. C. McClurg.

Grey, Charlotte. 2002. *Flint and Feather: The Life and Times of E. Pauline Johnson, Tekahionwake*. Toronto: HarperFlamingo Canada.

Griswold, Rufus. 1850. "Frances Sargent Osgood." *International Monthly Magazine of Literature, Science and Art* 2, no. 1 (December): 131–40. ProQuest. https://search.proquest.com/docview/90621266?accountid=7098.

Hamlin, Kimberly A. 2017. "Gender." In *A Companion to the Gilded Age and Progressive Era*, edited by Christopher M. Nichols and Nancy C. Unger, 87–101. Hoboken, NJ: Wiley Blackwell.

Hartman, Saidiya. 1996. "Seduction and the Ruses of Power." *Callaloo* 19, no. 2 (Spring): 537–60.

———. 1997. *Scenes of Subjection: Terror, Slavery, and Self-Making in Nineteenth-Century America*. New York: Oxford University Press.

H. D. (Hilda Doolittle). 1986. *H. D.: Collected Poems, 1912–1944*. Edited by Louis L. Martz. New York: New Directions.

Helfenstein, Ernest [Elizabeth Oakes Smith]. 1844. "Genius Exempt from Ordinary Laws." *Godey's Magazine and Lady's Book* 28 (February): 98–99.

Heydrick, Benjamin A. 1900. "Intensive Study of Lyric Poetry." *Chautauquan: A Weekly Newsmagazine* 31, no. 6: 617–20. American Periodicals. https://search.proquest.com/docview/125211698?accountid=7098.

Hilkey, Judy Arlene. 1997. *Character Is Capital: Success Manuals and Manhood in Gilded Age America*. Chapel Hill: University of North Carolina Press.

Ho, Janice. 2011. "The Crisis of Liberalism and the Politics of Modernism." *Literature Compass* 8, no. 1: 47–65.

Hoberek, Andrew. 2016. "'But—What Can Anyone Do about It?': Modernism, Superheroes, and the Unfinished Business of the Common Good." *Journal of Modern Literature* 39, no. 2: 115–25.

Hoffman, Tyler. 2011. *American Poetry in Performance: From Walt Whitman to Hip Hop*. Ann Arbor: University of Michigan Press.

Homestead, Melissa. 2005. *American Women Authors and Literary Property, 1822–1869*. New York: Cambridge University Press.

Hopkins, Frances Anne. 1874. *Minnehaha Feeding Birds*. Painting. Reprinted in *I'm Not Myself at All: Women, Art, and Subjectivity in Canada*, by Kristina Huneault, 96. Montreal: McGill-Queen's University Press, 2018.

Hoxie, Frederick E. 2001. *A Final Promise: The Campaign to Assimilate the Indians, 1880–1920*. Lincoln, NB: Bison Books.

Hutchens, John K. 1942. "Miss Millay's New Poem." *New York Times,* October 25, X12.

I. F. 1924. "When Edna St. Vincent Millay Recites Her Poems and Acts a Play." *Christian Science Monitor,* February 29, 6. ProQuest Historical Newspapers. https://search.proquest.com/docview/510927834?accountid=7098.

Independent. 1928. "New Books in Brief Review." October 6, 333.

Jablonsky, Thomas J. 2017. "The Midwest and Far West during the Gilded Age and Progressive Era." In *A Companion to the Gilded Age and Progressive Era,* edited by Christopher M. Nichols and Nancy C. Unger, 58–70. Hoboken, NJ: Wiley Blackwell.

Jackson, Timothy F. 2008. "Selected Lyrics and Dramatic Verse of Edna St. Vincent Millay: A Critical Edition." PhD diss., Boston University. UMI, 3314032.

Jackson, Virginia. 1998. "Longfellow's Tradition; or, Picture-Writing a Nation." *Modern Language Quarterly* 59, no. 4 (December): 471–96.

———. 2005. *Dickinson's Misery: A Theory of Lyric Reading*. Princeton, NJ: Princeton University Press.

———. 2008. "Who Reads Poetry?" *PMLA* 123, no. 1: 181–87.

———. 2011. "The Poet as Poetess." In *The Cambridge Companion to Nineteenth-Century American Poetry,* edited by Kerry Larson, 54–75. New York: Cambridge University Press.

Jackson, Virginia, and Yopie Prins. 1999. "Lyrical Studies." *Victorian Literature and Culture* 7, no. 2: 521–30.

———. 2013. General introduction to *The Lyric Theory Reader: A Critical Anthology,* edited by Virginia Jackson and Yopie Prins, 1–10. Baltimore: Johns Hopkins University Press.

Johnson, E. Pauline. 2002. *E. Pauline Johnson, Tekahionwake: Collected Poems and Selected Prose.* Edited by Carole Gerson and Veronica Jane Strong-Boag. Toronto: University of Toronto Press.

Johnson, Robert. 1995. "A Moment's Monument: Millay's Sonnet and Modern Time." In *Millay at 100: A Critical Reappraisal,* edited by Diane P. Freedman, 117–41. Carbondale: Southern Illinois University Press.

Johnson, Walter. 1999. *Soul by Soul: Life inside the Antebellum Slave Market.* Cambridge, MA: Harvard University Press.

Johnston, Sheila M. F. 1997. *Buckskin and Broadcloth: A Celebration of E. Pauline Johnson Tekahionwake.* Toronto: Natural Heritage Books.

Jones, Manina, and Neal Ferris. 2017. "Flint, Feather, and Other Material Selves: Negotiating the Performance Poetics of E. Pauline Johnson." *American Indian Quarterly* 41, no. 2 (Spring): 125–57.

"J. S." 1852. "Evenings with Some Female Poets." *American Whig Review* 9, no. 3 (March): 210–18.

Kateb, George. 1995. *Emerson and Self-Reliance.* Thousand Oaks, CA: Sage Publications.

Kazin, Michael. 2017. "Why the Gilded Age and Progressive Era Still Matter." In *A Companion to the Gilded Age and Progressive Era,* edited by Christopher M. Nichols and Nancy C. Unger, 450–53. Hoboken, NJ: Wiley Blackwell.

Keese, John. 1843. "To the Reader." In *The Sinless Child and Other Poems,* by Elizabeth Oakes Smith, edited by John Keese, vii–xii. New York: Wiley and Putnam.

Keller, Betty. 2015. *Pauline: A Biography of Pauline Johnson*. Halifax: Formac Publishing.

Kete, Mary Louise. 2000 "Gender Valences of Transcendentalism: The Pursuit of Idealism in Elizabeth Oakes-Smith's 'The Sinless Child.'" In *Separate Spheres No More: Gender Convergence in American Literature, 1830–1930*, edited by Monika M. Elbert, 245–60. Tuscaloosa: University of Alabama Press.

Keyser, Catherine. 2007. "Edna St. Vincent Millay and the Very Clever Woman in *Vanity Fair*." *American Periodicals* 17, no. 1: 65–96.

———. 2010. *Playing Smart: New York Women Writers and Modern Magazine Culture*. New Brunswick, NJ: Rutgers University Press.

Kimber, Marian Wilson. 2016. "In a Woman's Voice: Musical Recitation and the Feminization of American Melodrama." In *Melodramatic Voices: Understanding Music Drama*, edited by Sarah Hibberd, 61–82. New York: Routledge.

Kramer, Dale. 1940. "Main Street in 1940: Sigourney, Iowa." *Forum and Century* 103, no. 4 (April): 166–73.

Lawrence, Bonita. 2004. *"Real" Indians and Others: Mixed-Blood Urban Native Peoples and Indigenous Nationhood*. Lincoln: University of Nebraska Press.

Lears, T. J. Jackson. 1983. "From Salvation to Self-Realization: Advertising and the Therapeutic Roots of the Consumer Culture, 1880–1930." In *The Culture of Consumption: Critical Essays in American History, 1880–1980*, edited by Richard Wightman Fox and T. J. Jackson Lears, 1–38. New York: Pantheon Books.

Levine, Alan, and Daniel Malachuk. 2011. Introduction to *A Political Companion to Ralph Waldo Emerson*, edited by Alan Levine and Daniel Malachuk, 1–42. Lexington: University Press of Kentucky.

Library of Congress. 1911a. *Catalogue of Copyright Entries, Part 1, Group 2: Pamphlets, Leaflets, Contributions to Newspapers or Periodicals, Etc.; Lectures, Sermons, Addresses for Oral Delivery; Dramatic Compositions; Maps, 8, no. 2*. Washington, DC: Government Printing Office.

———. 1911b. *Catalogue of Copyright Entries, Part 1, Group 2: Pamphlets, Leaflets, Contributions to Newspapers or Periodicals, Etc.; Lectures, Sermons, Addresses for Oral Delivery; Dramatic Compositions; Maps, 8, no. 3*. Washington, DC: Government Printing Office.

Literary World. 1884. "Table Talk." *Literary World: A Monthly Review of Current Literature* 15, no. 19 (September 20): 308.

Loeffelholz, Mary. 2004. *From School to Salon: Reading Nineteenth-Century American Women's Poetry*. Princeton, NJ: Princeton University Press.

Longfellow, Henry Wadsworth. 1842. "Maidenhood." *Southern Literary Messenger* 8, no. 1 (January): 57.

———. 1891. *The Song of Hiawatha*. Illustrated by Frederick Remington. New York: Houghton Mifflin.

Lootens, Tricia. 2016. *The Political Poetess: Victorian Femininity, Race, and the Legacy of Separate Spheres*. Princeton, NJ: Princeton University Press.

Luhrs, Marie. 1926. "Hearts and Flowers." *Poetry: A Magazine of Verse* 27, no. 5: 281–82.

Lundy, Benjamin. 1845. *The Poetical Works of Elizabeth Margaret Chandler: With a Memoir of Her Life and Character*. Philadelphia: T. E. Chapman.

Lush, Paige Clark. 2008. "The All American Other: Native American Music and Musicians on the Circuit Chautauqua." *Americana: The Journal of American Popular Culture, 1900 to Present* 7, no. 2 (Fall). EBSCOhost. http://www.americanpopularculture.com/journal/articles/fall_2008/lush.htm.

Lustig, R. Jeffrey. 1986. *Corporate Liberalism: The Origins of Modern American Political Theory, 1890–1920*. Berkeley: University of California Press.

Lyon, George W. 1990. "Pauline Johnson: A Reconsideration." *Studies in Canadian Literature / Études en Littérature Canadienne* 15, no. 2. https://journals.lib.unb.ca/index.php/SCL/article/view/8124/9181.

MacKay, Ruth. 1944. "White Collar Girl." *Chicago Daily Tribune*, December 15, 21.

Maddox, Lucy. 2005. *Citizen Indians: Native American Intellectuals, Race, and Reform*. Ithaca, NY: Cornell University Press.

Maggor, Noam. 2017. "American Capitalism: From the Atlantic Economy to Domestic Industrialization." In *A Companion to the Gilded Age and Progressive Era*, edited by Christopher M. Nichols and Nancy C. Unger, 205–14. Hoboken, NJ: Wiley Blackwell.

Mamdani, Mahmood. 2015. "Settler Colonialism: Then and Now." *Critical Inquiry* 41, no. 3 (Spring): 596–614.

Mao, Douglas, and Rebecca L. Walkowitz, eds. 2010. *Bad Modernisms*. Durham, NC: Duke University Press.

McClay, Wilfred. 1994. *The Masterless Self: Self and Society in Modern America*. Chapel Hill: University of North Carolina Press.

McDonald, Robert M. S. 2001. "Early National Politics and Power, 1800–1824." In *A Companion to 19th-Century America*, edited William L. Barney, 5–18. Malden, MA: Blackwell.

McGill, Meredith. 2003. *American Literature and the Culture of Reprinting, 1834–1853*. Philadelphia: University of Pennsylvania Press.

———. 2012. "Frances Ellen Watkins Harper and the Circuits of Abolitionist Poetry." In *Early African American Print Culture*, edited by Lara Langer Cohen and Jordan Alexander Stein, 53–74. Philadelphia: University of Pennsylvania Press.

McGill, Meredith, Scott Challener, Isaac Cowell, Bakary Diaby, Lauren Kimball, Michael Monescalchi, and Melissa Parrish. 2015. "Genre and Nationality in Nineteenth-Century British and American Poetry." In *Teaching Transatlanticism: Resources for Teaching Nineteenth-Century Anglo-American Print Culture*, edited by Linda Hughes and Sarah Robbins, 164–80. New York: Oxford University Press.

Milford, Nancy. 2002. *Savage Beauty: The Life of Edna St. Vincent Millay*. New York: Random House.

Mill, John Stuart. 1976. "What Is Poetry?" In *Essays on Poetry*, edited by F. Parvin Sharpless, 3–22. Columbia: University of South Carolina Press.

———. 2002. *The Basic Writings of John Stuart Mill: "On Liberty," "The Subjection of Women," and "Utilitarianism."* New York: Modern Library.

———. 2003. *Autobiography*. Project Gutenberg. Accessed September 30, 2019. www.gutenberg.org/cache/epub/10378/pg10378-images.html.

Millay, Cora Buzzell. 1889. "Good-night." *Maine Farmer*, October 10, 4.

Millay, Edna St. Vincent. 1910. Diary, vol. 3. Edna St. Vincent Millay Papers, box 94, folder 13. Manuscript Division, Library of Congress, Washington, DC.

———. 1940. "There Are No Islands, Any More." *New York Times*, June 14, 3.

———. 1952. *Letters of Edna St. Vincent Millay*. Edited by Allan Ross Macdougall. New York: Harper.

———. 1956. *Collected Poems*. Edited by Norma Millay. New York: Harper.

Miller, Cristanne. 2012. *Reading in Time: Emily Dickinson in the Nineteenth Century*. Amherst: University of Massachusetts Press.

———. 2016. "Chronology I: American Women Poets, 1900–1950." In *A History of Twentieth-Century American Women's Poetry*, edited by Linda A. Kinnahan, 41–55. New York: Cambridge University Press.

Miller, J. Hillis. 1965. *Poets of Reality: Six Twentieth-Century Writers*. New York: Atheneum.

Mills, Charles W. 2008. "Racial Liberalism." *PMLA* 123, no. 5 (October): 1380–97.

Mitchell, Koritha, ed. 2018. *Iola Leroy; or, Shadows Uplifted*. Peterborough, ON: Broadview Press.

Mitchell, W. J. T., and Barbara Kruger. 1991. "An Interview with Barbara Kruger." *Critical Inquiry* 17, no. 2 (Winter): 434–48.

Monroe, Harriet. 1918. "Review: First Books of Verse." *Poetry: A Magazine of Verse* 13, no. 3: 167–68.

———. 1924. "Comment: Edna St. Vincent Millay." *Poetry: A Magazine of Verse* 24, no. 5: 260–66.

Monture, Rick. 2014. *We Share Our Matters: Two Centuries of Writing and Resistance at Six Nations of the Grand River*. Winnipeg: University of Manitoba Press.

Moore, Charles. 1915. "The Lyric Lord." *The Dial: A Semi-Monthly Journal of Literary Criticism, Discussion, and Information* 59, no. 705 (November): 401–3. American Periodicals. https://search.proquest.com/docview/89677218?accountid=7098.

Moore, Marianne. 1994. *Complete Poems*. New York: Penguin.

Morse, Samuel F. B. 1829. *Amir Khan, and Other Poems: The Remains of Lucretia Maria Davidson . . . With a Biographical Sketch*. New York: G. & C. & H. Carvill.

"Mrs. L." 1865. "Mrs. Frances E. W. Harper on Reconstruction." *Liberator* 35, no. 9 (March): 35. ProQuest. https://search.proquest.com/docview/91123851?accountid=7098.

Neal, John. 1843. "Elizabeth Oakes Smith." In *The Sinless Child*, by Elizabeth Oakes Smith, edited by John Keese, xv–xxvi. New York: Wiley and Putnam.

News and Observer (Raleigh, NC). 1888. "Linguistic Work at the University." September 29, x.

Nichols, Christopher M., and Nancy C. Unger, eds. 2017. "Introduction: Gilded Excesses, Multiple Progressivisms." In *A Companion to the Gilded Age and Progressive Era*, 1–4. Hoboken, NJ: Wiley Blackwell.

Oakes Smith, Elizabeth. 1843. *The Sinless Child and Other Poems*. Edited by John Keese. New York: Wiley and Putnam.

———. 1845. *The Poetical Writings of Elizabeth Oakes Smith*. New York: J. S. Redfield.

———. 1851. *Woman and Her Needs*. New York: Fowlers and Wells.

———. 1887. "Man and Woman." *Boston Investigator*, March 30, 2.

———. 1994. "A Human Life: Being the Autobiography of Elizabeth Oakes Smith; A Critical Edition and Introduction." Edited by Leigh Kirkland. PhD diss., Georgia State University. UMI, 1994.9518227.

———. n.d. Papers. MssCol 2780. Manuscripts and Archives Division, New York Public Library.

Onuf, Peter S. 2012. "American Exceptionalism and National Identity." *American Political Thought* 1, no. 1 (Spring): 77–100.

Orvell, Miles. 1989. *The Real Thing: Imitation and Authenticity in American Culture, 1880–1940*. Chapel Hill: University of North Carolina Press.

Osgood, Frances Sargent. 1850a. "Laborare Est Orare." *Raleigh Register*, July 13, 1850, n.p.

———. 1850b. *Poems*. Philadelphia: Carey and Hart.

———. 1859. "Labor." *Ohio Farmer*, October 8, 328.

———. 1914. "Selections from 'Laborare Est Orare.'" *Christian Science Monitor*, January 5, 17.

Palgrave, Francis Turner. 1992. *The Golden Treasury: The Best Songs and Lyrical Poems in the English Language*. New York: Penguin Classics.

Parker, Sarah. 2016. "Publicity, Celebrity, Fashion: Photographing Edna St. Vincent Millay." *Women's Studies* 45, no. 4: 380–402.

Parks, Edd Winfield. 1930. "Edna St. Vincent Millay." *Sewanee Review* 38, no. 1: 42–49.

Patterson, Cynthia Lee. 2016. "'Hermaphroditish Disturbers of the Peace': Rufus Griswold, Elizabeth Oakes Smith, and Nineteenth-Century Discourses of Ambiguous Sex." *Women's Studies* 45 (August): 513–33.

Patterson, Martha, ed. 2008. *The American New Woman Revisited: A Reader, 1894–1930*. New Brunswick, NJ: Rutgers University Press.

Pender, [Mrs.] Frederick W. 1905. *His Exceptional Mother-in-Law*. New York: Edgar Werner.

———. 1911. *Ojistoh: Illustrated Indian Woman Monologue*. New York: Edgar Werner.

Peterson, Carla. 1995. *"Doers of the Word": African-American Women Speakers and Writers in the North (1830–1880)*. New York: Oxford University Press.

Phillips, Ruth B. 2001. "Performing the Native Woman: Primitivism and Mimicry in Early Twentieth-Century Visual Culture." In *Antimodernism and Artistic Experience: Policing the Boundaries of Modernity*, edited by Lynda Jessup, 26–49. Toronto: University of Toronto Press.

Piatote, Beth H. 2011. "Domestic Trials: Indian Rights and National Belonging in Works by E. Pauline Johnson and John M. Oskison." *American Quarterly* 3, no. 1 (March): 95–116.

———. 2013. *Domestic Subjects: Gender, Citizenship, and Law in Native American Literature*. New Haven, CT: Yale University Press.

Poe, Edgar Allan. 1895. "Elizabeth Oakes Smith." In *The Works of Edgar Allan Poe*, edited by Edmund Clarence Stedman and George Edward Woodberry, vol. 3, 301–14. Chicago: Stone and Kimball.

Prins, Yopie. 2008. "Historical Poetics, Dysprosody, and *The Science of English Verse*." *PMLA* 123 (January): 229–34.

———. 2012. "Poetess." In *The Princeton Encyclopedia of Poetry and Poetics*, 4th ed., edited by Stephen Cushman et al., 1051–54. Princeton, NJ: Princeton University Press.

Pulitano, Elvira. 2003. *Toward a Native American Critical Theory*. Lincoln: University of Nebraska Press.

Putzi, Jennifer. 2012. "'Some Queer Freak of Taste': Gender, Authorship, and the 'Rock Me to Sleep' Controversy." *American Literature* 84, no. 4 (December): 769–95.

Rabiee, Robert Yusef. 2016. "Feudalism, Individualism, and Authority in Later Emerson." *ESQ: A Journal of Nineteenth-Century American Literature and Culture* 62, no. 1: 77–114.

Ray, Angela. 2006. "What Hath She Wrought? Woman's Rights and the Nineteenth-Century Lyceum." *Rhetoric and Public Affairs* 9, no. 2: 183–214.

Rees, J. D. 1874. "English Lyrical Poetry." *Littell's Living Age* 122, no. 1572: 95–208. American Periodicals. https://search.proquest.com/docview/90416081?accountid=7098.
Richards, Eliza. 2004. *Gender and the Poetics of Reception in Poe's Circle*. New York: Cambridge University Press.
———. 2012. "Voice." In *The Princeton Encyclopedia of Poetry and Poetics*, 4th ed., edited by Stephen Cushman et al., 1525–27. Princeton, NJ: Princeton University Press.
Riding, Laura, and Robert Graves. 1927. *A Survey of Modernist Poetry*. London: William Heinemann.
Robbins, Sarah. 2002. "'The Future Good and Great of Our Land': Republican Mothers, Female Authors, and Domesticated Literacy in Antebellum New England." *New England Quarterly* 75, no. 4 (December): 562–91.
Robbins, Sarah Ruffing. 2017. *Learning Legacies: Archive to Action through Women's Cross-Cultural Teaching*. Ann Arbor: University of Michigan Press.
Robinson, Daniel. 1995. "Reviving the Sonnet: Women Romantic Poets and the Sonnet Claim." *European Romantic Review* 6, no. 1: 98–127.
Ronda, Margaret. 2013. "Georgic Disenchantment in American Poetry." *Genre* 46, no. 1: 57–78.
Rosenbaum, Susan B. 2007. *Professing Sincerity: Modern Lyric Poetry, Commercial Culture, and the Crisis in Reading*. Charlottesville: University of Virginia Press.
Rottenberg, Catherine. 2014. "Happiness and the Liberal Imagination: How Superwoman Became Balanced." *Feminist Studies* 40, no. 1: 144–68.
Rubin, Joan Shelley. 2007. *Songs of Ourselves: The Uses of Poetry in America*. Cambridge, MA: Harvard University Press.
Russell, David. 2013. "Aesthetic Liberalism: John Stuart Mill as Essayist." *Victorian Studies* 56, no. 1: 7–30.
Ryan, Alan. 1998. "Liberalism." In *A Companion to Contemporary Political Philosophy*, edited by Robert E. Goodin and Philip Pettit, 291–311. Malden, MA: Blackwell.
Sanborn, Geoffrey. 2005. "Mother's Milk: Frances Harper and the Circulation of Blood." *ELH* 72, no. 3 (Fall): 691–715.
Schell, Stanley, ed. 1911. *Werner's Readings and Recitations No. 48*. New York: Edgar S. Werner.
Schwartz, Barry. 1991. "Iconography and Collective Memory: Lincoln's Image in the American Mind." *Sociological Quarterly* 32, no. 3: 301–19.
Shamir, Milette. 2006. *Inexpressible Privacy: The Interior Life of Antebellum American Literature*. Philadelphia: University of Pennsylvania Press.
Shklar, Judith. 1989. "The Liberalism of Fear." In *Liberalism and the Moral Life*, edited by Nancy L. Rosenblum, 21–38. Cambridge, MA: Harvard University Press.
Simonds, Arthur Beaman. 1894. *American Song: A Collection of Representative American Poems, with Analytical and Critical Studies of the Writers*. New York: G. P. Putnam's Sons.
Simpson, Audra. 2014. *Mohawk Interruptus*. Durham, NC: Duke University Press.
Sklansky, Jeffrey. 2002. *The Soul's Economy: Market Society and Selfhood in American Thought, 1820–1920*. Chapel Hill: University of North Carolina Press.
Socarides, Alexandra. 2017. "Making and Unmaking a Canon: American Women's Poetry and the Nineteenth-Century Anthology." In *A History of Nineteenth-Century American Women's Poetry*, edited by Jennifer Putzi and Alexandra Socarides, 186–202. New York: Cambridge University Press.

———. 2018. "The Poetess at Work." In *The Cambridge Companion to the Literature of the American Renaissance*, edited by Christopher N. Phillips, 128–41. New York: Cambridge University Press.

Sorby, Angela. 2005. *Schoolroom Poets: Childhood, Performance, and the Place of American Poetry, 1865–1917*. Durham: University of New Hampshire Press.

Sorisio, Carolyn. 2010. *Fleshing Out America: Race, Gender, and the Politics of the Body in American Literature, 1833–1879*. Athens: University of Georgia Press.

———. 2011. "Playing the Indian Princess? Sarah Winnemucca's Newspaper Career and Performance of American Indian Identities." *Studies in American Indian Literatures* 23, no. 1 (Spring): 1–37.

Spires, Derrick. 2019. *The Practice of Citizenship: Black Politics and Print Culture in the Early United States*. Philadelphia: University of Pennsylvania Press.

Stanbrough, Jane. 1993. "Edna St. Vincent Millay and the Language of Vulnerability." In *Critical Essays on Edna St. Vincent Millay*, edited by William B. Thesing, 213–28. New York: G. K. Hall.

Stanton, Elizabeth Cady, Susan Brownell Anthony, and Matilda Joslyn Gage, eds. 1881. *History of Woman Suffrage*. Vol. 1. New York: Fowler and Gage.

Strobel, Marion. 1921. "A Flourish of Trumpets." *Poetry: A Magazine of Verse* 19, no. 3: 151–54.

Strong-Boag, Veronica, and Carole Gerson. 2002. *Paddling Her Own Canoe: The Times and Texts of E. Pauline Johnson (Tekahionwake)*. Toronto: University of Toronto Press.

Sweet, Timothy. 2002. *American Georgics: Economy and Environment in American Literature, 1580–1864*. Philadelphia: University of Pennsylvania Press.

Tate, Allen. 1993. "Miss Millay's Sonnets." In *Critical Essays on Edna St. Vincent Millay*, edited by William B. Thesing, 61–64. New York: G. K. Hall.

"Tekahionwake." Promotional Bill for the American Chautauqua Tour, June, 1907. 1907. Joseph Keppler Jr. Iroquois Papers, Collection Number 9184, box 3. Division of Rare and Manuscript Collections, Cornell University Library, Ithaca, NY.

Tetrault, Lisa. 2015. *The Myth of Seneca Falls: Memory and the Women's Suffrage Movement, 1848–1898*. Chapel Hill: University of North Carolina Press.

Thain, Marion. 2007a. *"Michael Field": Poetry, Aestheticism and the Fin de Siècle*. New York: Cambridge University Press.

———. 2007b. "Poetry." In *The Cambridge Companion to the Fin de Siècle*, edited by Gail Marshall, 223–40. New York: Cambridge University Press.

Threadcraft, Shatema. 2016. *Intimate Justice: The Black Female Body and the Body Politic*. New York: Oxford University Press.

Trachtenberg, Alan. 2004. *Shades of Hiawatha: Staging Indians, Making Americans, 1880–1930*. New York: Hill and Wang.

Tuchinsky, Adam. 2016. "'Woman and Her Needs': Elizabeth Oakes Smith and the Divorce Question." *Journal of Women's History* 28, no. 1 (Spring): 38–59.

Tucker, Herbert. 1985. "Dramatic Monologue and the Overhearing of Lyric." In *Lyric Poetry: Beyond New Criticism*, edited by Chaviva Hosek and Patricia Parker, 226–43. Ithaca, NY: Cornell University Press.

Tuckerman, Henry Theodore. 1842. "Keats." *Southern Literary Messenger* 8, no. 1 (January): 37–41.

———. 1843. "Literary Portrait." In *The Sinless Child,* by Elizabeth Oakes Smith, edited by John Keese, xxvii–xxxii. New York: Wiley and Putnam.

———. 1850. *The Optimist.* New York: G. P. Putnam.

Untermeyer, Louis. 1993. "Edna St. Vincent Millay." In *Critical Essays on Edna St. Vincent Millay,* edited by William B. Thesing, 115–20. New York: G. K. Hall.

Vanity Fair. 1920. "Poems by Edna St. Vincent Millay." 15, no. 3 (November): 49.

Vermont Chronicle. 1832a. "Essay on Lyric Poetry." August 24, 136.

———. 1832b. "Essay on Lyric Poetry." September 14, 148.

Viehmann, Martha L. 2012. "Speaking Chinook: Adaptation, Indigeneity, and Pauline Johnson's British Columbia Stories." *Western American Literature* 47, no. 3: 258–85.

Vizenor, Gerald. 1994. *Manifest Manners: Narratives on Postindian Survivance.* Middletown, CT: Wesleyan University Press.

Walker, Cheryl. 1991. *Masks Outrageous and Austere: Culture, Psyche, and Persona in Modern Women Poets.* Bloomington: Indiana University Press.

Walker, Susan. 1842. "Female Influence: In Seven Chapters." *Southern Literary Messenger* 8, no. 1 (January): 25–37.

Warner, Charles Dudley. 1897. *Library of the World's Best Literature.* Vol. 41. New York: International Co.

Warwick, Diana. 1923. "Life and Letters." *Life,* December 13, 20.

Wayne, Tiffany. 2005. *Woman Thinking: Feminism and Transcendentalism in Nineteenth-Century America.* Lanham, MD: Lexington Books.

Weaver, Jace. 1997. *That the People Might Live: Native American Literatures and Native American Community.* New York: Oxford University Press.

Welke, Barbara. 2010. *Law and the Borders of Belonging in the Long Nineteenth Century United States.* New York: Cambridge University Press.

Western Recorder (Utica, NY). 1825. "Poetry and Music: Lyric Poetry." August 16, 132. American Periodicals. https://search.proquest.com/docview/126894477?accountid=7098.

Wexler, Laura. 2000. *Tender Violence: Domestic Visions in an Age of U.S. Imperialism.* Chapel Hill: University of North Carolina Press.

Wheeler, Lesley. 2008. *Voicing American Poetry: Sound and Performance from the 1920s to the Present.* Ithaca, NY: Cornell University Press.

———. 2015. "The Formalist Modernism of Edna St. Vincent Millay, Helene Johnson, and Louise Bogan." In *The Cambridge History of American Poetry,* edited by Alfred Bendixen and Stephen Burt, 628–49. New York: Cambridge University Press.

Williams, Andreá N. 2014. "Frances Watkins (Harper), Harriet Tubman and the Rhetoric of Single Blessedness." *Meridians* 12, no. 2: 99–122.

Wilson, Ivy. 2001. *Specters of Democracy: Blackness and the Aesthetics of Politics in the Antebellum U.S.* New York: Oxford University Press.

Wolosky, Shira. 2003. "The Claims of Rhetoric: Toward a Historical Poetics (1820–1900)." *American Literary History* 15, no. 1: 14–21.

Wyman, Mary A. 1927. *Two American Pioneers: Seba Smith and Elizabeth Oakes Smith.* New York: Columbia University Press.

York, Lorraine. 2002. "'Your Star': Pauline Johnson and the Tensions of Celebrity Discourse." *Canadian Poetry* 51 (Fall/Winter). http://canadianpoetry.org/volumes/vol51/york.html.

Index

Note: Italic page numbers refer to illustrations.

www.ingramcontent.com/pod-product-compliance
Lightning Source LLC
Chambersburg PA
CBHW030354270326
41926CB00009B/1093

9781469659817